CONTRARY
CREEK

BITS OF GRACE

by Lanham Flynt

CONTRARY
CREEK

Printed in the United States of America

FIRST EDITION

Library of Congress Cataloging-in-Publication Data
Flynt, Lanham
        Bits of Grace / Lanham Flynt. – 1st ed.
        p. cm.
        ISBN 1-930899-03-3
Library of Congress Card Number: 00-107527

COVER DESIGN BY LANA KOVNER

Contrary Creek Publishers
3863 Southwest Loop 820 – Suite 105
Fort Worth, Texas 76133

This devotional book is dedicated with love and appreciation to the wonderful memory of Lanham Flynt, a godly husband and father, who was inspired by the Holy Spirit as he diligently studied God's Word. We will always remember his great wisdom and knowledge along with his gentle and uncritical spirit, and especially how he gave God the glory for all things. We will be forever grateful to him for being sensitive to God's inspiration and allowing Him to be his guide as he wrote *Bits of Grace*.

In loving memory,
Charlotte, Karan, Kathy & Lana

BITS OF GRACE

by Lanham Flynt

LET HIM GUIDE US AS WE WRITE

Here with verse we tell His story,
As we give our God the glory.
He's directing, we're projecting,
What He means to you and me.
And the purpose of these writings,
Is to help us with our sightings,
Of His living, loving, giving.
For believing, we're receiving,
Throughout all eternity,
Life with Him eternally.

As we're writing, and we're living,
We can sense His Spirit giving,
With connection, a direction,
With regard to what we write.
So by writing, we are saying,
We're responding by obeying,
And our citing in our writing,
Is from scripture's holy light.
Christ in action is impaction,
And we pray each day and night,
Let Him guide us as we write.

STATEMENT OF FAITH AND DIRECTIVE

I believe that Jesus Christ, the second Person of the Trinity (God incarnate), walked this earth as a man and paid the full penalty for all our sin (past, present and future) when He shed His blood upon the cross. He arose that we might have eternal life in and through Him. We receive His life (eternal life) when we in simple faith exercise our belief and put our trust in Christ alone. We are reconciled to God the Father through Christ's death, and that when we repent and place our trust in Christ we are immediately sealed with the indwelling Holy Spirit, a deposit guaranteeing us eternal life. We are justified (judged righteous) in the eyes of God the Father because we are given the "righteousness of Christ." We are imputed His righteousness and God the Father sees us through the blood of Jesus, which washed us white as snow.

God's provision for us is to live eternally as "joint heirs" with Jesus in the Kingdom of God. This is a gift. We can't buy it and we can't earn it. We can only thankfully receive it and accept it, after which we are "sanctified" by God. The word "sanctification" means to be "set apart." We are set apart by God to do good works.

As Christians we reside in a state of sanctification, but we also are being sanctified (being made holy) by God on a daily basis. There are times when we don't feel very holy and we struggle, fret and worry, but we can take comfort in God's promises. Two of His most profound promises that have given me comfort are that "He who began a good work in you will carry it on to completion until the day of Christ Jesus" (Philippians 1:6) and "My grace is sufficient for you" (2 Corinthians 12:9).

Let each of us appropriate this grace freely given us through Christ and the indwelling Holy Spirit (the third Person of the Trinity). Let us realize and remember God's unconditional love for us through Christ, and let His indwelling Spirit guide and direct us as we pass His love on to others. Our prayer is that by God's grace, we will let Him guide us daily and live His life through us, that we might be an example to others and consequently be used by God to bring others into this living, loving relationship with our Lord Jesus Christ.

Some portions of the following are dated, since this was written by Lanham Flynt prior to his death December 5, 1997. However, the editors felt it important to retain the author's thoughts.

GOD CANNOT BE OUTMANEUVERED

Some portions of the following are dated, since this was written by Lanham Flynt prior to his death December 5, 1997. However, the editors felt it important to retain the author's thoughts.I am living proof that "God cannot be outmaneuvered." I firmly believe that when we accept Christ, God has a plan and a purpose for our life. We may delay it, resist it, prolong it, or with stubborn resistance postpone it. But His ultimate purpose for our life will be implemented.

I accepted Christ as my personal Savior when I was 9 years old. When I was in my late teens I felt a call to serve in the ministry in some capacity. During that period of time and into my early 20s I successfully resisted that call – not only with delaying tactics but with a attitude of self-sufficiency and self-importance. What I did not comprehend at that time was that regardless of our determination to resist His will, and despite any tactics we might use, GOD CANNOT BE OUTMANEUVERED.

In my mid 20s, I married a beautiful Christian girl and from that union we were blessed with three beautiful daughters, who in turn have blessed us with seven beautiful grandchildren.

I launched into the business world with supreme self-confidence, fought many business battles – won some, lost some – but the most powerful motivating factor in my life was the desire to be financially successful. I didn't call this "pride" – I called it "ambition for success" or the "American way." But God had other plans for my life. After many years of prideful endeavor, much resistance, planned procrastination and outright rebellion, I surrendered. I needed some "resting from the testing."

When we moved to Dallas in 1971, my wife, Charlotte, became active in Christian Women's Club. I didn't know exactly what was happening to her, but I thought she was going off the deep end with religion. It seemed that each time I came home the radio would be tuned to some religious program with some preacher preaching a sermon. To this day a standard joke in our home is that in the past I asked her to "turn it off,' and now I ask her to "turn it up." You see, the Lord can work miracles.

In the mid '80s the Lord gave me a burning desire to study the Bible. Since that time I have been rising each day between 3 a.m. and 5 a.m. to pursue that study until about 7 a.m. To some, the sequence of Bible study, which I believe was directed by the Lord when I began, might seem rather unusual, even extraordinary. However, the Lord knew my character traits better than I did. I had and still have an insatiable desire to find the answer and solution to any given problem. I began the study of eschatology.

Now, eschatology is a very complex and controversial subject. Many of our Christian brothers and sisters are not in agreement with regard to interpretation of the scriptures in this area. And, even though I have a definite opinion with regard to interpretation, I believe that the end result (the fact that we will be with the Lord forever) far outweighs in importance the sequence in which these events transpire. But I also believe the Lord was using my curiosity to trigger a study of the scriptures.

While engrossed in the study of eschatology, I read a book written by Walter Martin entitled, *The Kingdom of the Cults*. This triggered an in-depth study of the difference between Christianity and cultic beliefs. With so much in-depth study of the New Testament, there began to emerge the true meaning of the grace of God through our Lord Jesus Christ.

During this initial study period, I seemed to spend every spare moment studying the Bible, reading Bible commentaries or tuning into Christian broadcasting stations. I was fortunate (or was it by the Lord's direction?) to tune into stations that presented Christian teachers, such as Chuck Swindoll and Dr. Charles Stanley, who taught the message of grace through Jesus Christ. There developed within me an intense desire to search the scriptures for "the truth." And truth is found in the scriptures with the direction of the indwelling Holy Spirit.

That was exciting. I almost couldn't wait for each morning to arrive, so that I could get up and explore the abundance of God's love, mercy and grace. I discovered the unconditional love of God through Jesus Christ, who paid the full penalty for our sin. Christ's blood has cleansed us, so that when we, by faith, accept Him, we have His righteousness imputed to us and we receive His life. A life in Christ begins when we accept it and never ends – a life eternally with our Lord.

My wife, Charlotte, and I are members of Prestonwood Baptist Church. Two or three years after I began this in-depth study of scriptures, we were blessed to have Jack Graham begin his ministry in our church. His sermons contain and convey the pure gospel of the grace of God. Charlotte and I are also members of a rather large Sunday School Class at Prestonwood. We have approximately 150 members.

Several years ago Ed Moore returned to teach our class. Ed is a dedicated Christian teacher who is also an ordained minister. As I continued my study, Ed and I had many conversations regarding the love, grace and mercy of God – and in general, what Christianity is all about. He was a great encourager.

Ed's occupational pursuits involved him with other churches, so he was unable to teach our class every Sunday. My surprise was almost indescribable when He asked me to teach in his absence. I felt completely inadequate, but I elected to make myself available with complete dependence on the Lord. Teaching has been an exhilarating experience, and my search for truth in the scriptures has been even more pronounced and intense.

Since I am still engaged in a full-time vocation, my study periods remain before 7 a.m. each day. While I was studying one morning in mid 1992, the Lord seemed to group some words together for me that rhymed. Consequently, that morning I wrote my first poem. Six months later, I wrote two more. Then in 1993, there began a continuous, almost gushing outpouring of Christian "truths" that I felt compelled to arrange in poetic verse. I wrote 120 "long" poems in 1993. Almost without exception, each poem was written at "one sitting," each before 7 a.m. This has to be an inspiration from the Lord, because I know absolutely nothing about poetry. I believe that the Lord is using me through these means to help spread the gospel.

In whatever manner each of us serves the Lord, I believe the Lord, together with the indwelling Spirit, uses people to give us inspiration and direction. While I have already mentioned some of the people who originally gave me direction and inspiration via radio and/or television, our pastor at Prestonwood, Jack Graham, has continually blessed us with the gospel of grace. And Ed Moore has also been superlatively supportive. And last, but not least, I want to mention my family, and especially my wife, Charlotte. She has continually been encouraging me and has been so prayerfully supportive. Her middle name should be "Barnabas." I am and shall ever be eternally grateful for her encouragement. We now have no disagreement whatsoever when a Christian teacher is teaching on the radio. We don't "TURN IT OFF," we "TURN IT UP."

My hope and sincere desire is that this publication in some small way will be an inspiration to each of you. For those of you who do not know Christ intimately as your personal Savior, I hope you will find the truth of the gospel and the plan of salvation that is available for you. And, I hope, you will exercise saving faith and receive eternal life with Him. To those who are Christians, my hope and desire is that this daily devotional – written in both prose and poetry – will be helpful and encouraging. I hope it will remind each of us of the unconditional love, grace and mercy of God, through our Lord Jesus Christ, who not only gives us an eternity with Him, but also gives us sufficient grace to travel down this highway of life. His grace is sufficient. This publication is, to me, an overwhelming endorsement that GOD CANNOT BE OUTMANEUVERED.

Some of the acknowledgements, too, are dated, since they were written by Lanham Flynt prior to his death. However, since they were written by Lanham, the editor felt the wording should not be changed.

Acknowledgements

I would like to extend my deepest thanks and appreciation to so many people who gave encouragement, who extended their help and loyalty, and who made such special contributions to my writing in some form or another. Very often they didn't even know about it, but by just being there when I needed them passed the love of God through our Lord Jesus Christ on to me and to others.

To my wife, Charlotte, beautifully Christian, inside and out, my staunchest supporter, always graciously giving encouragement almost on a 24-hour basis. Without Charlotte, there would be no ***Bits of Grace***.

To my three beautiful Christian daughters – Karan, Kathy and Lana – who from a distance gave the same quality encouragement given by their mother.

And, to the many members of my family, all Christians, who were also supportive and encouraging: Karan's family, husband Rick, son Trent and daughters Tonya and Tricia Stone and her husband Ed Stone, and two great grandsons, Zack and Jake; Kathy's husband Mike, daughter Angela, and son Adam; and Lana's husband Gary and son Russell and daughter Kristel.

Charlotte's mother, Nettie Routh Moss, went home to be with the Lord September 11, 1995, but before her passing she was a tremendous encourager.

Charlotte's sisters, Louise Miller and Arlene Johnson (and husband Doug) have been very supportive and encouraging.

Acknowledgements

Dr. Chuck Swindoll and Dr. Charles Stanley who graced those Christian radio stations with the message of God's grace for so many years, and still do, gave me a tremendous desire to study the scriptures – to find out more and more about the grace of God through our Lord Jesus Christ.

Dr. Jack Graham, our pastor at Prestonwood Baptist Church, who since becoming our pastor, has preached the grace message and has enhanced my desire to learn more and more about His saving grace and the sufficiency of His grace.

Clarice Langran and husband John have also been great encouragers. Clarice, who has taught the Bible for 50 or more years, encouraged me to teach a small Bible study in our real estate office early in the day before the real estate office came alive; thus my first Bible study teaching.

Ed Moore, an ordained minister who returned to teach our Sunday School class at Prestonwood Baptist Church. The Agape Class, with approximately 150 members, encouraged me and gave me the opportunity to teach our class on the Sundays that he was not available. I shall be forever grateful to Ed for that opportunity. It has been a real blessing to me.

It is so difficult to name a particular person or just a few people in our Agape Sunday School class, because every one of them as so special to both Charlotte and me. However, Byron and Helen Rippy, our Christian friends for so many years, have always been completely supportive and are now so encouraging with regard to my writing and this manuscript.

Our entire class is really a family, and you can almost literally "feel" the love of Christ emanating from this group of saints. We are so fortunate to be members of the Agape Class.

Dr. Harry Piland and wife, Pat, have given such a tremendous amount of encouragement to me personally regarding my writing. They have read the entire manuscript, and are in process of showing it to others. Dr. Piland and Pat have had quite an interesting life. Harry's life's work has been for the Lord, with Pat by his side. He is a teacher, a preacher and an author. He was one of the very first ministers to go to Russia to help the Christian churches spread the gospel. He teaches in the Baptist seminary in Fort Worth and in schools in Tennessee and other states, in special meetings in various states all over the country and has preached and is continuing to preach at various churches and Christian institutions. He has authored and is teaching many facets of communication skills involving the operation of churches and Sunday schools. He has lectured all over the world and in every state in the United States. We met Dr. Piland and his wife Pat rather late in life, but these Christian friends have absolutely destroyed the myth that longevity has to be a factor in genuine Christian love and friendship. Our special friendship attests to the fact that we have all received that seal, the promised Holy Spirit, who is a deposit guaranteeing our inheritance. We are all one in Christ, and there are no words sweeter, nor is any other friendship greater than one centered around Jesus. We appreciate their encouragement but most of all, we value their friendship.

FOR REFERENCES THE FOLLOWING WERE USED:

Bible Translations – NIV, KJV, Williams, Beck, NAS and Amplified.
The Kingdom of the Cults by Walter Martin
Footsteps of the Messiah by Arnold G. Fruchtenbaum
Things to Come by J. Dwight Pentecost
The New Bible Dictionary by J. J. Douglas and others
Expository Dictionary of New Testament Words by W.E. Vine
Expository Dictionary of Biblical Words by W.E. Vine
Exhaustive Concordance of the Bible by James Strong
Analytical Concordance to the Bible by Robert Young
My Utmost For His Highest by Oswald Chambers.
The Bible Knowledge Commentary by Dallas Seminary Faculty
Various Tyndale New and Old Testament Commentaries

To the many who have helped me with this endeavor and have not been recognized, please forgive me. It was not intentional.

Again, to my wife, Charlotte, your middle name really should be "Barnabas."

THE BEGINNING

"In the beginning was the Word, and the Word was with God, and the Word was God. He was with God in the beginning." – John 1:1-2

As we begin a New Year, perhaps we should turn our eyes up yonder, and reflect on the awesome wonder of God's creation.

UP YONDER

Let us turn our eyes up yonder,
As we view God's awesome wonder,
Thoughts assembling, hearts a-trembling,
As we see what God has done,
For exhibit of creation,
Gives our hearts a pure elation,
While reviewing, and pursuing,
As on earth our race is run,
For with passion, and compassion,
God has given us His Son,
And through Christ, our race is won.

In this passage of scripture (John 1:1-2) we are told that in the very beginning there existed with God the Word who, in fact, was God. The Word, the second Person of the Trinity, ultimately came to this earth and manifested Himself in the flesh as Jesus Christ (John 1:14). The glory of God was beheld in Christ, and He was full of grace and truth.

As we begin our New Year, let us reflect on the beginning of creation, and how God with His ultimate wisdom, His all powerful presence, and His immense love for each of us, made provision for us to be with Him for eternity. He sent His only Son to shed His blood on a cross that we might be cleansed of our sins when we put our faith in Jesus Christ. Let us begin this New Year in awesome wonder of the love of God for each one of us. We, who are Christians, are privileged almost beyond human comprehension. We will spend an eternity with our Lord.

JESUS RECEIVES THE SPIRIT

"As Jesus was coming up out of the water, He saw the heavens being torn open and the Spirit descending on Him like a dove. And a voice came from the Heaven, 'You are My Son, whom I love; with You I am well pleased.'" – Mark 1:10-11

LIKE A DOVE

Once, upon this earth, so darkened,
Like a dove, God's Spirit harkened,
With decision, and provision,
Then descended on His Son.
As He came up from the water,
Spirit filled, the Master Potter,
Made a blessing, we're confessing,
Christ our Lord, the only one,
That God gave us, who can save us.
He's our Lord, whose work is done,
Jesus Christ, God's only Son.

This scripture reveals how Jesus received the Holy Spirit (third Person of the Trinity) from God the Father. This has special significance for each one of us who are Christians. In the Old Testament, we read that at various times God's Spirit would descend upon people of His choosing, however there is one very drastic difference. In the Old Testament, at God's discretion, this was a temporary situation, but when the Spirit of God the Father descended on His Son, this was a permanent situation.

What is so exciting to those of us who are Christians, that this same life-giving Holy Spirit is immediately received by us when we believe, and put our trust in Jesus. Having believed, you were marked in Him with a seal, the promised Holy Spirit, Who is a deposit guaranteeing our inheritance until the redemption of those who are God's possession – to the praise of His glory (Ephesians 1:13-14). When we accepted Jesus Christ as our Savior, we were immediately indwelt with this permanent life-giving Spirit. This is a deposit guaranteeing an eternity with our Lord. Also, just as this Spirit equipped Jesus for His work on this earth, His Spirit also equips us. May each one of us listen to this directing Spirit, and be filled with His spiritual power, the enabling power of the Holy Spirit.

January 3

GOD'S RAINBOW OF GRACE

"But He said to me, 'My grace is sufficient for you, for my power is made perfect in weakness.'" – 2 Corinthians 12:9

AFTER THE STORM

The storms in our life, seem awesome indeed,
They lash us wherever we go.
They batter and ram us, and leave us in need,
But, after the storm, God's Rainbow.
For, we have a hope, a shelter of love,
God's promise to all who believe,
It's that Rainbow of Grace that comes from above
That Rainbow of Hope we receive.
Though storms in our life, are awesome indeed,
And lash us wherever we go,
Let us never forget, in our time of need,
That after the storm, God's Rainbow.

We can take so much comfort in God's words; "My grace is sufficient." Whatever the circumstances, regardless of the magnitude of the storm we see brewing on the horizon, even if we are in the very midst of severe turbulence that is distressing to our soul, we know that God's grace is sufficient through Jesus Christ, our Lord.

After the great flood, God gave Noah the rainbow as a sign that the earth would forever be saved from destruction by flooding. How much more God gave each one of us who are Christians? We have God's rainbow of sure hope, our Lord Jesus Christ, who will not only provide for our eternity, but will be the rainbow in our lives, always providing the calm that follows each storm. God's rainbow of grace, our Lord Jesus Christ, is more than sufficient for all our needs. His power is made perfect in our weakness.

DO NOT WORRY

"Therefore do not worry about tomorrow, for tomorrow will worry about itself. Each day has enough trouble of it's own." – Matthew 6:34

HIS GRACE WILL BE OUR STRENGTH

Tomorrow is full of sorrow,
But tomorrow never comes.
So, today, let us not borrow,
From tomorrow, pain that numbs.
Let us live each day with gladness,
And depend on Him above,
For He'll take away our sadness,
And replace it with His love.
For His love's a revelation,
In it's depth, and width and length,
He not only gives salvation,
But His Grace will be our strength.

Jesus tells us, "Do not worry about tomorrow." What a great teaching this is, and what great insight Jesus had, for He knows what we are thinking. When we worry, it is always in anticipation of, or in fear of, something that will, or will not, happen in the future, or as Jesus said, "tomorrow." We never worry about yesterday, except how the events of yesterday might affect what we fear might happen, or not happen, tomorrow.

I believe this is one of the most difficult of all of the commandments of our Lord for us to keep. It seems that our very nature just "searches" for something to worry about. There is a solution, but it is not found within our nature, but rather in the nature of the indwelling Spirit of Christ. We simply need to say, "Lord, I can't handle it, but I know you can, and I know you will." In order for us to do this, we must believe that God's grace is sufficient in all situations, and HIS GRACE WILL BE OUR STRENGTH.

ETERNAL SECURITY

"My sheep listen to My voice; I know them, and they follow Me. I give them eternal life, and they shall never perish; no one can snatch them out of My hand. My Father, Who has given them to Me, is greater than all; no one can snatch them out of My Father's hand. I and the Father are one." – John 10:27-30

HE WON'T LET GO

We hear His voice; He knows us well,
We're saved by faith, and this we tell:
We follow Him, and ever live,
Eternal Life is His to give.
We're in His hand, He holds us tight,
He won't let go, we're in the light.
No one can snatch us from His hand,
So, no one will, for no one can.
The Father gave, us to the Son,
Through Christ our earthly race is run.
The hands of Both, hold us so tight,
We feel the love, the grace, the might
That God, Himself, through Christ our Lord,
Gave each of us, We're His to guard.

Eternal life is forever, and ever, and ever. Eternal life is not something that is temporary, and Christ promised us eternal life with Him. He also assures us that both He and the Father have Their hands securely around us, and They will not let go.

There seems to be a misconception by so many Christians that we should be trying our best to work and hang onto God, and that if we can just be good enough, then everything will be okay. We are not hanging on to God. God has His hands wrapped securely around us. We were not saved because we were good enough. We were saved because Jesus paid the sin debt that we owed at the cross, and we put our faith in Him. As Christians, through Christ, we have been adopted as sons and daughters into the family of God the Father. THERE IS NO GREATER SECURITY.

January 6

CHRIST IS THE CHIEF CORNERSTONE

"Consequently, you are no longer foreigners and aliens, but fellow citizens with God's people, and members of God's household, built on the foundation of the apostles and the prophets, with Christ Jesus, Himself as the chief cornerstone." – Ephesians 2:19-20

OUR CORNERSTONE

Our cornerstone is massive rock,
Embedded, "oh so deep."
It will hold us tight, and safe, and lock,
Our souls, therein to keep.
The grace of God is not a whim,
The love of God is real.
Let's live this life with eyes on Him,
Our hope, our joy, our seal.
Let's share His love, as we progress,
Let's share it while we can,
This Cornerstone that we confess,
God's precious gift to man.
Our Cornerstone goes "oh, so deep,"
The bedrock all sufficed,
To heal our wounds, our souls to keep,
Our Cornerstone is Christ.

In this passage of scripture, Paul is using the cornerstone as an illustration of how Christ, and only Christ, holds together the body of Christ, the church. The massive stone architecture of that era required the cornerstone as a structural necessity. Without the all-important cornerstone, a building could not stand. Without Jesus Christ, there is no church.

A disturbing trend that seems to be more and more prevalent in some churches today is the adherence to, and the participation in, such a variety of endeavors that somewhere along the line our Lord Jesus Christ is relegated to a position of secondary importance. As important as some of these endeavors and activities may be, it is imperative that we keep Christ as the Chief Cornerstone.

GRACE WOULD NO LONGER BE GRACE

"And if by grace, then it is no longer by works. If it were, grace would no longer be grace." – Romans 11:6

BY GRACE ALONE

I wonder, Lord, how well we learn,
And trust alone, in Your return.
You walked this earth, a little while,
And walked for us, that extra mile.
For each of us, You bore the cross,
And died for us, "oh, what a loss,"
But rose again, that we might be,
Forever Yours, eternally,
So, as we run, this earthly race,
Let us depend upon Your Grace.
Let's keep our eyes, upon Your Son,
By Grace alone, OUR RACE IS WON.

With reference to eternity, we have two choices. Either we can try to work our way to Heaven, or we can accept His saving grace by exercising faith in our Lord Jesus Christ, and rely on His ability. In this verse, we observe a great truth; grace and works don't mix, so we really don't have two choices if we want to spend an eternity with our Lord. We can't work hard enough, we can't get clean enough and we can't be good enough to earn our way to Heaven. When we exercise faith in Christ, His blood cleanses us. GRACE AND GRACE ALONE SAVES US.

THE FRUIT OF THE SPIRIT

"But the fruit of the Spirit is love, joy, peace, patience, kindness, goodness, faithfulness, gentleness and self-control." – Galatians 5:22-23

"I am the vine, you are the branches. He who abides in Me, and I in him, bears much fruit; for without Me you can do nothing." – John 15:5

LET US PLANT A TREE

Let us plant a little tree today, beside the raging streams,
Of life with all its problems, its shattered, broken dreams.
Let us plant a tree of caring, for those we know in pain,
Whose life seems now in shambles, and clouded dark with rain.
Let us water it with kindness, and nurture it with love,
And fertilize with goodness that comes from Him above.
Let us add a little patience, with gentleness in tow,
As faithfully we water, and see it grow and grow.

Let us prune it with a little joy, and peace and self-control,
And keep our eyes on Him above, who sanctifies our soul.
The tree we plant and water, and nurture with our love,
Is merely a reflection, of Him who reign above,
Who causes growth to follow, spreading branches to the sky,
The fruit of His eternal love, produced by Him on high.
Let us plant a tree for Him today, with love, and joy and laughter,
A beacon full of grace and truth, for those who follow after.

We are either led by the Spirit, and enjoy the fruit of the Spirit, or we are led by our sinful nature, and the Spirit's fruit is not produced. We know that the Lord produces the fruit of the Spirit through us, but we also know that we control the key that unlocks this production of spiritual fruit. Romans 8:5 tells us:

"Those who live according to the sinful nature have their minds set on what that nature desires; but those who live in accordance with the Spirit have their minds set on what the Spirit desires."

Our prayer is that the Lord will give us the strength, the courage and the direction to keep our eyes focused on Him, and let the Vine produce fruit through the branches, and all spiritual fruit produced will be for the glory of our Lord, Jesus Christ.

January 9

I SEEK NOT TO PLEASE MYSELF

"For I seek not to please Myself, but Him who sent Me." – John 5:30b

LORD, HELP US DO YOUR WILL

Lord, we pray that while we're learning,
You imbue us with a yearning,
With a burning, glowing yearning,
In our heart to do Your will.
Let us be in You abiding,
With the knowledge of Your guiding,
And with fervor, never swerver,
But be working here until,
We are captured, or we're raptured,
And at last our soul is still,
Lord, please help us do Your will.

This scripture is a graphic illustration of a very important Christian precept. When Jesus walked this earth He was all man, but He was also all divine. Although He had the power to call multiple legions of angels to do His bidding, (Matthew 26:53), He chose to be obedient to the Father. His first, foremost and only wish was to please the Father. In John 4:34, Jesus tells us that His food is to do the will of the one who sent Him (God the Father) and to finish His work.

Our prayer is that we who are Christians will have the same attitude that Jesus had – that we lovingly and willingly, might diligently seek to please the Lord, even when it seems not so pleasing to us. We ask that the Lord not only instills in us a desire to please Him, but that He also gives us the determination to carry through and finish whatever task He gives us. Then, perhaps, we can say, "Lord, we don't seek to please ourselves, and LORD, PLEASE HELP US DO YOUR WILL."

NEVER WILL I LEAVE YOU

"Never will I leave you; never will I forsake you." – Hebrews 13:5b

WE KNOW HE'S ALWAYS THERE

Let's review our situation, as we ponder our salvation,
For we ponder the wonder, of our Lord, who gave His all.
For that miracle of rising, set our soul to realizing,
That His rising was revising, then He issued us a call,
And His living, was the giving, of His life to one and all,
Who responded to His call.

By His mercy, He's providing, a new home for our residing,
And with mingling, and with tingling, we can feel His loving care.
So, as on this earth we travel, by His grace, let us unravel,
For our brothers, and for others, how, in love and grace we fare.
For abiding, we're residing, in His tender, loving care,
For we know He's always there.

God will never leave nor forsake us, the saints. We have His promise. We also have the indwelling Holy Spirit to guide us and comfort us along the way. There are many religions on this earth with various beliefs, professions of love, and instructions regarding how to live. These religions all have something in common. You work to obtain salvation, or to attain some degree of excellence. If you work hard enough, you make it, if you don't backslide. If you don't work hard enough, you don't make it.

Webster's Dictionary defines religion as a "system of beliefs and practices relation to the sacred, and uniting its adherents in a community." Christianity is unique, in that even though it is a system of beliefs, and even practices in some instances are prevalent, the bottom line is a personal relationship with the Lord Jesus Christ. In Christianity, we don't earn our salvation, rather, we accept the free gift of God's grace through our Lord Jesus Christ, and by faith we are saved. We know that our Lord will never leave us nor forsake us, and with the enabling of the indwelling Holy Spirit, we eliminate all conjecture. WE KNOW HE'S ALWAYS THERE.

January 11

DON'T LET US MESS IT UP

"Ask and it will be given to you. Seek and you will find, knock, and the door will be opened unto you." – Matthew 7:7

KNOCK, AND IT SHALL BE OPENED

Eternal life is for the meek, and given when we ask,
And found in Christ when ere we seek, by faith His life at last.
We're safe in Christ, our life secure, our knock was heard, we know,
But, now we have this earthly tour – from here, where do we go?

We ask, and seek, and knock and tell Him how we need His grace.
He opens other doors as well, in each and every case.
The door He opens midst our strife, may seem to interrupt,
But Lord, we pray, with all our life, don't let us mess it up.

We asked for eternal life, and it was given to us, for as we sought it in meekness, we found it in Christ. We knocked, and the door was opened unto us for all eternity. Now, having received eternal salvation, all we have to do is finish this earthly tour. Sounds simple, doesn't it – but is it? Absolutely not.

We are not promised a trouble-free life, but we are promised a solution for our problems. We are not promised a rose garden, but even at times when all seems to be going great, God may test and strengthen our character with the thorns on the rose bushes. His grace amidst all our strife is the solution.

We are more teachable when we realize we cannot control a situation. When we are meek, God can use us. In the midst of our earthly strife, He will open doors of opportunity for us to serve Him. Our prayer is "Lord, when You give us an opportunity to serve you, PLEASE, DON'T LET US MESS IT UP."

THE SEED OF THE GOSPEL

"I planted the seed, Apollos watered it, but God made it grow." – 1 Corinthians 3:6

A BUMPER CROP OF GOODNESS

The fruit of God's eternal love, is evident in all,
Who walk by faith, in Christ alone, and meekly heed His call.
Sufficient grace is His to give, to each and everyone,
Who yields to Him, and does His work, until God's will is done.

Through each and every Saint alive, He works to pass it on,
That all might hear, those words so dear, that Jesus Christ be known.
So we, ourselves, replant the seed, that other might receive,
The message of eternal life, for those who do believe.

The fruit of God's eternal love, will multiply and yield,
A bumper crop of goodness, throughout the entire field,
If planted with His loving care, and watered with His grace,
He uses arms, legs and us in each and every case.

When Christ walked this earth, He personally spread the gospel. He also gathered around Him apostles and disciples. And after His death and resurrection, and just prior to His ascension into Heaven, He gathered the eleven around Him and gave them specific instructions to "Go into all the world and preach the gospel to all creation." (Mark 16:15) The eleven received their "marching orders" then and today the same marching orders are applicable to those of us who are Christians.

The scope of our sphere may be limited to somewhat less than all creation, but within our sphere, we are the only arms, legs and voice that Jesus has. It is not only an opportunity for us to plant the seed of the gospel; it is an obligation. This commandment from our Lord does give us the opportunity to plant the seed of the gospel with love, water it with grace and watch God make it grow into A BUMPER CROP OF GOODNESS.

I AM THE LIGHT OF THE WORLD

"I am the Light of the world. Whoever follows Me will never walk in darkness, but will have the light of life." – John 8:12

THE LIGHT OF THE WORLD

The Light of the world, came down to unfurl,
His light, midst a world dark with sinning.
He came that he might, with His life, give light,
For He was the Word, the Beginning.

The world stood amazed, but most only gazed,
For the darkness enshrouded their vision,
And throughout the night, their eyes saw no light,
And on earth, they made no decision.

Even though God sent His only Son to this earth to be the Light of the world, the world not only rejected Him, they crucified Him on a cross.

"And the Word became flesh and dwelt among us, and we beheld His glory, glory as of the only begotten of the Father, full of grace and truth." (John 1:14)

"The light shines in the darkness, but the darkness has not understood it." (John 1:5)

John made these statements just a few years after Jesus finished his work here on earth.

The vast majority of the world has not changed. The darkness continues to either make no decision, or persist in an absolute rejection of Jesus Christ. We are so fortunate as Christians because we follow Christ. We will never walk in darkness because we have the light of Life. We made a decision to put our trust in our Lord, Jesus Christ, and that was by far the most important decision anyone living on this earth could ever make. We have, with His indwelling Spirit, the very life of Christ giving us life and that life will extend beyond the grave, giving us an eternity with our Lord. Our prayer is that the Lord will use us in some small way, that perhaps we can be beacons of light in the darkness.

THE ONE AND ONLY GOSPEL

"I am astonished that you are so quickly deserting the One who called you by the grace of Christ, and are turning to a different gospel, which is really no gospel at all." – Galatians 1:6-7

TIL WE SEE THE SETTING SUN

For, the dove of God descended,
And the Word of God befriended,
With the living and the giving,
Of God's Spirit to the Son.
And, our Lord will have it always,
From the earth to Heaven's hallways,
And believing, we're receiving,
This same Spirit from the Son.
So, let's teach it, and let's preach it,
'Til our time on earth is done,
'Til we see the setting sun.

Paul was not gently admonishing the Galatians for listening to and believing a distorted version of the gospel. He was condemning their actions. In fact, in Galatians 1:8, Paul was so adamant and unyielding in his defense of the gospel that he said, "Even if we, or an angel from heaven should preach a gospel other than the one we preached to you, let him be ETERNALLY CONDEMNED." So intense was Paul in his defense of the gospel that in Galatians 1:9 he, for the second time, gave these instructions: "As we have already said, so now I say again; if anybody is preaching to you a gospel other than what you accepted, let him be ETERNALLY CONDEMNED."

There is an extremely important lesson for us to learn as we read these passages of scripture. Paul would go to great lengths to present himself in a manner that he would be acceptable to those he was trying to reach with the gospel, but, he was absolutely immovable and unrelenting regarding the truth of the gospel. There was, and is, one gospel, and one gospel only. As we endeavor to tell others about the saving grace of Christ, let us take a page out of Paul's book and be absolutely sure that there is no distortion of the gospel. Let us teach the ONE AND ONLY GOSPEL, THE SAVING GRACE OF OUR LORD JESUS CHRIST WHEN WE EXERCISE BELIEF IN, AND PUT OUR TRUST IN CHRIST. THERE IS NO OTHER GOSPEL.

THE WISE AND FOOLISH BUILDERS

"Therefore, everyone who hears these words of Mine and puts them into practice is like a wise man who builds his house on rock." – Matthew 7:24

LET'S BUILD OUR HOUSE ON ROCK

We build on rock, or build on sand,
The one will fall, the other stand.
Our faith in Christ, will all suffice,
But not the land, that's filled with sand.
But if our house, is built on rock,
A house that He, can guard and lock,
His grace is ours, His mercy towers,
And He will lock our house on rock.

When Jesus was teaching, He used parables and illustrations so that His listeners could better understand and comprehend the meaning of His teaching. Jesus ends a portion of scriptures we identify as the "Sermon on the Mount" (Matthew 5-7) with an illustration concerning the wise and foolish builders. Thus, it appears to be somewhat of a recap of the entire text of the sermon in where Jesus admonishes His listeners to be wise and put His words into practice. His teaching in these three chapters covers many subjects, and Bible scholars the world over continue to try to interpret the entire meaning of what Jesus is telling us. However, one interpretation that cannot be refuted is that if we build our house (PUT OUR FAITH) on anything or anybody other than Jesus Christ, our house will fall (WE WILL NOT BE SAVED).

As Christians, our house is built on the SOLID ROCK. Our house is built on the saving grace of Jesus Christ.

A PROMISE FROM OUR LORD

"To him who overcomes, I will give the right to eat from the tree of life, which is in the paradise of God." – Revelation 2:7b

THE TREE OF LIFE

A seed is not a seed, until you sow it,
A tree is not a tree until you grow it,
But the Seed of Life, which the Lord has sown,
And the Tree of Life, which the Lord has grown,
Was prepared for us, and through Him received,
When we trusted Him, and in Him believed.

Once again, we have another promise from our Lord. Those who overcome, that is, those who put their complete trust in the Lord Jesus Christ for their salvation, will have the right to eat from the tree of life in the paradise of God. That is, they will enjoy a living eternity with our Lord.

In Genesis, when Adam and Eve ate the forbidden fruit, God banished them from the garden so that they could no longer eat the fruit from the tree of life. When Adam fell, the whole world fell, and all mankind inherited His sinful nature. God hates sin but not the sinner. God loves us, but God is a just God, therefore He sent His only Son to die on a cross as a blood sacrifice to erase the sins of those that would believe and have faith in Jesus Christ.

This passage of scripture tells us that since we exercised faith in God's only Son, we now can look forward to eternal life with Him. Moreover, the fruit from the tree of life will be available to us forever, and ever and ever, throughout all eternity. WHAT A PROMISE THIS IS.

THE BOASTFUL PRIDE OF LIFE

"For all that is in the world, the lust of the flesh, and the lust of the eyes, and the boastful pride of life, is not from the Father, but is from the world." – 1 John 2:16

OUR RICHES TURN INTO DITCHES

Our ego is pride, and pride is a ride,
A ride that will dump us in ditches,
And pride is a sin, a sin that's within,
And within our soul, it bewitches.
We first grab the wheel, we're ready to deal,
We can throw a strike with our pitches.
For, we stand so tall, and we know it all,
We forget – this road has its ditches.

How prideful we are, we power this car,
On the road to fame, and to riches.
As others can see, we drive fast and free,
Til we crash, and land in the ditches.
We're cut and we're bruised, our energy used,
By ourselves, we can't sew the stitches.
We're down in the ditch, and we're still not rich,
Our riches have turned into ditches.

The sin of pride was the downfall of Lucifer (Satan), and it was the downfall of Adam and Eve. Each placed self ahead of obedience to God, hence, the downfall. Even though we, as Christians, have eternal security with our Lord, as we drive down life's highway, we have a tendency to become comfortable and complacent with our ability to navigate. We don't need any help from anyone. We can do it by ourselves. We know what we're doing. Then, all of a sudden, our car swerves and we land in a real deep ditch and we can't get out. Our riches have turned into ditches. At this point, our ego begins to shrink for we begin to understand that perhaps it is possible that we can't do it by ourselves. This may be exactly where God wants us, because, as we realize how powerless we are, we suddenly become teachable, and therein do we truly find God's riches.

January 18

FROM DITCHES TO RICHES

"Let him who boasts, boast in the Lord, for it is not the one who commends himself who is approved, but the one the Lord commends." – 1 Corinthians 10:17-18

GOD'S RICHES IN THE DITCHES

The ride filled with pride, was not by His side,
Our race, and our every endeavor,
Were powered by pride, throughout the ride,
Our dependence on Him was never.
But, mercy and grace, through Him will take place,
Our Glorious Lord, who does love us.
He'll give us His Hand, and see that we land,
On our feet; He's standing above us.

He must be amused, to see us defused,
With the pride of self, which still haunts us.
But, now we are meek, and it's Him we seek,
And that's exactly where He wants us.
So, now when we ride, He rides by our side,
And though we may still find the ditches,
With love, joy and peace, and mercy's release,
God's riches are found in the ditches.

In our pursuit of this world's riches, our old sinful nature impress upon our minds how we should be commended for doing such a good job. Our ego begins to enlarge, and we begin to take pride in our personal accomplishments. Just about that time, when we are speeding down the highway of life, our car swerves into a real deep ditch, and we can't get out of it. Our ego is shattered, and then, sometimes in desperation, we turn to the Lord for help. That is when we find God's real riches. When everything was going our way, we were not very teachable. Now that we are in this deep ditch, we begin to be real teachable. We learn about God's grace, joy, peace and His release of mercy to us. We begin to understand just how much God loves us, and we begin to have a very personal relationship with our Lord, Jesus Christ. Some of us even thank Him for the ditches, because in all areas of our life, we begin to realize that God's true riches are found in the ditches.

I HAVE FOUGHT THE GOOD FIGHT

"I have fought the good fight, I have finished the race, I have kept the faith." – 2 Timothy 4:7

THE GOOD FIGHT

While we're here, let's tell the story, of the Grace of God in Glory,
Who has fashioned, with compassion, life for us for evermore.
Let us run our course by feeding, what the world is sorely needing.
With His ration, of compassion, Let's pass on His love and more,
To our brothers, and to others, and through us, let His love pour,
Never-ending love, and more.

As we see our highway ending, and we see God's skyway pending,
Let's be striving, and be driving, that the Good Fight might be fought.
Let's not let our work diminish, let's not stop until we finish,
With our brothers, and with others, let our life not be for naught.
Let's be teaching, and be reaching, and we'll know by souls we sought,
That "The Good Fight" has been fought.

In this passage of scripture, Paul knew that he was reaching the end of the course. His race was almost finished. He was giving the last instructions to Timothy, who was like a son to him. He was exhorting Timothy to "preach the word," to spread the gospel of Jesus Christ. He also warned Timothy that a time was coming when men would not want to hear sound doctrine, but he charged Timothy to continue preaching the truth. He knew he was going to die in the very immediate future, and he was giving Timothy a blueprint of his ministry to follow. "I have fought the good fight, I have finished the race; I have kept the faith." Paul continues his dissertation with, "Now there is in store for me the crown of righteousness, which the Lord, the righteous Judge, will award me on that day."

None of us knows how many more days we have on this earth. The Lord can call us home at any moment. But while we are here, let us with all earnestness say, WE HAVE FOUGHT THE GOOD FIGHT. WE HAVE FINISHED THE COURSE. WE HAVE KEPT THE FAITH. ETERNITY IS ONLY A HEARTBEAT AWAY.

UPON THIS ROCK

"And I tell you that you are Peter, and on this rock I will build my church, and the gates of Hades will not overcome it." – Matthew 16:18

CHRIST IS THE ROCK

In a rock are we embedded,
And we know where we are headed,
For believing, we're receiving,
Life with Christ eternally.
From this rock we'll not be taken,
Nor can Christ, the Rock, be shaken,
For His shielding, is unyielding,
With His grip on you and me.
All efficient, all sufficient,
And with Him we'll ever be,
Throughout All Eternity.

In this passage of scripture the word used for Peter in the Greek is "Petros," but the Greek word for rock is "petra." There has been some misunderstanding concerning this passage. There is a vast difference in the meaning of "petros," as opposed to "petra." "Petros" denotes a detached, movable stone – a rock none the less, but a loose rock. The word "petra" denotes a foundational mass of immovable rock. Jesus was calling Peter a rock, but a loose rock. When He made reference to "this rock," He was describing the gospel, and the gospel is Jesus Christ, the immovable Rock. Jesus was referring to Himself.

Today, let us thank God for Christ, the immovable Rock, The foundation upon which we as Christians stand, and for His gospel which has provision for an eternity of fellowship with our Lord.

MY PEACE I GIVE YOU

"Peace I leave with you, My peace I give you. I do not give to you as the world gives. Do not let your hearts be troubled, and do not be afraid." – John 14:27

OUR SEARCH FOR PEACE

Our search for peace, within our heart,
Will cease, and fail, and fall apart,
Unless we keep, our eyes on Christ,
The One whose work has all sufficed.

"My peace I give you." What a glorious promise from our Lord. Also, Philippians 4:7 tells us that the peace of God, which transcends all understanding, will guard our hearts and our minds in Christ Jesus.

In our hectic, everyday activities, sometimes we have a tendency to forget this promise of peace from our Lord. We have our minds, and sometimes even our hearts, geared so strenuously toward the activities of the world that we lose the peace that our Lord has promised us. But regardless of our circumstances, regardless of the storm clouds that are raging in our lives, the peace that transcends all understanding is ours for the asking. We focus our eyes and our minds on Christ, and something supernatural begins to happen. To the very core of our being, we can feel His peace, and our hearts will almost be bursting with thanksgiving for what our Lord means to us.

OUR SEARCH FOR PEACE WILL SUCCESSFULLY END WITH OUR LORD JESUS CHRIST.

THE SECOND COMMANDMENT

"Love the Lord your God with all your heart and with all your soul and with all your mind. This the first and greatest commandment, and the second is like it; love your neighbor as yourself." – Matthew 22:37-39

LET'S LOVE OUR NEIGHBORS

The time of His return, should not be our concern,
The fact we know He will, gives each of us a thrill.
But, love of Christ demands, that we hear His Commands,
And love our neighbors true, with Grace and Mercy too.

We are commanded to love the Lord, and those of us who are Christians have His Spirit indwelling us as a guide and a comforter. We know we love the Lord, but is our love a passive love? How do we gauge the actual intensity of our love for Him?

His second greatest commandment was for us to love our neighbor as ourselves. And within the sphere of this commandment, we can be sure ours is an active, fervent love for the Lord if we have an intense desire to love our neighbor, then convert the passive to the active by compassion and good deeds. In Matthew 25:40, Jesus says, "The King will reply; 'I tell you the truth, whatever you did for the least of these brothers of mine, you did for me.'" It is our prayer that when we see the King, we can truly say that we loved our neighbors as ourselves.

January 23

NOTHING CAN SEPARATE US

"For I am convinced that neither death nor life, neither angels nor demons, neither the present nor the future, nor any powers; neither height nor depth, nor anything else in all creation, will be able to separate us from the love of God that is in Christ Jesus, our Lord." – Romans 8:38-39

HIS LOVE IS A REVELATION

Let us live each day with gladness,
And depend on Him above,
For He'll take away our sadness,
And replace it with His Love.
For His love's a revelation,
In it's depth, and width, and length,
He not only gives salvation,
But His Grace will be our strength.

What a promise this is. Regardless of where we are; regardless of our circumstances; nothing in this universe, nor even in all creation, can separate us from the love of God that is in Christ Jesus our Lord. God's love for us was evidenced by the gift of His Son because this is God's nature. As Vines tell us:

"It was an exercise of the Divine will in deliberate choice, made without assignable cause save that which lies in the nature of God Himself. This is agape-love that expresses the deep and constant love and interest of a perfect Being towards entirely unworthy objects. As unworthy as we are, we are the recipients of the greatest gift, God's love through our Lord Jesus Christ, and the good news is that nothing can separate us from that love."

HE WHO BEGAN A GOOD WORK

"He who began a good work in you will carry it on to completion to the day of Christ Jesus." – Philippians 1:6

HE WILL GUIDE OUR TOUR

Our future life is His to guard,
For we obtained, through Christ, our Lord,
Eternity, with Him on high,
Our soul, with Him will never die.

We have God's love, His grace, His peace,
He holds us now, and won't release,
We're in His hands, His grip is sure,
Forever will He guide our tour.

We, as human beings, even though we are Christian human beings, continue to fall into negative emotionalism when things go wrong. We are confronted with negative situations that seemingly have no solutions. In our own strength, we don't know what to do; we don't know which way to turn. Our powerlessness is from fear, a dread of what will happen. Negative emotionalism begins to push faith to one side in order to gain center stage. At that precise time we should, with all expediency, focus our attention on the promises of God.

This particular promise of God is awesome in scope. As weak and fragile and powerless as we are in our own strength, we have God's promise that since we accepted Jesus Christ as our Savior (1 John 3:2), that when He appears we shall be like Him. Then in Philippians 1:6 we have His promise to complete the good work in us even unto the day our Lord returns. What a glorious promise this is.

January 25

MY YOKE IS EASY

"Come to Me, all you who are weary and burdened, and I will give you rest. For my yoke is easy, and my burden is light." – Matthew 11:28, 30

NO LOAD IS TOO HEAVY FOR THE LORD

No load's too heavy for the Lord,
His strength is all-efficient.
His love for us is our reward,
His grace is all-sufficient.
Let's take His yoke upon us,
And let Jesus lead the way,
For His Mercy is a bonus,
And His love is ours today.

When Jesus spoke these words and referred to a yoke, we need to take note of exactly what was happening. He was speaking primarily to Jews who were under the Law. Not only were they under the Law, but the Pharisees were laying heavy burdens on them by their misguided interpretation of the Law. They were demanding meticulous obedience to manmade laws, and indeed this was a yoke.

The yoke Jesus offered was loyalty to the person of our Lord Jesus Christ, not strict adherence to a set of manmade rules. How different His yoke was. His yoke was, and is, a yoke of love.

Today, as we observe legalism in action in some churches, there seems to be a demand to obey manmade rules instead of having a personal love relationship with the Lord Jesus Christ. Instead of fear, Jesus wants us to experience the exhilarating sensation of being in love with Him. HIS YOKE IS EASY.

NO FEAR IN LOVE

"There is no fear in love, but perfect love drives out fear, because fear has to do with punishment. The one who fears is not made perfect in love." – 1 John 4:18

THROUGH FAITH, NOT FEAR

Through Faith, not fear, while we're down here,
Our eyes will peer, our ears will hear,
His message clear, we know He's near,
Indwelling here, We're His to rear.

Christ is the key, for you and me,
His love is free, and through Him we,
On bended knee, rely that he,
With us will be, eternally.

"There is no fear in love" – This great invigorating truth is for Christians only, because the love depicted here is identified as "perfect love," and that is the completed love of Jesus Christ. We have placed our complete trust in Him; consequently, our eternity is secure. This fact should dominate our thinking.

It is impossible for perfect love and fear to live in the same house. One will have to go. The non-Christian has no choice because his eternity is not secure in Christ, hence the occupant in his house cannot be perfect love, but his house will very comfortably accommodate fear. Why, as Christians, do we also make our house very comfortable for fear, instead of perfect love?

The answer to this is our mindset. We alone control what we are thinking. The old adage, "garbage-in, garbage-out," is extremely applicable in this instance. If we constantly focus our minds on our problems, those problems will magnify and multiply, then worry becomes a very deep-seated fear. But if we focus our minds on our Lord Jesus Christ and what His perfect love has done, and is doing for us, almost supernaturally we experience His peace in our life.

Let us focus our minds on Christ, so that the occupant of our house will not be fear, but will be the PERFECT LOVE OF OUR LORD JESUS CHRIST.

January 27

WHEN I AM WEAK

"For when I am weak, then I am strong." – 2 Corinthians 12:10b

STRENGTH IN WEAKNESS

Weakness makes us strong,
When we admit we're wrong,
And put our trust completely in the Lord.
Our life is turned around,
Newborn Faith is found,
The Joy of life through Christ, is our reward.

The point in time, and the circumstances under which Paul gives us this message are as follows: Paul had a "thorn in his flesh," some physical ailment that apparently was either very painful or something that he believed would severely hinder his ministry. We do not know what this thorn in the flesh was, but we do know that he asked the Lord to remove it three times, and the Lord's reply was "no," but the Lord gave him an explanation. Paul was told the Lord's grace was sufficient and that His power was made perfect in Paul's weakness (2 Corinthians 12:9).

Only when we fully realize that we are weak, will the Lord use us with His power. We must divest ourselves of any trace of pride in order to be used by the Lord to the utmost. The weaker we are, that is, the more we realize our personal limitations and depend upon His strength, the stronger we will be, because we will be using His strength and His power, instead of depending on our own. In our weakness, our prayer is that the Lord will use us in His strength.

January 28

THE JOY OF FAITH

"May the God of hope fill you with all joy and peace, as you trust in Him, so that you may overflow with hope by the power of the Holy Spirit." – Romans 15:13

FAITH BRINGS JOY

We struggle here today,
Strife along the way,
A testing in this life that we receive.
Things that so annoy,
But things that turn to JOY
When faith is placed in Christ, and we believe.

When we place our faith in the Lord, we not only receive eternal life, but we become eligible to receive the peace and the joy of Christ. There is a vast difference between being happy and being joyful. Happiness is a temporary emotion that we experience because of some happening or event that has transpired. For a short time, we are elated because things seem to have gone our way. The next thing that happens that does not go our way causes our happiness to disappear. It quickly vanishes and we find ourselves in a state of depression.

Joy and peace come from the indwelling Spirit. We should reflect on the awesome love God has for us through Jesus Christ, and that we will spend eternity with him. If we will just focus our eyes and our minds on Him instead of spending our time struggling with, and worrying about our current problems, He not only will furnish the solution, but will give us the peace and joy that surpasses all understanding. This joy is not something that can be altered by circumstances, for we know He lives, and He lives in us. Since we have exercised faith in Christ, we can have the peace and joy of Christ, if we will but focus our minds on Him. Christ is the reason and the only reason for our joy.

January 29

IN ALL THINGS, GOD

"And we know that in all things God works for the good of those who love Him, who have been called according to His purpose." – Romans 8:28

ALL THINGS WORK FOR GOOD

All things work for good – That good is understood,
When we rely on Him for all our needs.
Faithful, Loving care – the cross He had to bear,
The price He had to pay for all our deeds.

Romans 8:29 tells us, "For those God foreknew, He also predestined to be conformed to the likeness of His Son, that Christ might be the firstborn among many brothers." This means that when we exercised faith in Jesus Christ, we became members of God's family.

When we face trials and tribulations, and we seek a solution through prayer, sometimes it is exceedingly difficult for us to understand that God is working for our good. We pray for a solution, and frequently the answer to our prayer is not the solution we are seeking. We usually want an immediate solution to our immediate problem, but God, with His infinite wisdom, looks beyond the immediate need to our ultimate good. With our finite minds, how difficult it is for us to understand what our ultimate good is, but God knows, and acts accordingly.

How many times have we uttered a prayer to our Lord for an immediate solution, been disappointed with His answer, then later realized that He indeed has infinite wisdom and His answer to our prayer exceeded all of our expectations? As we grow in our Christian experience with the Lord, we begin to realize and understand more and more that God does indeed work for our good through our Lord Jesus Christ.

THE SHED BLOOD OF CHRIST

"Without the shedding of blood, there is no forgiveness." – Hebrews 9:22b

THERE'S A REASON

There's a reason for His Dying,
To cleanse our sins, and make us pure.
His blood was shed upon that tree,
That we might have eternity,
When we, in faith, accept His call,
Then we receive His Grace, His All.

With this statement, "Without the shedding of blood, there is no forgiveness," the writer of Hebrews is stating a fact that was well known by the Jewish people under the Law. On the tenth day of the seventh month, Israel observed it's most solemn holy day, the Day of Atonement. On this day, the high priest, after offering a blood sacrifice for himself, offered a second goat as a blood sacrifice for the people. The writer of Hebrews is establishing a principle that is true under the New Covenant, except that with our new High Priest, the Lord Jesus Christ. Christ, as our High Priest, had no sin so there was no need for Him to cleanse Himself. Our High Priest offered Himself as a blood sacrifice for those who, by faith, accepted Him.

Under the Old Covenant, there was atonement for sins. The word atonement was the Hebrew word "kaphar," which means to cover. Under the New Covenant, the word used is propitiation, which is the Greek word "hilaskomai," meaning, "to take away." There is a vast difference between sins being temporarily covered and sins being permanently removed.

Since God established that "without the shedding of blood, there is no forgiveness," let us be forever thankful for the cleansing blood of our Lord Jesus Christ; knowing that when we accepted His call, we also received His grace, His all.

SALVATION FOR BELIEVERS

"I am not ashamed of the gospel, because it is the power of God for salvation of everyone who believes." – Romans 1:16

GOD'S SALVATION

As we ponder God's salvation,
Let our hearts, with great elation,
Feel the rapping, and the tapping,
Of God's love upon our door.
Let us feel His mighty power,
When on earth our days go sour,
And be thankful, for the bank full,
Of His love and grace, and more.
Let our story be His glory,
Thanking Him, whom we adore,
Thanking Him forever more.

This scripture goes immediately to the truth of the gospel, "...the power of God for salvation of everyone who believes." It does not say, "everyone who works," but "everyone who believes." As crystal clear as the scripture is regarding our salvation, if we conducted a survey, even among Christians, and asked the question, "Do you believe you are going to Heaven?" The vast majority would reply, "I will if I am good enough" or "I will if I work hard enough." The truth of the matter is that none of us are good enough and none of us can work hard enough. Romans 3:23-24 tells us that all have sinned and fallen short of the glory of God and that we are justified by HIS GRACE. Ephesians 2:8-9 tells us, "For it is by grace you have been saved, through faith, and this not from yourselves, it is the gift of God, NOT BY WORKS, so that no one can boast."

God loved us so much that He made a love offering for us in the person of Jesus Christ. By a simple act of faith in Him, we receive salvation through eternity without having to earn it. The gospel is the absolute power of God to give us this glorious gift when we exercise faith in our Lord. WHAT A GIFT THIS IS.

February 1

THE POOR IN SPIRIT

"Blessed are the poor in spirit, for theirs is the Kingdom of Heaven." – Matthew 5:3

WE PONDER OUR LIMIT

Each hour and each minute, we ponder our limit,
As we stand on the threshold of time,
A struggle within us, a grace there to win us,
A Love that's so great, it's sublime.
We fall down and recover, as grace we discover,
God's gift to those who believe,
His kindness and virtue, a faith that we nurture
A life that is ours to receive.

Chapters 5, 6 and 7 of Matthew contain teachings of Jesus in the Sermon on the Mount. The very first utterance by Jesus in chapter 5 was "Blessed are the poor in spirit, for theirs is the Kingdom of Heaven." So that we can properly interpret this passage, let us consider the circumstances when Jesus spoke this truth. The Pharisees had added manmade rules and regulations that had transformed Jewish faith into a matter of religious rituals instead of faith in God. They wanted to know that they had worked hard enough and had been good enough to enter the Kingdom of Heaven.

Beginning with this very first beatitude, Jesus is teaching them that the pride of self-accomplishment, whatever the extent, is not the answer. To be "poor in spirit," to realize our own inadequacy and to place our dependence on the Lord, is the answer. This applies to our salvation as well as to our everyday living. The Pharisees taught an outward adherence to their rules and regulations. But Jesus was teaching about inner qualities, about what should really be in our heart. So today as WE PONDER OUR LIMIT, let our prayer be that we fully realize that in and of ourselves, we reached our limit long ago. But the love, the grace and the mercy that the Lord has for each one of us is UNLIMITED, and through Him, ours IS the KINGDOM OF HEAVEN.

PEACE IN CHRIST

"I have told you these things, so that in Me you may have peace. In this world you will have trouble, but take heart; I have overcome the world." – John 16:33

HIS PEACE RETURNS

The shadows fall, the light will dim,
The peace we have seems to depart,
But if we keep, our eyes on Him,
And know His love, within our heart,
His peace returns, His love so bright,
Will light our path, and show the way,
Though shadows fall, we see the light,
And then our night, turns into day.

The word "peace" used in the Old Testament was the word "shalom," which means "well being, completeness and soundness." In the New Testament, the word "peace" embodies not only those characteristics, but assumes a higher, spiritual connotation because it is a gift from God. The scriptures use this word in harmony with grace, life and righteousness.

The message for us as Christians is this:

First, Christ provided us with a solution for our sins, and by believing, our eternity is secure with him. Thus, we know that we will have the ultimate victory through Him.

Second, because of this knowledge of ultimate victory, even though this world will bring us our share of troubles, we can be assured that He has overcome the world (defeated Satan at the cross) and that IN HIM we also have His power to defeat Satan.

Jesus tells us that in Him, we may have His peace. What a glorious promise this is. Our prayer is, "Lord, help us keep our eyes and our mind focused on You, so that Your peace will be our constant companion. And even if we temporarily see the shadows fall and the light dim, we know that all we need to do is turn to You and let Your light turn our night into day. And we will experience a return of Your peace, which surpasses all understanding."

February 3

GOD'S ULTIMATE promise

"No eye has seen, no ear has heard, no mind has conceived what God has prepared for those who love Him." – 1 Corinthians 2:9

WHAT WILL HEAVEN BE LIKE?

Lord, what will Heaven be like? Will we –
Ride a bike, take a hike, smile and dream, eat ice cream,
Laugh and play, have our way, get some rest, have Your best?
Lord, we know in Heaven, we will –
Sing with glee, when we see, bow and be, at Your knee,
Sing Your praise, as we gaze, on Your face, know Your Grace,
And, Lord, we know in Heaven we will, for an eternity –
Be Your child, reconciled, have Your Love, from above,
See Your face, know Your Grace, Mercy too, BE WITH YOU.

What a wonderful, glorious promise this is. In this scripture, we are given assurance that Heaven is nothing like we have ever seen or heard on this earth. In fact, we are told that we cannot even imagine what God has prepared for those who love Him, that our finite minds cannot conceive of the glory that awaits us in Jesus Christ.

There is another important truth in this scripture. The scripture reads "...what God HAS PREPARED," not "will prepare." When we exercised our belief and faith in Christ, our reservation for a permanent dwelling place with our Lord was permanently confirmed. In John 14:1, Jesus says, "In My Father's house are many mansions; if it were not so, I would have told you. I go to prepare a place for you."

There has been much speculation about what Heaven will be like, and where it will be. As Christians, we can let our imaginations run rampant even with joyful extremism, and our minds still cannot conceive the magnitude of the glory of God with His preparations for us. As to the speculation concerning where Heaven is located, we know one thing for sure. The location may be a mystery, but Heaven is wherever Jesus is, and God's ultimate promise is that we will spend an eternity with Him. What a glorious and magnificent promise this is for those of us in Christ.

February 4

THE RAPTURE

"For the Lord Himself will come down from Heaven with a loud command, with the voice of the archangel, and with the trumpet call of God, and the dead in Christ will rise first. After that, we who are still alive and are left will be caught up together with them in the clouds to meet the Lord in the air, and so we will be with the Lord forever." – 1 Thessalonians 4:16-17

LORD, HOW WILL YOU TAKE US THERE?

Will we go on wings, other things,
Float on air, do we dare,
Soar at last, "oh so fast, "
Zip through space, ultra pace?
Lord, how will you take us there?

The word "Rapture" is not found in the Bible. However, it is the word we use to describe the meaning of these verses in 1 Corinthians. The Latin word for "caught up" is "rapturo." Thus, when we use the term "Rapture," when we describe the moment when the dead and then the living will be "caught up" in the clouds (with new spiritual bodies) to meet the Lord.

This passage of scripture, along with 1 Corinthians 15, clearly differentiates between the Rapture and the return of Christ. What we designate as the Rapture is that moment in time when, if we are in Christ, whether living or dead, we will be caught up with Christ, and be given glorified bodies, then we will be forever with the Lord.

We understand the meaning of this scripture, but as to the specific mechanics utilized by the Lord to accomplish this, we can only let our imagination flow rampant as we ponder that glorious moment when we will be united with our Lord forever. It is not important whether we "soar at last, oh so fast, or zip through space, ultra pace." The truth that is so important to Christians is that we will be with our Lord for all eternity.

February 5

GOD IS LOVE

"If anyone acknowledges that Jesus is the Son of God, God lives in him, and he in God. And so we know and rely on the love God has for us. God is love. Whoever lives in love, lives in God, and God in Him." – 1 John 4:15-16

HEAVEN'S ROMANCE

Heaven's romance, is not by chance,
This romance with our Lord.
His love so great, He seals our fate,
We're always His to guard.

We hear His plea, believe and see.
We know His love is pure.
We hear His call, He gave his all,
We know His love is sure.

In these two verses, John tells us that we have God's Spirit indwelling in us and can confidently rely and depend on the love that God has for us.

We receive God's Spirit when we have faith that Jesus Christ is the Son of God and trust that His blood was shed for the propitiation of our sins. Then after acknowledging this conviction and faith in Him, we, have a heavenly romance with our Lord.

We realize, at least to some extent, the magnitude of God's love for us, and we are almost literally swept off our feet with this realization. God is love and we are overwhelmed with the awesomeness of His love for us. This romance we have with our Lord is love in its purest sense. The courtship began with his declaration of love for us, and we responded by having faith in Him. This romance with our Lord will continue and ultimately be brought to its unblemished, eternal fruition when we at last see our Lord face-to-face. We heard His call – He gave His all – We know His love is sure.

OUR DARKNESS TURNS TO LIGHT

"I am the light of the world. Whoever follows Me will never walk in darkness, but will have the light of life." – John 8:12

THE FUNNEL IN THE TUNNEL

Lord, our soul's inside a tunnel,
Squeezing down into a funnel,
And the tunnel, in the funnel,
Seems so dark we lose our sight,
But at tunnel's end our thirsting,
Will be quenched with brilliant bursting,
And your brilliance, and resilience,
And your loving strength and might,
Is Your gifting, and the lifting,
Of the darkness of the night,
For our darkness turns to Light.

In our daily walk on this earth, we encounter difficulties. When facing these obstacles, our difficulties are so acute that our very soul focuses only on the darkness. The funnel of the tunnel seems to be swirling ever downward into an even greater degree of darkness. But we need to remember that through our Lord Jesus Christ, there is light at the end of the tunnel. The old adage suddenly becomes a reality.

Jesus has told us that He is the LIGHT OF THE WORLD. Whenever our focal point is Jesus Christ, the darkness disappears and we can see the light at the end of the tunnel.

Most of us have a tendency to worry, to be overly concerned about circumstances. Frequently our concern is so intense that it seems our very soul is consumed with fear and apprehension. The solution for this condition is not found within us, but it is found in the loving grace and mercy of Jesus Christ. Not only are we promised an eternity with Him, but we are also promised that as we follow Him, we will receive the light of life. When we keep our eyes focused on Jesus, instead of our circumstances, the funnel in the tunnel becomes loses its power. The downward plunge into darkness suddenly erupts with a brilliant bursting of light, the Light of the World, our Lord Jesus Christ.

WHO CAN BE AGAINST US?

"If God is for us, who can be against us?" – Romans 8:31

LET IT COMMENCE

God's Universe, His heavenly Realm,
To finite minds, will overwhelm,
The stars we see, up in the sky,
Seem so remote, so far, so high.

As small as we, may seem to be,
In this great realm, we cannot see,
To God, through Christ, we stand so tall,
For by our Faith, we have it all.

Through God's great Love, and through His Son,
He fought our fight, the battle's won,
And with His Life, we stand immense,
Whatever comes LET IT COMMENCE.

This could possibly be THE MOST reassuring verse in the entire Bible. "IF GOD IS FOR US, WHO CAN BE AGAINST US." I purposely deleted the question mark after this scripture; there is a reason. This is a STATEMENT OF FACT. It is truth. If we are in God's corner, it makes absolutely no difference who the adversary is. God is omnipotent (all powerful), He is omniscient (all knowing) and He is omnipresent, (present everywhere).

When we accepted Jesus Christ and put our complete trust in Him, we were automatically placed in God's corner. All of His power, all of His knowledge and His continuing presence was immediately made available to us. What can we possibly fear in this life or our life hereafter? He has already fought our fight with the death and resurrection of Jesus Christ. OUR BATTLE IS WON, and not only do we have an eternity with our Lord to look forward to, but also IN THIS LIFE, WITH HIS LIFE, WHATEVER COMES, LET IT COMMENCE.

GOD GIVES ETERNAL LIFE

"God has given us eternal life, and this life is in His Son. He who has the Son has life. He who does not have the Son does not have life." – 1 John 5:11-12

A LIFE NEVER ENDING

The light of the world, came down to unfurl,
His light, midst a world dark with sinning.
He came that He might, with His Life give Light,
For He was the Word, The Beginning.

The Light of the World, came down and unfurled,
The message of Grace He is sending.
By Faith we believed, and then we received,
Through our Lord, A LIFE NEVER ENDING.

"He who has the Son, has life." This is not only a marvelous promise from God, but we have God's pledge and assurance that when we exercise our faith, believe in and put our trust in Christ, this state of being will immediately exist. This life we receive through Christ is not something that will occur in the future. This scripture is not dealing in future tense, but rather in present tense.

Our eternity with our Lord does not begin when we die; it has already begun. It began the instant we exercised saving faith in Jesus Christ. We have His life right now, and this life that we possess through our Lord is a life that cannot be extinguished, even by death, because: The Light of the world, came down and unfurled, the message of grace He is sending. By faith, we believed, and then we received, through our Lord, A LIFE NEVER ENDING.

February 9

HE FIRST LOVED US

"We love because He first loved us. If anyone says, 'I love God,' yet hates his brother, he is a liar. For anyone who does not love his brother, whom he has seen, cannot love God, whom he has not seen." – 1 John 4:20

PASS IT ON

With death did He cleanse, the stigma of sins,
And He rose that we might keep living.
With all our sins waived, eternally saved,
By Faith we accepted His Giving.

We hold His love dear, His message is clear,
We're to "PASS HIS LOVE ON" to another,
To those whom we meet, and those whom we greet,
And to all our sisters and brothers.

There is absolutely no room for error concerning the interpretation of this scripture. We are clearly told that God loved us before we loved Him. In fact, He loved us to such an extent that He sent His only Son to this earth to suffer the pain and the humiliation of the cross in order to give us the opportunity to spend eternity with Him. What a gift this is. However, we are told to love our brother, and to love our neighbor as ourselves. How can this possibly become a reality?

Some of our neighbors, and yes, even some of our brothers and sisters in Christ at times appear to be not so lovable. In fact, at times some of them seem to be absolutely unlovable. But even though our old sin nature strains to be released with the venom of retaliation, we have a Helper Who consistently gives us the strength and the wisdom we need to meet each situation head-on and react with agape-love. This Helper is the indwelling Spirit of Christ.

Agape love is not an emotional love, and it is not love in the same sense that we associate with family. However, through our Lord, it can encompass the emotions. But agape-love is shown by our unselfish actions toward others, without any thought of benefit for ourselves. The Lord gives us this quality with His indwelling Spirit. Consequently, our attitude and actions toward others can directly display our love for God. Our prayer is that our Lord will give us the guidance and grace to realize His great love for us and to pass it on to others; To those whom we meet, and those whom we greet, and to all our sisters and brothers.

February 10

THE ANCHOR

"We have this hope as an anchor for the soul, firm and secure." – Hebrews 6:10

"…it is impossible for God to lie…" – Hebrews 6:18

CHRIST IS THE ANCHOR

Christ is the anchor for our soul, an anchor, firm and deep.
We're held by Him as storms unfold, our soul is His to keep.
Our ship will toss, and rock and roll, the tempest hits with force;
The only line we have to hold, to keep our soul on course,
Is Christ, who calms the wind and waves, The One whose love is kind,
The One, and only one who saves and gives us peace of mind.
CHRIST IS THE ANCHOR for our soul, in Him we have the best.
Our ship may toss, and rock and roll, but He will give us rest.

The writer of Hebrews uses this verse as an illustration of the certainty of God's promise. In verse 18, we are reminded that it is impossible for God to lie. Knowing this, we have the absolute certainty of our hope in the Lord Jesus Christ, our Great High Priest who will not only save our soul but will be the anchor for our soul.

In this life, our ship will not always have smooth sailing. On our course, we often detect a shift of the wind that spawns a storm that floods our ship with a torrid pelting of rain midst the intense turbulence and swelling waves. The storms completely engulf us. Our very soul is not only adrift; it is in the very midst of a pounding tempest intent on destroying us. We need an anchor, and we need it right now.

This is the GOOD NEWS. We have an anchor, and that anchor is JESUS CHRIST. We encounter the life that Christ has for us in the midst all the storms and the turbulence. However bleak and dismal tomorrow may look, drop your anchor in the bedrock of the love of God. Let Christ keep you firm and secure through the storm. As you see the waves subside and again experience the calm that follows the storm, thank Him for the ensuing peace you receive. CHRIST IS THE ANCHOR FOR OUR SOUL. IN HIM, WE HAVE THE BEST.

THE CRUCIFIXON

"Then Pilate took Jesus and had Him flogged. The soldiers twisted together a crown of thorns and put it on His head. They clothed Him in a purple robe and went up to Him again and again, saying 'Hail, King of the Jews,' and they struck Him in the face. Finally Pilate handed Him over to them to be crucified."
– John 19:1-3, 16

PAIN AND HUMILIATION

The pain He had, the agony,
The crown of thorns, humility,
The spittle there, upon His face,
This Lord of ours, they did abase.
But through it all, He passed the test,
And when they laid Him down to rest.
He rose again, to live anew,
He gives us life, and mercy, too.
We owed a debt; we could not pay,
Immersed in sin, there was no way,
Except for Him, Who loves us so,
He paid a debt, He did not owe.

When we hear the word "crucifixion," do we as Christians really understand the agony, the pain and the suffering that Jesus endured for us? They spit on Him, put a crown of thorns on His head and mocked Him. He endured the torment and the anguish of the cross for you and me, and did it voluntarily. Matthew 6:53 tells us He could at once have more than 12 legions (72,000) angels at His disposal to rescue Him. Instead, He chose to fulfill the scriptures and suffer the agony of the cross for you and me.

Jesus personally made the blood sacrifice that the Father required so that we might be cleansed of sin with His blood, and by faith be saved and spend an eternity with Him. This was God's plan. Jesus, God the Son, willingly obeyed God the Father and suffered the indignity of the cross in order that we might inherit eternal life with Him.

All of us have sinned and fallen short of the glory of God, but thanks be to Jesus Christ, WE HAD A DEBT WE COULD NOT PAY, AND HE PAID A DEBT HE DID NOT OWE, OUR SIN DEBT. This remarkable truth is a glorious example of God's love for us.

February 12

LET US DO GOOD

"Therefore, as we have the opportunity, let us do good to all people, especially to those who belong to the family of believers." – Galatians 6:10

A STUMBLING BLOCK, OR STEPPING STONE?

A Stumbling Block, A Stepping Stone,
Which one are we, you and me --?
Does His love through us shine bright?
Do they see in us, His light?
Do we try to do what's right?
Is the love of Christ passed on?
Do we live like we're alone?
Do we let His grace be known?
Which one are we, can they see?

In this verse, Paul was exhorting the Galatians to love one another, to do good to all people, especially to those who belong to the family of believers. We are also commanded by our Lord to love our neighbor. The word "neighbor" seems to be quite comprehensive in scope, and all encompassing with regard to those we know or meet. That being said, in this verse Paul gives a special admonition with regard to actions toward fellow Christians.

To set the stage for his exhortation, let us briefly review what was happening. Paul had given the Galatians the gospel. In his absence, false teachers were giving instructions that the gospel was not enough and that some rituals must be observed and work added to complete God's work. Many of these new Christians were believing what these false teachers were teaching. Paul was so enraged with this situation that he actually pronounced the strongest curse conceivable (eternal damnation) on anyone who taught anything other than the gospel of grace. To teach that one must work to gain salvation is, in effect, saying that Jesus dying on the cross was necessary, but not enough.

In our individual walk with the Lord, we encounter both new and seasoned Christians. By our actions we can both support and sustain one another, especially the new Christians who perhaps need some degree of special guidance. This places us in the position of being either a "stumbling block" or a "stepping stone." WHICH ONE ARE WE, YOU AND I? CAN THEY REALLY SEE?

February 13

ASK, SEEK AND KNOCK

"Ask and it will be given you; seek and you will find, knock, and it will be opened to you." – Matthew 7:7

WITH A KNOCK UPON HIS DOOR

Now, regardless of our gender,
He's the giver and the sender.
He's the Healer, and the Sealer,
Of our soul for evermore.
In His mercy, grace and splendor,
To each saint, He'll always render,
With His feeding, and His leading,
All His tender love, and more,
For believing, we're receiving,
WITH A KNOCK UPON HIS DOOR,
LIFE WITH HIM, FOREVERMORE

In this passage of scripture, we can very easily perceive a dual significance in the teaching of Jesus. With respect to eternal salvation, we ask, we seek and we knock by exercising saving faith in our Lord Jesus Christ. This is a "grace gift" that we receive when we put our complete trust in the Lord. However, in this particular passage of scripture, Jesus is urging us to pray. This instruction is issued in present imperative, and Jesus allegorically summarizes in subsequent verses how earthly fathers, though stained with evil, want the very best for our children. How much MORE then will our heavenly Father, who is inherently good, want they very best for His children?

Routinely we, as fathers, have good intentions and desire to give good gifts to our children, but so often don't have the resources. Moreover, the gifts we would like to give may, or may not, be best for our children. But, our heavenly Father not only knows what we truly need, but He also has the resources to fulfill that need.

He wants us to ask, and seek and knock. This communication with our Father is through prayer. When we ask within that spiritual realm, it is given to us; when we seek, it is found; and when we knock, it is opened unto us. Not only "with a knock upon His door, did we receive life forevermore," but we are told to continue to ask, and seek and knock with an unrelenting persistence and the spiritual gifts of God the Father will be ours.

February 14

MAY YOU REJOICE

"May you rejoice in the wife of your youth." – Proverbs 5:18

AN ANGEL IN DISGUISE

If I were to paint a portrait, of an angel in disguise,
I'd look no farther, for that trait, than in one I know, so wise,
In ways of tender, loving care, always giving those in need,
An angel's love, a trait so rare, and it's done in word and deed.

A beauty seen, within, without, It's a beauty, 'Oh so rare,'
It's what God's love is all about, and her countenance, so fair,
I know this angel in disguise, I've known her most my life.
My love for her soars to the skies; for this Angel is my Wife.

On Valentine's Day, our thoughts seem to turn to yesteryear. We begin to relive the events, and almost literally feel the tingle of excitement we felt when we first met the one who would become our spouse, and who would share the remainder of our life with us.

God designed and promulgated marriage. In Genesis 2:24 we are told that a man shall leave his own father and mother, and unite with his wife and the two will become one flesh. Marriage is the most intimate, most sacred and holiest relationship we will experience on this earth, except for our spiritual relationship with our Lord. When both husband and wife are Christians, this union can blossom into an exhilarating experience. We know there will be times of stress, moments of anxiety and days when the pressure mounts. But we know that as we separately grow with the Lord, we in unison grow in the Lord. Neither stress, nor anxiety, nor pressure will be intense enough to dislodge us from the peace that we receive through Christ. A good, virtuous, loving Christian wife should be treasured above all things on this earth, for she has a beauty that is not merely on the outside, but also on the inside. She is truly "an angel in disguise."

GLORIFY THE FATHER

"Let your light so shine before men, that they may see your good works, and glorify your Father in Heaven." – Matthew 5:16

OUR REASON FOR BEING

There's a reason for our being,
To glorify the Lord we love.
The scripture says, and tells to me,
To live a life, that others see,
With love and grace, He gives to each,
When they reside, within His reach.

What is the real reason for our being? Is it to be competitive in the business world? Is it to accumulate a great fortune? Is it to be the most scholarly? Is it to realize all our personal desires? Is it to be the very best husband or wife, father or mother that we can possibly be?

No.

Though some of these things are worthy, some perhaps even exemplary, none of these things are our ultimate reason for being.

The basic reason for our being is to glorify God. It's that simple. We don't accomplish this with lip service, but by letting Christ live His life through us. We have a choice: first, whether or not to accept, and put our faith in Christ for our eternity and second, whether or not to yield to Christ and let Him live His life through us. The Christian glorifies God by crucifying self and yielding totally to the leading of the indwelling Holy Spirit. This usually does not occur immediately in the lives of Christians.

When we are born again, we are immediately sanctified (set apart) by God to do good works (Ephesians 2:10). Ephesians 1:6 promises that we will one day be like Christ. However, the sanctifying process is a day-by-day, lesson-by-lesson process. The more we yield ourselves to Christ, the more Christ can work in our lives to sanctify us.

With the guiding power of the Holy Spirit, and with a yielding of our spirit, may our words and especially our actions and good works, bring glory to the Father. This is the basic and primary reason for our existence, our very being – to glorify God, through Jesus Christ. Our prayer is that this is accomplished expeditiously in the lives of each and every Christian, and that God will receive all of the glory.

OUR TESTING

"No discipline seems pleasant at the time, but painful. Later on, however, it produces a harvest of righteousness and peace for those who have been trained by it." – Hebrews 12:11

FROM TESTING TO RESTING

Lord, we ask, please let us rest from the testing.
Our soul is mired, our body aches, we're so tired.
We know, that in You only, are we nesting,
We pray, please turn our Testing into Resting.

None of us enjoy being on the receiving end of discipline. As children, we were disciplined by our parents, and even though it was for our own good, most of us just did not like it. Now, as sons and daughters of God the Father, we undergo His discipline and testing, also for our good, and we still don't like it, but we need to view this testing from God's perspective.

God disciplines us that we might share in His holiness. Through this testing, God teaches us. We might even refer to it as instructive and corrective training that prepares us for our Lord's work. In Hebrews 12:3 we are told to consider Him (Christ) who endured such opposition from sinful men, so that we will not grow weary and lose heart. Through our faith in Christ, and by the grace of God, we as Christians have an eternity with our Lord to look forward to. But if we are to serve Him now, I believe one of the very first things God wants us to learn is that there is absolutely no sufficiency in self, but there is complete sufficiency in Christ.

During our time of testing, we often reach that point where we cry out to God. We are so tired, our body aches, and our very soul seems mired in an avalanche of circumstances beyond our control. At that particular time we lift a prayer to our Lord and ask him to please "turn our testing into resting." I believe this is exactly where our Lord wants us to be. We become teachable when we are stripped of our pride and lose our self-confidence. Now the Lord can use us. Our prayer is that He will use each one of us to produce that harvest of righteousness and peace, and TO GOD BE THE GLORY.

February 17

ACCESS TO GOD

"Therefore, since we have been justified through faith, we have peace with God through our Lord Jesus Christ, through Whom we have gained access by faith into this grace in which we now stand and we rejoice in the hope of the glory of God." – Romans 5:1-2

HIS GRACE REALIGNED US

The past is behind us, there is nothing to change.
His Grace realigned us; He has widened our range,
To pass on His story, and the depth of His love,
And tell of His glory, from the Father above.

We have gained access to God's grace through Jesus Christ. By the simple act of faith in Christ we have been justified, and having been justified (declared righteous in the sight of God), we have access to peace with God. We enjoy peace with God because our future is secure. There is nothing that we can do to change the past. It is behind us; we only have today. But today, as we access God's grace through Jesus Christ, we discover a new way of life.

His grace has realigned our thinking, widened our range and broadened the scope of our understanding. We begin to comprehend the awesome spiritual power to which we have access through our Lord Jesus Christ. We start to realize the depth of His love, His mercy and His grace. We become available to be used by Him to spread the good news of the message of Jesus.

The past is behind us; there is nothing to change, but His grace has realigned us, and has widened our range, so let's pass on His story, and the depth of His love, and tell of His glory, from the Father above.

IT IS RAISED IMPERISHABLE

"So will it be with the resurrection of the dead. The body that is sown is perishable, it is raised imperishable." – 1 Corinthians 15:42

OUR FOUNTAIN OF YOUTH

The Fountain of Youth is searched for, indeed.
The search entails many cosmetics.
The search for our youth, quite often, we read,
Has little to do with genetics.

Though not so much fun, we walk and we run.
We work, and we do calisthenics.
We push up and down, and work 'til it's done,
'Til we almost strain our appendix.

But the Fountain of Youth that is ours though the Lord,
Has nothing to do with cosmetics,
For we are by grace, not only His ward,
But forever His through genetics.

For centuries, some have pursued that elusive, mythical, non-existent Fountain of Youth. Today, many of us are pursuing, to some degree, the fountain of youth. This striving determines what we eat, how we exercise and, of course for the ladies, what brand of cosmetics to use. So many, are on a crash course to look better, feel better and last longer. And though a touch of vanity might be involved, these efforts are admirable and the results are sometimes absolutely amazing. However, the only lasting fountain of youth is found through faith in Jesus Christ.

Though we may die and our bodies perish, at the Rapture we will receive a body that is absolutely imperishable, a body that will last us throughout all eternity. Can you imagine a body that not only will last forever, but also is pain free? You will find the only true Fountain of Youth in Christ. To God be the glory through our Lord and Savior, Jesus Christ.

February 19

THE FIRST FRUIT

"But the fruit of the Spirit is love." – Galatians 5:22

LORD, LET US LOVE

The Love of Christ, is ours, indeed,
His Love for you and me.
He saves our soul, and meets our need,
Whatever that may be.

So, not by fear, but free in grace,
Please let us work until,
His very Life, do we embrace,
And work to do His will.

In this scripture, the word "fruit" is singular, yet it encompasses nine specific fruits of the spirit. In Galatians 5:16, the Apostle Paul tell us to "live by the Spirit." We must note here that fruit is not produced by the branches, but by the life and strength of the vine acting through the branches (John 15:5). Our Lord is the vine; we are the branches. This fruit produced by the vine through the branches is the manifestation of our surrender and obedience to the will of the indwelling Holy Spirit.

"Love" is the very first of the nine virtues listed because God's love is the foundation upon which all virtue is produced (John 3:16 and 1 John 4:10). When we live by the Spirit, agape-love is evident in our attitude and actions toward others. Without agape-love, none of the other spiritual fruit could be produced. The fruit of the Spirit validates the existence of the Spirit of Christ dwelling within us. SO, NOT BY FEAR, BUT FREE IN GRACE, PLEASE LET US WORK UNTIL – HIS VERY LIFE DO WE EMBRACE, AND WORK TO DO HIS WILL.

THE SECOND FRUIT

"But the fruit of the Spirit is love, joy…" – Galatians 5:22

OUR JOY

The Grace of God is not a whim,
Our Joy through Christ is real.
Let's live this life with eyes on Him,
Our Hope, our Joy, our Seal.

In this scripture, the second fruit of the Spirit is "joy." First, the Apostle Paul listed the foundational virtue of love, then immediately after, Paul listed joy. We may ask ourselves if Paul had any specific reason for making joy the second virtue listed. We don't know the answer to that question, but we do know that the one and only thing that can give us joy is our relationship with Jesus Christ. No other event, no other happening and no other circumstance can deprive us of the joy of Christ if we have a personal relationship with Him. The events of life may make us unhappy and cause us to be distracted by our circumstances, but if we focus our eyes and mind on Jesus, nothing can shatter that pure, exhilarating joy that we have in Jesus Christ.

The Grace of God is not a whim,
Our Joy through Christ is real.
Let's live this life with eyes on Him,
Our hope, our Joy, Our Seal.

THE THIRD FRUIT

"But the fruit of the Spirit is love, joy, peace..." – Galatians 5:22

HIS PEACE

God's Love gives us, through Christ, our Lord,
When we believe, with all our heart,
Eternal Life, as our reward,
And through His grace, we're set apart.

But while we're here, let's do our part,
Our trust in Him, is just a start,
Let's show the world, 'ere we depart,
His Peace resides, within our heart.

In John 14:27, Jesus said, "Peace I leave with you; My peace I give you. I do not give to you as the world gives." A short time before Jesus was crucified, He promised His disciples that the Father would send them a Counselor, the Holy Spirit (John 14:26), who would bring them peace.

There is a vast difference between the world's peace and the peace that Jesus gives. The world's peace is a temporary circumstance where things seem to be under our control and we experience a momentary feeling of well being. Then we are thrust into another set of circumstances and that worldly peace disappears real fast. Either anxiety or guilt replaces it and we seem to have no control over our emotions. But there is a solution, and that solution is the peace of God through Jesus Christ.

We know that love is God's foundational gift, but upon this foundation, the Christian also receives God's gifts of joy and peace. Have you ever encountered a Christian whom you knew was struggling with some extremely difficult situation, yet exuded such a spiritual peace that it seemed to be supernatural? Well, the peace of God through Jesus Christ is supernatural and it is a gift that can be observed by others, and in turn, strengthen their faith. Our prayer is THAT WHILE WE'RE HERE, WE DO OUR PART, OUR TRUST IN HIM WAS JUST A START, LET'S SHOW THE WORLD 'ERE WE DEPART, HIS PEACE RESIDES WITHIN OUR HEART.

THE FOURTH FRUIT

"But the fruit of the Spirit is love, joy, peace, patience…" – Galatians 5:22

GIVE US PATIENCE

Lord, give us patience, and give it right now,
That's what we ask for, the what and the how,
We don't want to wait, but have You endow,
This gift of the fruit, our gift You allow.

But, Your great time clock, is not always ours,
Yours may clock eons, while our clock devours,
Seconds and minutes, and last of all, hours,
And if not by then, our impatience towers.

"Patience" is truly a characteristic of God. The KJV renders it "long-suffering." The NAS renders it "perseverance." In God's dealing with mankind, He has poured out an abundance of patience and restraint because of His great love for us. In Romans 15:5, Paul's hope is that God will grant us a like-mindedness toward one another. And in the parable of the sower (Luke 8:15), Jesus tells us that the seed in the good ground represents the ones who have heard the word with an honest and good heart and, having heard it, keep it and bring forth fruit with patience.

The gift of patience comes from God through Jesus Christ. But to receive this gift, we must cooperate with God. We must open our hearts, keep our eyes on the Lord and let Him live his life through us.

As Christians, most of us desire this gift. In fact, we want patience and we want it RIGHT NOW. We are exceedingly impatient to have patience. I believe that God answers all of our prayers, but within His divine will, the answer is sometimes "yes," sometimes "no" and sometimes "wait." It seems that we have more difficulty with the "wait" answer than we have even with the "no" answer. Is God testing our patience? I believe He is. Our prayer is that through this testing, our impatience will evaporate and be replaced with God's patience through Jesus Christ.

THE FIFTH FRUIT

"But the fruit of the Spirit is love, joy, peace, patience, kindness..." – Galatians 5:22

LET'S SHOW KINDNESS

Lord, we pray that while we're learning,
You imbue us with a yearning,
With a burning, glowing yearning,
In our hearts to do your will.
Let's show kindness to our brothers,
And be gentle to all others,
And with fervor, never swerver,
But be working here until,
We are captured, or we're raptured,
And at last our soul is still.
Lord, please help us do Your Will.

The translates the word for the fifth fruit as "gentleness," while in the NIV, the NAS, and in most of the other versions, the word is interpreted as "kindness." This is an "action fruit." Whereas love, joy and peace deal primarily with our attitude toward God, and patience deals primarily with our attitude toward others, kindness describes the actions produced by a godly attitude. With respect to our attitude toward others, kindness is the "action-result" of an attitude of patience that is tempered with the love of God. We might even express it this way: Kindness is loving patience in action.

This is certainly God's attitude toward us. He has equipped us with the indwelling Holy Spirit to have this Christ-like attitude toward others. This attitude comes to actual fruition with our acts of kindness, or gentleness to others.

Our prayer is that the Lord will use us, and that our attitude will be such that the fifth fruit of the Spirit will be clearly visible and evident in our daily walk with Him.

THE SIXTH FRUIT

"But the fruit of the Spirit is love, joy, peace, patience, kindness, goodness…" – Galatians 5:22

HIS GOODNESS

Goodness understood, all things work for good,
If we just let the Lord show us the Way,
Spirit of the Son, ours, when we are one,
And let Him live His life through us today.

Grace not to condemn, trusting only Him,
Our weakness turns to strength from Him above,
Life is turned around, newborn faith is found,
His goodness is a "Fruit" He gives with love.

"Goodness" originates with God and is ours through Jesus Christ. In the New Testament, this word is used in conjunction with the regenerate person. It denotes and signifies a moral quality that is the antithesis of evil.

As with the other fruit of the Spirit, this fruit is also a gift from God through Jesus Christ. This gift cannot be earned and it is freely given, but we need to cooperate. In Romans 8:5, the scripture tell us that "those who live according to the sinful nature have their minds set on what that nature desires, but those who live in accordance with the Spirit have their minds set on what the Spirit desires." Consequently, we as Christians have an obligation to focus on the things of the Spirit. With this mindset, the Lord can use us. When we surrender to His will, His goodness will become a fruit of the Spirit in our life.

THE SEVENTH FRUIT

"But the fruit of the Spirit is love, joy, peace, patience, kindness, goodness, faithfulness..." – Galatians 5:22

FOR BY FAITH

As we travel down earth's highway,
Leading up to Heaven's skyway,
We're relying, on His dying,
And His rising from the grave,
For by Faith are we believing,
And His Life are we receiving,
And forever, and forever,
We'll be thankful that we gave,
His great ration, of compassion,
So, we know our souls he'll save,
And through Him, triumph the grave

The KJV translates the word for this fruit of the Spirit as "faith." In most of the other translations of the Bible the word is interpreted as "faithfulness." So that we can better understand the meaning of this scripture, let us review the circumstances in which it was written.

The Galatians had heard the message of the gospel from Paul and trusted in the saving work of Jesus. But in Paul's absence, false teachers had convinced the Galatians that the gospel was not enough. They taught the Galatians that they had to do certain works and observe certain rites in order to be saved. Paul, in no uncertain terms, proclaimed this new teaching to be a false gospel and condemned those who taught it.

The only thing that we do, in regard to our salvation, is exercise faith in Jesus Christ. And we do that only by the grace of God (Ephesians 2:8). God has provided for our eternity with the cleansing blood of Christ and with the resurrected life of Christ. We "walk by faith" and the grace of God permits us to have a personal relationship with Christ. By faith we are believing, and His life we are receiving, and we know our souls He'll save, and through Him, we will triumph the grave.

THE EIGHTH FRUIT

"But the fruit of the Spirit is love, joy, peace, patience, kindness, goodness, faithfulness, gentleness…" – Galatians 5:22

BE GENTLE

Lord, when in this life we're reeling,
With our soul in need of healing,
Please don't ration, your compassion,
But let meekness rule the day.
When we falter in our weakness,
Please produce in us a meekness,
For as weakness, turns to meekness,
In Your strength we do obey,
And for brothers, and for others,
Gentle love is our today,
As they pass along our way.

The word for "gentleness" is translated as "meekness" in the KJV Bible. This fruit of the Spirit is primarily a God-given natural disposition, as Vines describes it, an inwrought grace of the soul, and the exercises of it are first and foremost toward God. However, this Christ-like virtue gives the Christian both the desire and the capacity to withstand both insult and injury. Even in the face of ridicule or derision, this fruit of the Spirit enables us to harness the power and strength of our Lord and respond with gentleness and kindness.

In this world, our natural response to an injustice done against us or our family is to get even. But with this fruit of the Spirit, our Lord gives us both the inclination and the determination to return good for evil. He equips us to do unto others as we would have them do unto us. He equips us through meekness to have the power and strength to be gentle toward others. This is truly a God-given fruit of the Spirit.

February 27

THE NINTH FRUIT

"But the fruit of the Spirit is love, joy, peace, patience, kindness, goodness, faithfulness, gentleness and self-control." – Galatians 5:22

SELF-CONTROL

When we fall our soul is sinking,
Let's let Him revise our thinking,
Then our groping, turns to coping,
As we let Him be our guide.
Self control while we are living,
Is a product of God's giving,
But compliance, not defiance,
Is our mindset to abide,
Then our striving, turns to thriving,
As our Lord walks by our side,
And we're His, to steer and guide.

This ninth fruit of the Spirit is another gift from God. It is not directed toward God, nor toward man, but toward self. It is impossible for us to have Christ's kind of self-control without the indwelling spirit of Christ. But again, we must also cooperate. We need to have the correct mindset. We are told in Galatians 5:16 to "walk by the Spirit, and we will not gratify the desires of the sinful nature." In all probability, Paul was talking to the Galatians primarily about sexual matters, but self-control in all areas of our life is not only important, but also imperative to spiritual growth.

TONGUES OF FIRE

"They saw what seemed to be tongues of fire that separated and came to rest on each of them. All of them were filled with the Holy Spirit and began to speak in other tongues as the spirit enabled them." – Acts 2:3-4

A FIRE BEFORE UNKNOWN

Eternally, with Him we'll be.
His mercy, He'll not ration.
His love and grace, for you and me,
Shows us His great compassion.

And, our soul will feel His Glory,
And a fire before unknown,
Will burn to tell His Story,
And His Seed of Love is sown.

This scripture records the fulfillment of the promise Jesus made to His disciples in John 14:26. He told them that He was going to the Father, and that He would return, but He promised that while He was away, the Father would send them a Counselor in His name, the Holy Spirit.

It is interesting to see how fear prevailed among the disciples throughout the ordeal of the arrest, the trial and the crucifixion of Jesus. But, at the feast of Pentecost, something supernatural happened. What looked like tongues of fire appeared over each disciple as they received the promised Holy Spirit. And fear was no longer foremost in their thoughts. From that day forward, the scripture records the bravery of these disciples. Fear had turned to courage.

In our walk with the Lord, we probably did not see tongues of fire hover over us when we received the Holy Spirit. But as we receive the Spirit, we pray that there will be a supernatural fire, before unknown, that works in our soul, that makes us just burn to tell His story, and thus help plant the seed of the gospel for His harvest, and His glory.

March 1

THE ENGAGEMENT RING

"Having believed, you were marked in Him with a seal, the promised Holy Spirit." – Ephesians 1:13b

WE'RE ENGAGED TO OUR LORD

He seeks our hand, engagement band,
The ring to seal our heart.
We take this ring, then our souls sing,
And this is just the start.

Engagement here, a heavenly sphere,
Preview of things to be.
His promise made, our dowry paid,
His glory, ours to see.

John 3:29 says that "the bride belongs to the Bridegroom." The Bridegroom is Jesus Christ and we who are Christians are the brides. Ephesians 1:13-14 tells how we become permanently engaged to our Lord. He has extended us an invitation, and when we accept Him (that is, place our faith in Him), we immediately receive an engagement ring from Him (the promised Holy Spirit). This is His seal, guaranteeing that we will be with Him at the wedding feast at the end of the age.

Jesus used many parables while teaching. This enabled his listeners to understand the meaning of His words. Just as the people of that time understood agriculture (the vine and the branches), they also understood the betrothal, or engagement, period and the wedding ceremony. The bride-to-be could be almost completely sure that the wedding ceremony would take place. We, as Christians, can be completely sure that the wedding ceremony with our Lord will take place. Our dowry was paid in full at the cross, so our engagement here with Him is truly a heavenly thing, a preview of things to come – His promise made, our dowry paid, His glory, ours to see.

March 2

THE WEDDING BANQUET

"But while they were on their way to buy the oil, the bridegroom arrived. The virgins who were ready went in with him to the wedding banquet, and the door was shut." – Matthew 25:10

THE BRIDEGROOM'S FEAST

The courtship starts; He owns our hearts,
He sweeps us off our feet.
No hint of guile, His manner mild,
He is the Mercy seat.

The bridegroom's feast, feast without yeast,
The bride is at His side.
Betrothal ring, the angels sing,
This marriage will abide.

As we noted in yesterday's devotional, Jesus quite frequently taught in parables. In the parable of the ten virgins recorded in Matthew 25, the oil for the lamps is a metaphor for the saving grace of the Lord Jesus Christ. The virgins who had an adequate supply of oil for their lamps were ready for the bridegroom when he arrived, and they went in with him to the wedding banquet. The virgins who lacked a sufficient supply of oil for their lamps were turned away because the door was shut. No one knew exactly when the bridegroom would arrive. Some were prepared and some were not.

The message for us in this parable is that we don't know when the Lord will return, but when He does, there will no longer be time for us to exercise faith in Him and receive His saving grace. At the moment the Bridegroom comes, THE DOOR WILL BE SHUT.

We have the opportunity to exercise saving faith in the Lord at this moment, and this assures us of an eternity with Him. The person who says, "I will do it tomorrow" has no assurance that they will have a tomorrow. We only have today.

Our prayer is that the unsaved person will submit and yield to the summons of the Spirit today, exercise faith in Jesus Christ and receive the saving grace of our Lord for all eternity. We look forward to the Bridegroom's feast where we are at His side; the betrothal ring will become the wedding ring and the angels will sing because this marriage will last for all eternity.

March 3

LIVE AS CHILDREN OF LIGHT

"For you were once darkness, but now you are light in the Lord. Live as children of light." – Ephesians 5:8

THE LORD'S GREAT LIGHT

A lamp is not a lamp, until you light it.
A wrong is still a wrong, until you right it.
But the lamp of life, is the Lord's Great Light,
And the oil of love makes it shine so bright,
That our eyes can see, and our hearts can feel,
His mercy and grace, for His love is real.

Throughout the New Testament, the words "light" and "darkness" are used metaphorically; light denoting goodness and truth, while darkness represents evil, or the concealment of sin.

In this verse, Paul reminds the Christians of Ephesus that once they walked in darkness, but now through Jesus Christ, they are light. He admonishes them to act like it, to live their lives as children of light.

Paul's admonition was also directed to every person who has trusted the Lord for salvation. We had a choice when we exercised saving faith in Jesus Christ, and we also have choices as we live this Christian life.

The Lord's great light is truly the lamp of our life, and the oil of love supplied by Him makes our lamp glow, and shine so bright – that our eyes can see, and our hearts can feel, His mercy and grace, for His love is real. The darkness dissolves and becomes light when we let the Lord's light shine in our lives.

A SPRING OF ETERNAL WATER

"But, whoever drinks the water I give him will never thirst. Indeed, the water I give him will become in him a spring of water, welling up to eternal life." – John 4:14

THE GIFT OF LIFE

A gift is not a gift, until you give it,
A life is not a life, until you live it,
But the Son of God, is the Lord who gives,
And the Son of God, is the Lord who lives,
Through the hearts of saints, that the world might see,
All the Love and Grace, He gives you and me.

In this scripture, Jesus is explaining to the Samaritan woman that the water He gives, the Holy Spirit, is living water that will not only indwell the believer, but will become a spring welling up into eternal life. In John 10:10, Jesus says, "I came that they might have life, and have it more abundantly."

In this scripture, Jesus is also teaching that, in addition to salvation, when we put our trust and our faith in Him we also have the capacity to have a quality of life here on earth that it is impossible to have otherwise. He wants us to have abundant life now.

Salvation is a gift, and we receive that gift when we place our faith in Jesus. But we also have His indwelling Spirit to guide and comfort us in this life.

The Son of God is truly the Lord who gives, and He is also the Lord who lives, through the hearts of saints, that the world might see, all the love and grace He gives you and me. We who are Christians are truly blessed.

March 5

THE RACE

"Do you not know that in a race all the runners run, but only one gets the prize? Run in such a way as to get the prize." – 1 Corinthians 9:24

LET'S WIN THIS RACE

A race is not a race, until you've run it,
A win is not a win, until you've won it,
But the race for souls, which the Lord has run,
And the win for us, which the Lord has won,
Gives to each of us, who are His by grace,
The stamina needed, to win this race.

The Olympic games originated in ancient Greek culture and athletic games and races were common. The second most prominent ancient athletic contests were the Isthmian games held in Corinth every four years.

In this scripture, Paul used the imagery of the games to make a point. In each race, there was only one winner and one prize. That prize was simply a pine wreath. The athletes would very strenuously train, and train and train in order to win the pine wreath.

Paul exhorts the Christians of Corinth to live their lives in such a manner that their lives would glorify the Lord. He urges the Christians to set their minds on spiritual things instead of secular things, thereby training, with self-discipline, to win the prize. Their prize being the incorruptible crown of pleasing the Lord, not a corruptible pine wreath that wilts and dies. Every Christian can win this race if they train for it properly.

Paul wants us to set our minds on spiritual things (Romans 8:5) in order to let our spirit, indwelt by Christ, control and break through our sinful nature. He wants us to use every opportunity to serve the Lord in whatever capacity or dimension we find ourselves.

As we run this race here on earth, let us be ever mindful of what the Lord has done for us and use the stamina that He has given, not only run the race, but to win the race for Him.

March 6

JESUS, THE LIGHT OF LIFE

"I am the light of the world. Whoever follows me will never walk in darkness, but will have the light of life." – John 8:12

THE SONG OF LIFE

A bell is not a bell, until you ring it.
A song is not a song, until you sing it.
But, the bell of life, which the Lord has rung,
And the song of life, which the Lord has sung,
Gives to each of us, who are His to hold,
The brightness to see, all His grace unfold.

In this scripture, the Jewish people understood exactly what Jesus was saying. In fact, the Pharisees challenged him about it. In their wandering in the wilderness for forty years, God provided a cloud for shade each day and a pillar of fire by night to light up the sky and guide them. The festival of Tabernacles memorialized this act of God through the lighting of giant lamps in the women's court of the temple in Jerusalem.

During this feast, Jesus now declares to them that He is the Light of the world and that whoever follows Him will not only never walk in darkness, but will have His life. This was His declaration that salvation was to be found in and through Him only, and that whoever put their trust in Him would have eternal life. This, of course, was also a declaration of His deity.

When we put our faith in Jesus, His indwelling Spirit provides us with knowledge of His truth, and the Light of the world will so illuminate our path that we never again have to walk in darkness. What a magnificent gift this is.

March 7

ETERNITY WAS GAINED

"The angel said to the women, 'Do not be afraid, for I know that you are looking for Jesus, Who was crucified. He is not here; He has risen, just as He said.'" – Matthew 28:5-6

HIS SEED OF LOVE WAS SOWN

Upon a cross, for you and me,
His body wrecked and pained,
But midst His pain, eternity,
For you and me was gained.
Upon that cross, His blood was poured.
They placed Him in a grave.
But from that grave, His body soared,
And by His life, He'll save
Those who by faith, in Him believe,
And trust in Him alone.
Eternal life, we then receive.
His seed of love was sown.

In Romans 5:10, Paul tells us that "if, when we were God's enemies, we were reconciled to Him through the death of His son, how much more having been reconciled, shall we be saved through His life?"

The cleansing blood of Christ was poured out upon that cross for you and me. The agony and the anguish He suffered was His "love-gift" to sinners. Whosoever believed in Him would be cleansed and their sins and any stigma related to their sins would be taken away, thereby enabling them to be saved by His life.

Jesus truly sowed a seed of love on a cross for you and me. His body wrecked and pained, but midst His pain, eternity, for you and me etenity was gained.

March 8

WE'RE NOT ALONE

"But a time is coming, and has now come, when you will be scattered, each to his own home. You will leave Me all alone. Yet, I am not alone, for my Father is with Me." – John 16:32

WE'LL NEVER WALK ALONE AGAIN

We'll never walk alone again.
Our Lord walks by our side.
He gives us strength; He holds our hand,
His love so great, He died –

Let's thank Him for His gift of Grace,
His life and Deity.
For His great strength, what 'ere we face,
He gives to you and me.

In this scripture, the disciples have just told Jesus that they believe He has come from God, to which Jesus responded in John 16:31 – "You believe at last." These words could also be translated, "Do you now believe?" Even through the disciples were sincere in their affirmation of belief, Jesus knew their limitations. For not until after the resurrection and the advent of the Spirit did these disciples manifest complete faith. Jesus continued his response by telling them that they would desert Him, but that His heavenly Father would not. In Hebrews 13:5 we are told that our Lord will never leave us, nor forsake us.

Jesus knew that the disciples would fail Him but He knew His Father would not. The lesson in these scriptures is so clear. Others will fail us and we will fail each other, but our Lord will never fail us. What a comforting truth this is, for we know that no matter what our circumstances might be, despite the pain, the anxiety or any anguish we might face, our Lord is with us. His Spirit dwells within us and He walks beside us. So we know beyond any shadow of a doubt, that we'll never walk alone again. What a gracious gift this is from our Lord.

March 9

THE VICTORY

"Jesus said, 'Father, forgive them for they know not what they are doing.' Jesus called out with a loud voice, 'Father, into Your hands I commit My spirit.'" – Luke 23:34, 46

THE TRIBUTE ON THAT HILL

For upon that hill was rising,
Such a tribute, and a sizing,
That was seeming to be beaming,
With a blazing glow of grace.
For, the cross that Christ would die on,
And the one that we rely on,
Is the Story of His Glory.
We can almost see his face,
With it's anguish, as we languish,
With the truth of His abase,
Which has given us God's grace.

Just before the death of Jesus, darkness reigned over the whole land for three hours from noon to 3 p.m. Then, when Jesus voluntarily died and committed His Spirit to the Father, the scriptures tell us that the curtain of the temple was torn in two from top to bottom, the earth shook, rocks split and tombs broke open. The people were terrified and exclaimed that surely this was the Son of God.

When I visualize that cross on the hill enshrouded in darkness, I know that the very earth shook. But since this was God's victory over sin and death through Jesus Christ, I envision the cross as a tribute to our Lord.

The curtain of the temple divided the Holy Place from the Most Holy Place that only the chosen priest could enter. This curtain was torn in two from top to bottom, indicating that God had torn the curtain. This event symbolized that Jesus had made it possible for all of us to have direct access to the God instead of going through the priestly system.

Though Christ suffered anguish upon that cross, He emerged triumphant and we bask in the radiance of His grace. Even though darkness prevailed for a little while, our Lord prevails forever, and that cross seems to beam with a blazing glow of the radiance of His everlasting mercy and grace, to the glory of God the Father.

THE RIGHTEOUS SHALL LIVE BY FAITH

"For in the gospel, a righteousness from God is revealed, a righteousness that is by faith, from first to last, just as it is written: 'The righteous shall live by faith.'" – Romans 1:17

BY FAITH WE ACCEPTED HIS GIVING

With death did He cleanse, the stigma of sins,
And He rose that we might keep living.
With all our sins waived, eternally saved,
By Faith, we accepted His giving.

Christians have a righteousness that is from God, a righteousness that is impossible for us to earn. We now possess the same righteousness that our Lord Jesus Christ has. This may be difficult for us to believe, but it is absolutely true. God the Father sees us through the blood of Jesus. His blood shed on that cross has changed us and washed us white as snow.

We are told in this scripture that we have a righteousness that is from God, and this righteousness is ours because of our faith in Jesus Christ. In and of ourselves, our goodness is as "filthy rags," but God has made provision to cleanse us and give us eternal life when have faith in His Son.

God has indwelt our spirit with His Spirit. Even though we still have our old sinful nature, His Spirit constantly urges us to take control of ourselves so that we can do good works in the power of the Spirit and produce good fruit. God has given us this mercy and grace because we have exercised faith in Jesus Christ, God's only Son.

The righteous live by faith, so faith is the one and only way we are to live our life. We walk by faith, knowing that God wants the very best for us, and when we are distressed with adversity, we know that "all things work for good for those who love the Lord." Our prayer is that the Lord will extend to each one of us a sufficient amount of His grace so that we can gracefully walk by faith all the days of our life. To God be the glory.

THE WAY, THE TRUTH AND THE LIFE

"I am the way, and the truth and the life. No one comes to the Father except through Me." – John 14:6

A LIFE NEVER ENDING

Christ came to this world,
Came down and unfurled,
The message of grace He is sending.
By faith we believed,
And then we received,
Through our Lord, a life never ending.

This is the sixth of the seven "I Am" statements made by Jesus, and recorded in the book of John, the other six being found in John 6:35; 8:12; 10:7-9; 10:11,14, 24-30; 11:25 and 15:1-5.

In each and every one of these "I Am" statements, Jesus is proclaiming Himself to be deity, and He is defining His role in the process of salvation, being the very embodiment of God the Father. Jesus tells us that He is not only truth and life, but He is the way to salvation. He then declares that He is the only way when He says, "No one comes to the Father except through me." This statement by Jesus absolutely eliminates all other avenues of access to God the Father. There is no other way.

Even within the realm of Christianity, if the question is asked, individual Christians regarding their assurance of personal salvation, so many times their response is, "I hope so… I am trying… If I am good enough, I'll make it." This is a direct contradiction of the grace message of our Lord. We can't work hard enough and we can't work long enough to achieve salvation. It is a free grace gift from God the Father when we put our faith in His only Son, Jesus Christ.

FOR CHRIST CAME TO THIS WORLD, CAME DOWN TO UNFURL, THE MESSAGE OF GRACE HE IS SENDING – BY FAITH WE BELIEVED, AND THEN WE RECEIVED, THROUGH OUR LORD, A LIFE NEVER ENDING.

March 12

I HAVE OVERCOME THE WORLD

"I have told you these things, so that you may have peace. In this world you will have trouble. But take heart; I have overcome the world." – John 16:33

LORD, IT'S SO COLD DOWN HERE

Lord, sometimes it seems so cold, down here,
As circumstances start to take their toll, down here,
So many things in life, we can't control, down here,
The things that seem to make us not so bold, down here,
And challenges, that try to change our goal, down here,
And sometimes, all we do is what we're told, down here,
So often, we just seem to lose our hold, down here,
And we just wait to see Your love unfold, down here,
And, we're for sure, no longer on a roll, down here.
Lord, sometimes it seems so cold, down here.

Have you ever had the distinct feeling that your circumstances were out of control and that no matter what you do or say, nothing seems to change? Have you ever faced a situation that seemed to have no solution? If you haven't yet had this experience, you probably will. Jesus, in this passage of scripture, has promised that "in this world we will have trouble." The good news is that He has also promised us a solution, and He is that solution.

Jesus tells us that He "has overcome the world." He accomplished this with his ordeal on the cross and His victory over sin and death. He tells us to "take heart," to be courageous and rejoice in His victory. His victory is our victory.

In an exposition of the scriptures by the Dallas Theological Seminary faculty, this truth was recorded. Believers have a dual existence. They are in Christ, and in this world. The world system continually exerts a hostile pressure, but Christ has overcome the world system, and so can we when we completely put our trust in Him. He has promised that in Him we can find peace. Our prayer is that when our circumstances in this world seem out of control, when, in this world it seems so cold down here, we lift our eyes heavenward, set our minds on Jesus and receive His very warm promise of peace, regardless of our circumstances. Jesus Christ is the ultimate solution to any problem we will ever encounter in this world. What a promise this is.

A GIFT FROM GOD

"Therefore, if anyone is in Christ, he is a new creation; the old has gone, the new has come. All this is from God who reconciled us to Himself through Christ, and gave us the ministry of reconciliation." – 2 Corinthians 5:17-18

WE'RE RECONCILED

A gift from God, we're reconciled,
To Him through Christ, the One defiled,
Who shed His blood, upon that tree.
He shed His blood, for you and me.

Nowhere in the New Testament does it ever say that God is reconciled to man. Instead, the New Testament teaches that man is reconciled to God. However, God took the initiative with this reconciliation. Through the propitiatory sacrifice of Christ, initiated by God, the person who exercises faith in Christ is thereby automatically delivered from the just wrath of God because of their sins. The enmity and hostility of men toward God disappears when this reconciliation occurs. God's righteousness is vindicated and man's sins are dealt with through Jesus Christ. There is no longer a sin barrier between God and man. The blood of Jesus has washed away the stain and stigma of sin, reconciling us to God and helping prepare us for a "ministry of reconciliation."

When we are reconciled to God, we are prepared with the presence of the indwelling Spirit to let the Lord use us to pass the message of the gospel on to others, and attempt to persuade them to also become reconciled to God. Our ministry of reconciliation is to invite others to repent of their sin and accept God's provision for eternal life. Our prayer is that God will use each one of us in this ministry of reconciliation to His glory.

ANOTHER GIFT FROM GOD

"This righteousness from God comes through faith in Jesus Christ to all who believe. There is no difference, for all have sinned and fall short of the glory of God, and we are justified freely by his grace, through the redemption that came by Christ Jesus." – Romans 3:22-24

WE'RE JUSTIFIED

A gift from God, we're justified,
When we accept the One who died,
And place our trust in Him alone,
The Greatest Gift, we've ever known.

Perhaps the simplest way to illustrate what the word "justification" means is to imagine a trial in which we are the defendant, and the judge is all powerful. We are charged with a crime and, if convicted, we will receive the death penalty. We are guilty. We know we are guilty and have no hope. Suddenly, someone offers to take our place and the judge accepts the offer. In fact, the judge has personally arranged for that person to take our place. He then declares us acquitted and we are set free.

The judge is God. We are the defendants and our crime is sin. We know we are guilty, and the Judge is just. Therefore, we know that our crime must be paid for, and that penalty is death. Then something extraordinary happens. The Judge (God the Father) arranges for someone else to pay for our crime. God is just; therefore, our sin-debt must be paid. But He makes the arrangement for His Son to pay our debt in full and gives us a full and complete acquittal. God judges us righteous in His sight, because we have placed our faith in His Son, Jesus Christ. This is what justification means.

ANOTHER GIFT FROM GOD

"To the church of God in Corinth, to those sanctified in Christ Jesus, and called to be holy." – 1 Corinthians 1:2

WE'RE SANCTIFIED

A gift from God, we're Sanctified,
When we accept the One who died.
We're set apart to do His will
And by His grace, we're here until
He takes us through that pearly door,
At last with Him for evermore.

The word "sanctification" means "to be set apart." This scripture gives us a clear insight into the sanctification process. First, when we exercise faith in Jesus, we are immediately saved for all eternity, given an indwelling Holy Spirit and sanctified (set apart) by God to do good works. In fact, we are declared to be holy in God's sight and He calls us "saints."

There is a difference between our "state of sanctification" and the "process of sanctification." We are immediately placed in a state of sanctification (set apart for good works) when we accept Christ, and receive the indwelling Spirit. But now the more difficult process of sanctification comes.

Through the indwelling Spirit, we are guided into the truth of God's will, but our sin nature so often resists that will. We seem to have a constant tug of war between our spirit, which is controlled by God, and our soul, or nature, which is not. Even though we have been sanctified and judged holy in His sight, we must keep our minds and hearts set on spiritual things if we are to have God's spirit control our nature. Our prayer is that the Lord will give us the strength and the will to have His Spirit do the directing during this process of sanctification.

March 16

THE GIFT OF SALVATION

"Salvation is found in no one else, for there is no other name under Heaven given to men by which we must be saved." – Acts 4:12

OUR SALVATION

Salvation comes, when we put trust,
In Christ alone, this is a must.
No judgment now, He saves our soul,
Let's live for Him, that is His goal.
Eternal life, is His accord,
We're saved by faith, through Christ, our Lord.

The word "salvation" denotes both deliverance and preservation. When we trust Christ and believe that He died for our sins and arose to give us life, we receive this salvation. This salvation, the deliverance from the sin debt we owe, is preserved forever. It is a free gift from a righteous God acting in grace toward the undeserving sinner, who by faith puts his trust in the righteousness of Christ. God through Christ, thereby removing the guilty stain of sin, justifies us. Since Christ has made peace for us through His blood on the cross, and we have put our faith in Christ, God reckons to us the perfect righteousness of Christ. In that "reckoning," God forgives our sin, reconciles us to Himself and gives us salvation – not just a deliverance, but a preserved eternity with our Lord. What a glorious gift this is.

March 17

REDEMPTION IS OURS

"Christ redeemed us from the curse of the law by becoming a curse for us." – Galatians 3:13

"In Him we have redemption through His blood, the forgiveness of sins, in accordance with the riches of God's grace." – Ephesians 1:7

REDEEMED BY HIS BLOOD

Redeemed by blood, the blood He shed,
Upon that cross, till He was dead,
But from the grave, arose to give,
To each of us, His life to live,
The ransom paid, to set us free,
Was blood He shed, upon that tree.
The sin debt paid, for you and me,
Through faith gives us, eternity.

The Greek word, "apolytrosis," is the word used in Ephesians 1:7 for redemption. This is the strongest word that could possibly be used to describe the price paid in ransom to release the slave who was under condemnation, and who, after the ransom is paid, is set free. This word is so strong and so rare that while it is found ten times in the New Testament, but only eight times in all the rest of Greek literature. It means much more than mere deliverance from something or someone. It embraces the meaning of deliverance, but only after a ransom has been paid, and it then clearly means that the subsequent state is freedom for the slave.

We existed under the curse of the Law, under the curse of our sin debt. Being made a curse for us, Christ took our place and paid our debt with His blood. He bore our curse, paid our debt and redeemed us unto freedom in which we, as Christians, now stand.

So we can in all humility say, "The ransom paid to set us free, was blood Christ shed upon that tree; the sin debt paid for you and me, through faith, gives us eternity." That eternity is with our Lord.

THE GRACE OF OUR LORD

"The God of peace will soon crush Satan under your feet. The grace of our Lord Jesus be with you." – Romans 16:20

"My grace is sufficient for you, for My power is made perfect in weakness." – 2 Corinthians 12:9

HIS GRACE WILL BE OUR STRENGTH

A new life is what He gave us,
After dying on that tree,
And through faith His life will save us,
And for all eternity.

For His love's a revelation,
In it's depth, and width, and length.
He not only gives salvation,
But His grace will be our strength.

The word "grace" in theological terms is described as "unconstrained and undeserved divine favor or goodwill." Through the grace of God, we were provided redemption and salvation through Jesus Christ. Grace is God's favor toward us that is not and cannot be earned. Romans 5:2 tells us that this "grace position" in which we now stand was given us because of our faith in Christ. We don't work for it and we can't buy it – we can only thank God for it. Romans 11:6 tells us, "If by grace, then it is no longer by works; if it were, grace would no longer be grace."

Through the grace of our Lord, we are able to live each day with His peace in our heart. Because of His love and grace, we also have His mercy, and He makes us strong. Truly His love is a revelation in its depth, width and length, for He not only gives salvation – His grace will be our strength.

March 19

JESUS GIVES US THE COUNSELOR

"But, I tell you the truth; it is for your good that I am going away. Unless I go away, the Counselor will not come to you; but if I go, I will send Him to you." – John 16:7

HE'S WITH US, ALL THE WAY

That burning is the Spirit's fire,
He tells us where to go.
He lights the fire, He gives desire.
He sets our hearts aglow.

We're Spirit led, and Spirit fed,
He guides us day by day.
We're led and fed, until we're dead.
He's with us all the way.

The Counselor that Jesus was telling His disciples about before His crucifixion is the Holy Spirit, the third Person of the Trinity. He promised them that when He departed that He would not leave them by themselves, but would send them the Holy Spirit.

We have this same promise from Jesus. When we placed our faith in Christ, we immediately received the Holy Spirit. Ephesians 1:13-14 tells us that having believed, we were marked in Christ with a seal, the promised Holy Spirit, who is a deposit guaranteeing our inheritance until that final redemption by God, when He takes us home.

There is one God and one God only, and sometimes terminology concerning the Trinity becomes rather confusing. In an effort to clarify the matter, let me illustrate with a very simple analogy. An egg is an egg, and one egg is only one egg, but that egg is composed of three different things, the shell, the white and the yolk. God is one God and one God only, but the Trinity encompasses three distinct persons: God, the Father, God, the Son and God, the Holy Spirit. The Holy Spirit enters our life at the time of our conversion, and never leaves us. He is a constant companion and helps us get through some very disagreeable circumstances. He will not leave us, so we can say, with all candor that we're Spirit-led, and Spirit-fed, and He guides us day by day, and we're led and fed, until we're dead, for He's with us all the way.

March 20

NOW NO CONDEMNATION

"There is therefore now no condemnation for those who are in Christ Jesus, because the law of the Spirit of life has set you free from the law of sin and death." – Romans 8:1-2

HIS GRACE NOT TO CONDEMN

His grace not to condemn, trusting only Him,
Our weakness turns to strength from Him above.
His grace for us so great, grace that won't abate,
A peace and joy that comes from Him, with love.

In order to put this passage in proper focus, let's review Paul's thoughts in the seventh chapter of Romans. He had just stated that he had two laws at work within him: God's law in his inner being and another law at work in the members of his body. His concluding assessment of the problem was first, a statement, "what a wretched man I am," then a question, "Who will set me free from this body of death?" His follow-up answer to that question was, "Thanks be to God, through Jesus Christ, our Lord." We then have one of the most important and dynamic statements made in the entire Bible, beginning in the first verse of the eighth chapter of Romans.

"There is therefore, now, no condemnation for those who are in Christ Jesus, for the law of the Spirit of life in Christ Jesus has set us free from the law of sin and death." The word "now" indicates that we were under condemnation. Romans 3:23 tells us, "all have sinned, and fall short of the glory of God." The indwelling Holy Spirit has given us life instead of death, a life that began with our faith and will continue and sustain us unto an eternal extension of God's overwhelming love and grace to those in Christ. We thank God for this gift.

GOD MADE HIM TO BE SIN

"He made Him who knew no sin, to be sin on our behalf that we might become the righteousness of God, in Him." – 2 Corinthians 5:21

HIS BURDEN WAS OUR SIN

Now the One who had no sin,
Became sin, the sin of men,
Except for Him, this world was surely doomed.
On that cross He suffered so,
Jesus Christ, the One we know,
His burden, was our sin that He assumed.

For just a little while, Adam and Eve walked in that garden without sin. Then they sinned. From that time until the present, only one person has ever lived who did not sin, and that was Jesus Christ. Now, it's true that Jesus was deity, but He walked this earth as a man. He was tempted continuously by sin, just as you and I am, but He remained sinless. In order to fulfill the righteous requirements of God the Father, Jesus voluntarily went to that cross and shed His blood for the remission of our sins. Hebrews 9:22 tells us "without the shedding of blood, there is no remission of sin." This was God's law, and He was, and is, just. However, because of His love for us, He extended his grace to us. He sent His only Son to the cross so that His blood shed would be propitiation for our sin.

This act of love by which God the Father displays the magnitude of his love for us through Jesus. And because of His shed blood, and our faith in Him through the grace of God, we are now, and shall ever be throughout all eternity, members of the family of God.

March 22

FROM PRIDE TO MEEKNESS

"And the boastful pride of life is not from the Father, but is from the world." – 1 John 2:16

"Pride goes before destruction; a haughty spirit before a fall." – Proverbs 16:18

"Blessed are the meek, for they will inherit the earth." – Matthew 5:5

LET'S THANK HIM FOR THE VALLEYS

A mountaintop perch, so lofty, it seems,
We swell up with pride, and trust in our dreams.
But valleys below, God gives us to find,
A meekness through Him, and our peace of mind.

Thank God for valleys, the valleys below,
Valleys we're placed in, our soul there to grow,
Love so abundant, in times of distress,
Hearts overflowing, the meek have God's rest.

These scriptures teach us that pride and a haughty spirit are of the world, for they are certainly not of God. God wants our spirit to be characterized by meekness. Paul, in 2 Corinthians 12:10, tells us that when we are weak, then we are strong. We are strong in the Lord, because our weakness turns to meekness as we realize we can't do it on our own.

In this life, most of us have, at one time or another, been on a mountaintop perch. We had things going our way. Circumstances seemed to be completely under our control. From that lofty perch on the mountaintop, inhaling that rarefied air, we would swell-up with pride as we looked down into that valley below and marvel at our self-importance. About that time our lofty perch began disintegrating, and like an avalanche, began a slide all the way into the very bottom of that valley. We no longer had things under control. Our pride vanished real fast. This is exactly where God wants us to be. We're teachable now. In our weakness, our pride turns into meekness. Now we can be molded into the kind of person that God wants us to be. Our prayer is that in all areas of our life our pride turns to meekness, all for the glory of God.

March 23

NO SEPARATION

"For I am convinced that neither death nor life, neither angels nor demons, neither the present nor the future, nor any powers, neither height nor depth, nor anything else in all creation, will be able to separate us from the love of God that is in Christ Jesus, our Lord." – Romans 8:37-38

THERE IS NOW NO SEPARATION

There is now no separation,
For the love of God through Christ.
For the final reparation,
Was His death, which did suffice.
Now, our final destination,
Is to be with Him above.
For, through Him we have salvation,
And we have it through His love.

We, as Christians, should have a peace in our heart about our future, because we are promised an eternity with our Lord. At the Rapture, whether living or dead (1 Corinthians 15) we are promised a new imperishable spiritual body as we are transformed to a state of immortality. We might even describe it this way: We have a non-cancelable reservation to meet our Lord face-to-face and spend an eternity with Him. And even though this is exciting and comforting, most of us would prefer that this reservation not be activated into reality today or tomorrow, but at some time in the future.

What most of us fail to think about, or perhaps fail to comprehend, is that at the very moment of our conversion, we met our Lord face-to-face in Spirit, because at the precise instant that we put our faith in Him, His Spirit indwelt our spirit, never to leave us. Through His Spirit, we are guided, when we let Him guide, and we are comforted, if we let Him comfort. We actually possess a supernatural power through Him if we will only yield and use it. The good news is there is NOW, no separation from the love and the grace of God. He will never leave us, nor forsake us. We have His personal guarantee and promise. What more could we ever want?

MY SHEEP HEAR MY VOICE

"My sheep hear My voice, and I know them, and they follow Me." – John 10:27

WE HEAR HIS VOICE

We hear His voice, He knows us well,
We follow Him, and this we tell,
He gives us grace, and mercy, too,
He is our guide, what 'ere we do.
Because we knocked, upon His door,
He'll take us home, for evermore.

In the days of Jesus, there were many shepherds tending their flocks. During the day, the shepherd would lead his sheep to the greenest pastures available and the best water available, so that the sheep could graze and quench their thirst. The various flocks would often intermingle because there were no fences, as we know them today. As evening approached, the shepherd would then lead his sheep to a safe place. In order to lead his sheep from place to place, the shepherd would talk to them, and the sound and tone of his voice became very familiar to his sheep. The sheep knew his voice to the exclusion of all other voices, and they would follow only him. The sheep trusted their shepherd and knew that he wanted only the best for them. They also knew that as evening approached, he would lead them into a safe place.

In these scriptures, Jesus uses this analogy to illustrate the relationship He has with believers. When we focus our minds and our hearts on Jesus, we can almost literally hear His voice as he guides and directs us throughout the day. We trust Him. We know that He wants the very best for us. We also know that as our evening approaches, He will lead us into that eternal safe place, there to reside with Him for all eternity. What a great and caring Shepherd we have.

March 25

WHAT IS THAT TO YOU?

"When Peter saw Him, he asked, 'Lord, what about him?' Jesus answered, 'If I want him to remain alive until I return, what is that to you? You must follow Me.'" – John 21:22

WE FOLLOW OUR LORD NOW

We follow our Lord now, that was His command,
Though sometimes we stumble, He then takes our hand,
His grace is sufficient, our faith and our trust,
Are in Jesus only, 'til we become dust,
And whether we live then, or lie in our grave,
Our soul and our spirit are His there to save.

To set the stage for this passage of scripture, let us review what had just happened. After Peter's denial of Jesus three times before the crucifixion, our Lord has now risen and has just reinstated Peter, directing him to feed His sheep. Then Jesus told Peter that his life would also end on a cross. Peter then asked, "Lord, what about John?" In other words, "If I am going to die on a cross, how is John going to die?" This is a prime example of pride, jealousy and self-importance. Three of the disciples had already asked Jesus which one of them would sit on His right and which one on His left. The reply that Jesus gave Peter was essentially, "Tend to your own business." For He said to Peter, "What is it to you if I want him to even remain alive until I return? You just follow Me."

There is a great lesson in this scripture for each and every one of us. There may be times that we look at others and are tempted to compare ourselves with them, even though the Bible distinctly tells us not to. We may think the Lord has blessed someone else more than He has blessed us. This was exactly what was on Peter's mind when he asked Jesus what was going to happen to John. The admonition Jesus had for Peter is applicable for us today. We need to mind our own business and just follow Him. Jesus in Matthew 23:12 tells us, "Whoever exalts himself will be humbled, and whoever humbles himself will be exalted." Our prayer is that in humble meekness, we can serve our Lord all the days of our life, then join Him for an eternity of fellowship, all because of our faith, and the grace and mercy of our Lord.

March 26

YOU FOOLISH GALATIANS

"You foolish Galatians, who has bewitched you? Before your very eyes, Jesus Christ was clearly portrayed as crucified. I would like to learn just one thing from you. Did you receive the Spirit by observing the law, or by believing what you heard?" – Galatians 3:1-2

A LIFETIME CONTRACT

In the years that lie behind us,
And the time that lies ahead,
We reflect on how He signed us,
And His cost, the blood He shed.
Now, we're on His team forever,
And we strive to give our all.
We weren't signed for our endeavor,
But responded to His call.

The pure gospel is that salvation is by faith alone in Jesus Christ. Paul had preached the one and only pure gospel to the Galatians, but some false teachers had come after Paul and had taught that salvation is by faith in Christ PLUS obedience to the Law. Paul, in no uncertain terms, was telling them how foolish they were to let anyone sway them with a false gospel. His admonitions to the Galatians included a reminder of how they received the Holy Spirit. They did not receive the Spirit by observing the law, but by faith in Jesus Christ. The entire book of Galatians seems to be aimed at, and geared toward the presentation, explanation and clarification of the one and only pure gospel of salvation. Martin Luther's rediscovery of this truth brought about the Protestant Reformation. In the year 1517, Luther posted 95 theses on a church door in Germany, the primary thrust of these being justification by faith and faith alone.

The tragic truth is that even today some churches, and some church leaders, put so much emphasis on works that their message projects salvation and justification as being the end result of, not only faith in Christ, but good works and obedience to the law. This is tragic because it is an absolute distortion of the pure gospel. We receive the free gift of justification and salvation when we exercise our faith in Jesus Christ, and in Jesus Christ alone. In Christ, we have a lifetime contract. Now, we're on His team forever, and we strive to give our all. We weren't signed for our endeavor, but responded to His call. What a great and glorious gift this is.

TO MEET THE LORD

"And the dead in Christ will rise first. After that, we who are still alive and are left will be caught up together with them in the clouds, to meet the Lord in the air. And so we will be with the Lord forever." – 1 Thessalonians 4:16b-17

FACE TO FACE

Let's spend our days, and count the ways,
To thank Him for His grace.
For in the sky, we'll rise on high,
And meet Him, face to face.

In this chapter of 1 Thessalonians, and in chapter 15 of 1 Corinthians, Paul is describing what we call the "Rapture." This is a word from the Latin Vulgate meaning "caught up." This event is clearly not he same as the Second Coming of Christ. The Rapture precedes the Second Coming.

Paul had given the Thessalonians the gospel. Many had received the gospel and believed. They were excited about meeting the Lord. Then, as time passed, some of their brothers and sisters died and the Thessalonian Christians were concerned that the dead would miss this great event. In these scriptures, Paul is giving them assurance that those already in their graves would not only, not miss this event, but would, in fact, rise and meet the Lord first. Afterward, those still living will join them; all of them will be with the Lord forever. Also, in that instant, both the living and the dead in Christ will receive new imperishable spiritual bodies that will last for all eternity. This, again, is confirmation that we who are in Christ will spend eternity with Him.

Have you ever thought about what it will be like to meet our Lord face-to face, how rarefied the spiritual air will be at that time, the degree of exhilaration we will surely feel when that great event takes place and the new energized pain-free bodies we will suddenly have? How can we ever thank Him sufficiently for His grace? It's impossible but let's spend our days, and count the ways, to thank Him for His grace, for in the sky, we'll rise on high and meet Him FACE TO FACE.

March 28

FREEDOM IN CHRIST

"It is for freedom that Christ has set us free. Stand firm, then, and do not let yourselves be burdened again by a yoke of slavery." – Galatians 5:1

WE'RE FREE IN CHRIST

We're free in Christ, to do His will.
Our sins no longer hold us.
He guides us now, and will until,
His grace and mercy mold us.
Let us stand firm, do as He wills,
His Spirit lives inside us.
With love and grace, our soul He fills,
He's walking here beside us.

In Romans 1:17, we are told that the righteous will live by faith. Not only were we declared righteous in God's sight when we put our faith in Christ, and Christ alone, but we are instructed to live by faith. In this fifth chapter of Galatians, Paul was telling the Galatians that they were "free in Christ." They possessed the indwelling Holy Spirit; they knew they would spend eternity with the Lord, and their sins had all been forgiven, cleansing them of the guilt feelings so closely associated with sin. In other words, they were free. Free to serve the Lord, free to do whatever the Lord wanted them to do, not burdened by manmade directives from false teachers, but free to have a personal relationship with our Lord Jesus Christ.

Not only is our salvation and justification by grace given us through faith, but the sanctifying process is also accomplished the same way. We are sanctified (set apart) by God to do good works. As Paul was explaining to the Galatians, we are not to let anyone put us under a legalistic system of "do"-s and "don'ts." Our high priest is Jesus Christ and we have a personal relationship with Him. Let each one of us heed Paul's admonition to the Galatians. We are free in Christ to do His will. So let us stand firm, do as He wills, His Spirit lives inside us; with love and grace, our soul He fills, He's walking here beside us.

March 29

THE SON OF GOD

"As they were coming down the mountain, Jesus instructed them, 'Don't tell anyone what you have seen, until the Son of Man has been raised from the dead.'" – Matthew 17:9

THE SON OF MAN

The Son of God, the Son of Man,
The One who saves, the One who can.
God sent His Son that He might give,
His life to us that we might live.
He walked this earth, and then He died,
He rose again and death defied.
He did this all for you and me,
That we might have eternity.

Jesus quite often referred to Himself as the "Son of Man." This was a fulfillment of prophecy from Daniel 7:13. The Jewish people should have understood the significance of this fulfillment of Daniel's vision. Daniel said that one would come that would be like unto a "son of man," who would have eternal dominion over all nations. Jesus proclaimed Himself to be that Messiah, identifying Himself as deity, with the certainty of ultimate victory. Though He humbled Himself to become truly man, His have the ultimate victory.

Through the love and grace of God, Jesus came to this earth to go to the cross and die for our sins that we might be cleansed and made acceptable to God. Then He arose from the grave to give us His life, which we, by faith, now have, giving us an assurance of eternity with Him. The term, "Son of Man," also gives witness to the fact that Jesus has a very personal knowledge of each and every temptation that we might face. In our entire life, we will never face a temptation greater than those faced by Jesus, yet He remained sinless. Although He was God, He chose to walk this earth as a man, thereby identifying with each one of us personally. He went to the cross, suffered and died, then arose, the victor over death in order to give us life. He walked this earth, then He died. He rose again, and earth defied. He did this all for you and me, that we might have eternity.

March 30

DON'T COMPARE

"We do not dare to classify or compare ourselves with some who commend themselves. When they measure themselves by themselves, and compare themselves with themselves, they are not wise." – 2 Corinthians 10:12

DON'T COMPARE

Don't compare with one another,
With a sister or a brother,
But by living, let's be giving,
All the glory to the Lord.
Let's not work for man who sees us,
But be working hard for Jesus,
Then our living, will be giving,
All the glory to the Lord,
For His tender, loving splendor,
Will attest that we're His wards,
He's our Savior, and our Lord.

For those of us who are trying to live the Christian life, we have a two-fold message from Paul in this scripture. As we are told not to compare ourselves with others, the first, and obvious, message is that, the standards set by mortals do not in any way compare with the divine excellence of Christ. The second message we receive from this scripture is that if we do compare ourselves with others, we are not wise.

When we compare ourselves with others, we automatically place ourselves in one of two positions. We think that we are either better or worse than the one whom we are comparing ourselves with. If we think we are better, we just swell up with pride as we pat ourselves on the back, a condition not unlike that of the Pharisees during the ministry of Jesus. On the other hand, if we think we are worse, we become envious, so, which sin do we want, the sin of pride, or the sin of envy? The very obvious answer is that we want neither. Our prayer is that as we live this Christian life, we keep our eyes and mind set on Jesus, not on what others do. We might even say that in most instances, we need to mind our own business, so we tell ourselves: "Don't compare with one another, with a sister, or a brother, but by living, let's be giving, all the glory to the Lord, to our Savior and our Lord."

March 31

PRESS ON

"But I press on to take hold of that for which Christ Jesus took hold of me." – Philippians 3:12b

WE KNOW THE RACE IS WON

Lord, please use us as You will,
Your work, let us fulfill,
In You we do abide,
We're Yours to steer and guide.
Please tell us what to say,
Please use us day by day.
Lord, please use us as You will.
Please use us here until,
Your work through us is done,
We see the setting sun,
We know the race is won,
At last, we see Your Son.

As in other scriptures, Paul uses athletic imagery to illustrate the reality of the sanctification process. As if in a race, Paul, the coach, is urging the Philippians, the participants, to "press on," to love one another, to help each other, to spread the gospel, to live the Christian life, to win the race, to "take hold" and to strive for perfection. Paul also declares that he has not yet attained perfection, but that he is pressing on toward new spiritual heights. What a message this is for Christians. If we press on to take hold of that which our Lord Jesus Christ has given us, we set our eyes and minds on Him. His indwelling Spirit not only directs us, but gives us His sufficiency in order to complete the task. Have you ever felt a compulsive urgency to perform, what we might term, a very difficult task for the Lord? Our first impulsive thought is usually that we are not adequate, and we are absolutely correct. But He IS adequate, in fact, He is much more than adequate. He is superbly qualified.

Lord, in our own strength we can do very little. We know this. But our prayer to You this day is, "Lord, please give us Your strength to serve You. Then, please use us as You will, please use us here until, Your work through us is done, we see the setting sun, we know the race is won – AT LAST, WE SEE YOUR SON."

NO OTHER NAME

"Salvation is found in no one else, for there is no other name under Heaven given to men by which we must be saved." – Acts 4:12

OUR WORTH IS IN HIS NAME

When our playing days are finished,
And our life on this earth ends,
Then our worth is not diminished,
But a new life just begins.

So, our age and skills will never,
Be a factor in the game,
And we're on His team forever,
For "our worth" is in "His name."

In this passage of scripture, Peter is making perfectly clear the meaning and significance of the metaphorical quotation from Psalm 118:22, which pictures Christ as the "capstone" that the builders have rejected. Peter makes it perfectly clear that this Jesus, whom the Jews have rejected, is the Messiah and that the only way under Heaven that salvation can be accomplished is through Him.

Today, as in the days Peter was preaching the gospel, this truth still applies. There is one way, and one way only, to obtain salvation, and that is through faith in Jesus Christ. Once we exercise that faith, through His grace, we are on His team forever, beginning the very instant we place our trust in Him. The great thing about being on His team is that we don't have to "tryout" each year during preseason to see if our skills have eroded, to see if we can make the team. Our worth when we joined His team was not measured by skills. Our worth is in Him. And our worth in Him has not diminished, so our age and skills will never be a factor in the game, and we're on His team forever, for our worth is in HIS NAME.

April 2

IT IS FINISHED

"When He had received the drink, Jesus said, 'It is finished.' With that He bowed His head and gave up His Spirit." – John 19:30

WE'RE RELYING ON HIS DYING

Since that sin within the garden,
God devised for us a pardon,
And the warden, with the pardon,
Is His Son, who set us free.
For, His Son, the One God gave us,
Is the One God sent to save us.
We're relying, on His dying,
And His blood shed on that tree,
For the cleaning, and the gleaning,
He extended you and me,
Cleansing us, eternally.

When Jesus hung on that cross in physical agony, weighted down by the sins of the entire world, this scripture tells us that just before He gave up His Spirit, He uttered the words "it is finished." The Greek word he spoke was "tetelestai." According to the Bible Knowledge Commentary written by the faculty of Dallas Theological Seminary, this word was used on tax receipts that have been recovered from that time period. The word "tetelestai" was written across the receipts, meaning "paid in full," thus a twofold meaning of this last utterance of Jesus before His death.

Jesus came to this earth for one purpose, and one purpose only, to go to the cross and die for the sins of the world. He obeyed the will of His Father, even unto death. What He had come into this world to do, was now accomplished. The only perfect, all encompassing sacrifice was now being offered. This was His last act of submission to His Father's will, and at that moment, He gave up His Spirit.

We talk about salvation being free, and it is free to us when we put our trust in Jesus, but it was anything but free for Jesus. He suffered on that cross, enduring not only the physical agony, but also the spiritual agony as he was made sin on our behalf. He did this in order to cleanse us that we might be acceptable to God the Father. It was the only way, and we are eternally grateful. We are relying on his dying.

April 3

WITH THE LORD FOREVER

"And so we will be with the Lord forever." – 1 Thessalonians 4:17b

HE'LL SHOW US HEAVEN'S LAND

One day we'll look, and see His face,
And see His special smile,
His tenderness, His gift of grace,
He's loved us all the while.

He'll lift us up, and make us new,
And take us to the gate,
He'll welcome us, and take us through,
And we won't have to wait.

Our bodies there, will be brand new,
He'll take us by the hand,
With love, and grace, and mercy, too,
He'll show us Heaven's land.

The word "Heaven" in the Bible is translated primarily from two words, the first being the Hebrew word "Shamayim," and the latter, the Greek word "Ouranos" The first word is plural (the heavens), and the latter being singular, but is sometimes used in the plural sense. The Greek word for Heaven is used when describing the abode of God. This is the Heaven used so frequently in the New Testament, it is in fact at times is used as a reverent name for God. As an example, in Matthew, the "Kingdom of Heaven" and the "Kingdom of God" seem to have the identical meaning.

From the scriptures, we don't know exactly what to expect, except we are promised that it will far exceed any expectations that we might have. Can't you just see Jesus, with a smile on His face, ushering us through that gate, then taking us by the hand to give us a tour? We will have new bodies, so we won't get tired. There is no sadness there, only joy and peace, and we will have an eternity to explore the wonders there. We don't know exactly where it is, or exactly what to expect, but I personally look forward to Jesus taking me by the hand, and showing me Heaven's land. It has to be a glorious place, because that is where He is.

April 4

NO CONDEMNATION

"There is therefore now no condemnation for those who are in Christ Jesus. For the law of the Spirit of life in Christ Jesus has set you free from the law of sin and of death." – Romans 8:1

THERE IS NOW NO CONDEMNATION

Condemnation for our sinning,
Was erased with Jesus winning.
Death defying, after dying,
Was His gift to you and me.
For, in us He is now living,
With His Spirit freely giving,
Us direction, and protection,
As he walks with you and me,
Through His living, He is giving,
Us His life that sets us free,
Plus a great eternity.

Romans 8:1 is perhaps the one most dynamic and most prolific statement in the entire Bible: "There is now no condemnation." This scripture, resplendent with the essence of its message, gives us a promise of no condemnation, but the key word is "now." Now that we have believed, there is no condemnation. Now that we have accepted Christ as our Savior, we are no longer condemned. This scripture tells us that now we are set free by the Spirit of life in Christ Jesus.

We were dead in our sins, and lost. Because of the love of God the Father and His only Son for each one of us, a propitiation for our sins was effected on that cross, and we were given the opportunity to be saved through simple faith in Jesus. A just God satisfied his requirement of justice by substitution. He sent His only Son to the cross to pay our sin debt with His blood, and by simple faith in Jesus, we received not only His cleansing power, and His Spirit that set us free, but we received the promise of an eternity to be spent with Him. We might express it this way: "As He walks with you and me, through His living, He is giving, us His life that sets us free, plus a Great Eternity."

April 5

ABIDE IN ME

"Now you are clean through the word which I have spoken to you. Abide in Me, and I in you. As the branch cannot bear fruit of itself, except it abide in the vine, no more can you except you abide in Me." – John 15:3-4

STUMBLING BLOCK OR STEPPING STONE?

A Stumbling Block, a Stepping Stone,
Which one are we, you and me?
Does His love through us shine bright?
Do they see in us His Light?
Do we try to do what's right?
Which one are we, can they see?

A Stumbling Block, a Stepping Stone,
Which one are we, you and me?
Lord, please help us run this race,
That through us, they might embrace,
Your eternity of grace.
Please, let us be – you and me,
For Christ alone, a Stepping-Stone.

Which one are we? A stumbling block or a stepping stone? In this scripture, in an allegory, Jesus had just finished equating Himself with the vine, and believers with the branches. The vine produces fruit through the branches, however, if the branches do not abide in the vine, there will be no fruit.

There is speculation by some that these passages of scripture teach that you can lose your salvation. But this cannot be true because verse 3 clearly states that the believer is already clean, that is, he already has eternal life because of his belief in Christ. But to produce the fruit of the Spirit, he must let the Spirit of Christ flow through him.

This precise and distinct teaching tells us that in order to become the type of person Jesus wants us to be, one that He can use to enhance His ministry here on earth, we must, as branches, let the Vine, His Holy Spirit, flow through us.

The question that we need to ask ourselves is: In His ministry here on earth, are we a stumbling block or a stepping stone? Do we, by our words and our deeds, hinder the spreading of His gospel, or do we enhance it? A stumbling block or a stepping stone – Which one are we? Can others see?

April 6

ENOUGH TROUBLE

"Each day has enough trouble of its own." – Matthew 6:34b
"In this world you will have trouble." – John 16:33b

LIFE'S A BASEBALL GAME

Our life is like baseball, for we stand at the plate,
And our swing is too fast, or our swing is too late.
We blame it on pitches, as we look at the ball.
Our life is in shambles; we just don't like the call.

But, we have a Coach now, who will teach us to hit.
Regardless of pitches, He will help us to fit,
This life altogether, as we each come to bat,
Though seldom are pitches, down the middle and fat.

He'll help us with patience, and His grace we behoove.
He'll walk with us daily, and our swing He will groove.
So, when the bad pitches, come too fast or too late,
Let's let the Lord help us, as we stand at the Plate.

In these scriptures, Jesus has promised us that "in this world we will have trouble." He also tells us that each day has enough trouble of its own, so don't worry about tomorrow, but just take care of today.

When we first trusted Jesus, and accepted His saving grace, I am sure many of us, in reverie, looked forward to a trouble-free life, because at that time, "in Him" we had it all together. The truth is that in Him we do have it all together, not that problems in our life will suddenly disappear, but that He is the solution, for He promised us in 2 Corinthians 12:9 that His grace is sufficient.

Life is like a baseball game. We stand at the plate of life and look at pitches. Some are too fast, and some are too slow, and some are too high, and some are too low. In our own strength we swing, and our swing seems to either too fast or too slow, or we don't swing. We think it's a ball, then we don't like the call, but the good news is that in Christ we now have a coach who will teach us when and how to swing. Let's keep focused on Him, and He will groove our swing, so when the bad pitches, come too fast or too late, let's let the Lord help us, as we stand at the plate.

April 7

OUR ATTITUDE

"Your attitude should be the same as that of Christ Jesus." – Philippians 2:5

LET HIS LOVE BE SHOWING

Let our attitude while living,
Show the love that Christ is giving.
Let our brothers, and all others,
See the Lord in you and me.
Let the way our brother sees us,
Be consistent with our Jesus.
Let's be caring, and be sharing,
That the world out there might see,
He's the answer, our Enhancer,
And our Lord, He'll ever be,
Throughout all eternity.

Attitude is a mindset. We know what our attitude is, and God knows what it is, but we sometimes think that others don't know. But we're wrong. Our attitude becomes very apparent by our actions. To others, our attitude is not only what they hear, but also what they see.

In this passage of scripture, Paul is admonishing the Philippians to be humble in spirit, and to love and help one another. He tells them, and he is telling us, to have the same attitude Christ had when He was on this earth. Even though he was in very nature God, He humbled Himself and became a servant, obedient unto death on a cross.

As children of God, we need to strive to be humble, not only before God, but also in our relationships with others, especially with our brothers and sisters in Christ. Some have humility before God, but are not so humble when dealing with others. Pride in our relationships with others is evidence that there is something lacking in our relationship with the Lord. Jesus was the Son of God, yet He made Himself a servant. With His indwelling Spirit, we are equipped for obedience. Our prayer is that with His undergirding strength, we can have His attitude toward others, and that our brothers and all others, can see Him in you and me, for He's our Lord for all eternity.

OUR ANOINTING

"Now it is God who makes both us and you stand firm in Christ. He anointed us, set His seal of ownership on us, and put His Spirit in our hearts as a deposit, guaranteeing what is to come." – 2 Corinthians 1:21-22

USE IT OR LOSE IT

Our position in Christ is forever,
A position that no one can sever.
We're forever with Him, and it's never,
The result of our work or endeavor.

His anointing is ours, let us use it.
It was given through Christ, don't abuse it,
For He gives us His strength, don't refuse it.
But we use it for Him, or we lose it.

The word "anointed" used in this passage of scripture is the Greek word "chrio." This particular word limits the meaning to either sacred or symbolic anointings. When we placed our faith in Jesus Christ, we were anointed with the Holy Spirit – one anointing and one Spirit. This Spirit of Christ indwells the spirit of every believer and was received immediately upon conversion, never to depart. This Spirit of Christ gives us comfort, guides, directs and gives us His strength and power; at least, to the extent we will let Him. We hear people say, "be filled with the Spirit." This simply means, "we let Him." His Spirit is always there, but we have a choice whether to obey or disobey His guidance. When we obey, we supernaturally experience His joy and peace. We actually have Christ-power that enables us to let Him live His life through us. When we don't obey, though we are saved for an eternity with Him, we no longer have that Christ-power.

So, we know His Spirit will indwell the believer forever, and, His anointing is ours, let us use it, it was given through Christ, don't abuse it. For He gives us His strength, don't refuse it, but we use it for Him or WE LOSE IT.

April 9

IN A FLASH

"In a flash, in the twinkling of an eye, at the last trumpet, for the trumpet will sound." – 1 Corinthians 15:52

THE LAST TRUMPET

Our Lord is coming back, and we know it.
God's angel has his horn, and he'll blow it,
So the seed of His love, let us sow it,
If a weed's in our field, let us hoe it,
If our grass is too high, let us mow it,
We know we love the Lord, let us show it,
For His grace and mercy, He'll bestow it,
Eternally on us, and we know it.

The word "trumpet" was used both in the Old and New Testaments. In the Old Testament it signaled the appearance of God, and in both Testaments, it signals the summons to congregate, or come together. The Jews understood the meaning of the "the last trumpet," and so did the Greeks because of its military allusion. The "last trumpet" signaled the coming of the Lord to at last take the believers home, the last call for the assembled church. Paul tells us this will happen in a flash "...in the twinkling of an eye." We call it "the Rapture of the church."

We know the Lord is coming back, but we don't know when. And before God's angel blows that trumpet, we, as Christians, need to get our personal house in order, that the Lord might use us more effectively to sow the seed of the gospel and to pass His love on other others.

None of us know how much time we have left on this earth. There is no tomorrow; there is only today. The Lord could appear at any moment, or we could go to our grave at any time. Both of these possibilities can become reality in a flash, in the twinkling of an eye, so it behooves each one of us to let the Lord work through us today, before the angel blows that trumpet. We know we love the Lord, so let's show it. We will spend an eternity with our Lord, and we know it.

April 10

LIVE BY THE SPIRIT

"So I say, live by the Spirit, and you will not gratify the desires of the sinful nature." – Galatians 5:16

OUR BEHAVIOR

Let us trust only Christ, He's our Savior.
Life forever with Him, that's His favor
He's extended to us, He won't waver,
But, let's look at ourselves, our behavior.

Paul's admonition to the Galatians, and to us, is to "live by the Spirit." We who are believers are indwelt by the Spirit of Christ. We have this Spirit mingled with our spirit, giving us guidance and direction for our lives, but we also have residing within us another entity, our "sin nature." We are naturally sinners. We don't have to work at it, it comes naturally.

When we accepted Christ, we immediately received his Spirit as a deposit, guaranteeing our salvation. His Spirit will never leave us, and will give us guidance and direction all the days of our life. Thus, our spirit, indwelt by His Spirit, has the desire to live a life that is completely acceptable to and in accordance with His will. But we have a little problem. We still have that sinful nature to deal with. We are promised in the scriptures that we will never be tempted to sin beyond what we can bear. God will provide us with "a way out" (1 Corinthians 10:13). But we also have instructions regarding what we must do in order to refrain from sinning. We must set our minds on what the Spirit desires instead of what our sinful nature desires. We must release the Spirit and let it flow outward, crushing our sin nature and curbing our sinful desires until temptation begins to wane and His Spirit takes control of our soul.

We have this power through His indwelling Spirit. Our prayer is that we will set our minds, not on what our sinful nature desires, but on what the Spirit desires. Then, and only then, can we truly and effectively live by the Spirit.

THEY CRUCIFIED HIM

"And when they had mocked Him, they took off the purple robe and put His own clothes on Him. Then they led Him out to crucify Him." – Mark 15:20

HIS ANGUISH

'Twas the slighting, and the blighting,
That produced for us the lighting,
Midst the starkness, and the darkness,
Hung our Lord upon that tree.
Let's remember why He died there,
And let us, through Him abide there,
Through His living, and the giving,
Of His blood upon that tree.
For His giving, gives us living,
And His life is ours for free.
Our Lord died upon that tree.

As we walk down the pathway of the Christian life, there are many, many pitfalls and barriers on that path. We are misunderstood. Someone is taking advantage of us. We might even be accused of something we didn't do. The person, or persons, creating this crisis in our life are either completely without compassion or not understanding or perhaps in some instances are hatefully and spitefully vindictive. We don't want to "turn the other cheek." We don't want to walk that second mile. Our very nature wants to lash out. But we really do have a problem, and that problem is that we are supposed to be equipped with the nature of Christ. We are supposed to be "big enough," to be "Christ-like" enough to handle the situation properly. But instead we say, "It's just not fair."

When we think of fairness, let us look at what happened to Jesus. They scourged Him. They spat on Him. They mocked him, then they hanged Him on a cross to die in physical and spiritual anguish. Yet He said; "Father, forgive them for they know not what they do." So, when we want to retaliate, to get even, let's remember that our particular circumstance is but a small inconvenience compared to what He endured. Our prayer is that the Lord will give us some small portion of His forgiving nature, that when others see our reaction to an injustice, our actions might remind them of Jesus.

LITTLE CHILDREN

"Jesus said, 'Let the little children come to Me, and do not hinder them, for the Kingdom of Heaven belongs to such as these.'" – Matthew 19:14

PRECIOUS LITTLE CHILD

Precious little child residing,
With the love of Christ abiding.
See the lightness, and the brightness,
Of the little smiling face.
A reminder that we're knowing,
That in Christ the child is growing.
No denying, we're relying,
On our Lord with all His grace,
His great ration, of compassion,
And the strength of His embrace,
An extension of His grace.

The gospel teaches that until and unless we exercise faith in Jesus Christ, we are not saved. Is this the pure gospel? It certainly is. Is this the true gospel? Absolutely. So, if this is the true and pure gospel, what happens to little children who die before they are old enough to know who Jesus is, and/or what they need to do to be saved? Many Christians struggle with this question because there is no direct quote in the Bible addressing this specific circumstance. However this question is answered in so many ways in the Bible. In today's scripture, Jesus says that the Kingdom of Heaven belongs to such as these little children. In Matthew 18:1-3, Jesus, responding to the question of who would be the greatest in the Kingdom of Heaven, called a little child unto Him. He told His disciples that unless they became like little children, they would never enter the Kingdom of Heaven. We also know that God is just, gracious and merciful. We also know that Adam and Eve were in God's favor until they lost their innocence and sinned when they learned the difference between good and evil. They were not held responsible until they acquired that knowledge, and neither are little children held responsible until they have that knowledge. We call it "the age of accountability," that is, the time in their lives when they are mature enough to understand the gospel. Then, and only then, are they accountable. Before that time, they are under the umbrella of the love, mercy and grace of God.

DISEASE OF THE PHARISEES

"Everything they do is done for men to see." – Matthew 23:5

A LEGALISTIC FEVER

The Pharisees, had a disease,
A legalistic fever.
When in a crowd, they were so proud,
They hindered the believer.

They were precise, their hearts like ice,
A doctrine of requiring.
No faith that's true, no birth that's new,
Our Lord, they were defying.

Not all of the Pharisees were alike. There were some Pharisees who were converted. However, the vast majority rejected Jesus and called for His arrest, that ultimately led to His death.

The Scribes interpreted the written Torah, and the Pharisees administered "to the letter" the directives that they determined should be obeyed. They had arrived at a total of 613 commandments, 248 "do"-s and 365 "don'ts." They also precisely cited 39 acts that were prohibited on the Sabbath. They took God's law, compounded it with man's law, and called all of it "God's Law."

The system under which the Pharisees operated was strict obedience and adherence to the law. There was neither love, mercy, nor grace anywhere in sight. The most important thing was either "to do," or "not to do," as manmade law indicated, and as Jesus said, "everything they did was for men to see." They swelled up with pride as they outwardly put on a show for the people, yet inwardly they had no compassion, no love for others, no mercy in their hearts. They just presented a set of manmade rules, and required others to meticulously adhere to those rules, even though they themselves did not, except to pompously deceive others. We might say, they had a disease, an extremely acute case of "legalistic fever."

This is sad, but in some of our churches today, that same toxic, legalistic fever is rampant. More emphasis is placed on "do"-s and "don't"-s than on the love and grace of our Lord. Let us determine that if our temperature rises, our fever will be well within the realm of a personal relationship with our Jesus Christ, to Whom we give all the glory.

WOE TO THE PHARISEES – FIRST OF SEVEN

"Woe to you, teachers of the law and Pharisees, you hypocrites. You shut the Kingdom of Heaven in men's faces. You yourselves do not enter, nor will you let those enter who are trying to." – Matthew 23:13

THEY MISSED ETERNITY

Now, the Pharisees rejected,
Our Lord's call to the elected.
On reflection, this rejection,
Showed contempt for all to see
For the common people sought-to,
But the provision, of derision,
By their leaders made them be,
Indecisive, and divisive,
And their faith was not to be,
So they missed eternity.

There are only two conditions that are essential to salvation, repentance and saving faith. We must know we have a problem before we seek a solution. We must be sorry for our sins before we are capable of exercising saving faith.

The Pharisees rejected Jesus, their Messiah, and turned down His offer of the Kingdom of God. The not only personally rejected His offer, but through their hypocritical actions, they kept others from accepting Him. They continued to insist that the only way for salvation, the only basis for acceptance by God, was through the works of the law. This included all 613 commandments they believed were essential. Their personal rejection of the Lord, and their insistence on strict adherence to the law caused others to reject Christ.

Today, as in the days Jesus walked this earth, religious leaders exert an abnormal amount of influence over many, many people. We have seen examples of fallen pastors, and the havoc that was wrecked on their congregations when they "fell." The members of a congregation normally look to the pastor for leadership and guidance. This puts the pastor in a position to be looked upon and looked to for directives with regard to the gospel and the living of the Christian life. Our prayer is that whomever accepts a leadership role within a church family will not only preach and teach the gospel, but will do everything possible to ensure that their words and actions will not cause anyone to miss an eternity with the Lord. To God be the glory.

WOE TO THE PHARISEES – SECOND OF SEVEN

"Woe to you, teachers of the law and Pharisees, you hypocrites. You travel over land and sea to win a single convert, and when he becomes one, you make him twice as much a son of Hell as you are." – Matthew 23:15

THE ESSENCE OF PERVERSION

'Twas the essence of perversion,
That attended their conversion,
That conversion, was perversion,
That the Pharisees performed.
They would walk and they would travel,
With a mind set to unravel,
All the teaching, and the reaching,
That our Lord, with grace had formed
For abounding, and resounding,
Was a spate that they had formed,
As this legalism stormed.

This is the second of the seven "woes" Jesus pronounced on the Pharisees. With these woes, Jesus is condemning and denouncing false religions, specifically the religion the Pharisees were promoting. Jesus reiterates how zealous they were to gain converts. They would travel over land and across the sea to gain a single convert. Their zeal was hypocritical and misguided. Some of their converts had been pagans, and they insisted that these new converts, just as all Jewish believers, keep the entire letter of the law. Thus, they put this very heavy yoke upon the converts. But some of the converts became so zealous that they "out Phariseed" the Pharisees.

This is always a possibility, and in most instances, a probability when legalism is taught. Within the realm of legalism, a person compares himself to others. It becomes a contest to see who is the best, or the worst, as the case may be. This becomes a very fertile field for pride to flourish, and if not pride, self-condemnation. Neither has a place within the realm of God's kingdom. For in His kingdom, His love, His grace and His mercy, through our Lord Jesus Christ dominates.

If we see a "spate" of legalism forming, before it becomes full grown and storming, let's set our eyes and our mind on the pure gospel, and thank God for all of the blessings we have.

April 16

WOE TO THE PHARISEES – THIRD OF SEVEN

(Abbreviated) "Woe to you, blind guides, you say if anyone swears by the temple or by the altar, it means nothing. But if anyone swears by the gold of the temple, or by the gift on the altar, he is bound by his oath. You blind fools: which is greater; the gold, or the temple that makes the gold sacred, and the gift, or the altar that makes the gift sacred?" – Matthew 23:16-22

JUST A LEGALISTIC RULING

Just a legalistic ruling,
For the ones that they were fooling,
And their fooling, by this ruling,
Was their law they misapplied,
For in dealing with the masses,
And the Jewish lads and lasses,
There was urgence, for resurgence,
To their will, but they had lied,
And abounding, was astounding,
How our Lord, they had defied,
Blighting Him, before He died.

This third "woe" deals with integrity – integrity that the Pharisees did not have. Jesus points out the complete lack of character possessed by the Pharisees. When they took an oath, the validity of their intention to keep that oath depended upon who or what they swore the oath by. They, in fact, possessed a real tricky character. When they gave someone their word, whether or not they intended to keep their word depended on what or on whom they swore by. Jesus called them "blind guides," "blind fools" and "blind men."

The lesson for us is that our word should be our bond. We shouldn't need to have to swear by anything or on anyone in order to keep our word. This practice of the Pharisees was devious to the point of promoting lying to enhance self-interest. Our prayer is that we never, under any circumstance, let self-interest, or anything else, alter our integrity.

April 17

WOE TO THE PHARISEES – FOURTH OF SEVEN

"Woe to you, teachers of the law and Pharisees, you hypocrites. You give a tenth of your spices – mint, dill and cumin. But you have neglected the more important matters of the law – justice, mercy and faithfulness. You should have practiced the latter, without neglecting the former. You blind guides. You strain out a gnat, but swallow a camel." – Matthew 23:23-24

LET'S NOT MAJOR IN THE MINOR

Let's not major in the minor,
But, let's look at something finer,
For the minor, to the whiner,
Is an exercise of pride.
Let us look at our direction,
In our process of selection,
Not neglecting, but selecting,
Who we want to be our Guide,
For the major, is no wager,
But is Truth, who death defied.
Let His Spirit be our Guide.

The Pharisees lived and taught under "the Law." Part of it was God's Law as set forth in the "Torah," compounded and greatly expanded by their inter-pretation. A part of the Law had to do with tithing, and they meticulously and pridefully set aside a tenth of what they received as a tithe for the Lord. They were so pridefully meticulous that they even counted the leaves on the mint and dill they grew. In this scripture, Jesus is not telling them to ignore God's Law. He is calling them hypocrites because they are so pridefully engaged in legalism that they have no time, and probably no inclination, to pursue and practice the important things; justice, mercy and faithfulness.

Even though we may not be in a church that is inclined toward legalism, we must be careful how we spend our time, and extremely attentive regarding the importance we place on various interests and activities within our church home. Do we major in the minor? Do we attach more importance to the organization, or socializing, or "do"-s and "don't"-s than we do to our Lord? Our prayer is that regardless of how beneficial our church programs and activities may be, we will never put anything or anyone in front of our Lord. May we never "major in the minor," but continually major in Someone "much finer," Jesus Christ.

WOE TO THE PHARISEES – FIFTH OF SEVEN

"Woe to you, teachers of the law and Pharisees, you hypocrites. You clean the outside of the cup and dish, but inside are full of greed and self-indulgence. Blind Pharisee. First clean the inside of the cup and dish, and then the outside also will be clean." – Matthew 23:25-26

ALL THAT DIRT INSIDE

With self-love in their profession,
And the guile of their expression,
Their direction, and selection,
Was an exercise of pride.
They were wont to be selective,
With a narrow self directive,
For direction, and selection,
Made them look so clean outside,
But their striving, and their driving,
Covered all that dirt inside,
And their actions, we deride.

In this scripture, Jesus is dealing with the hypocrisy of the Pharisees, in that, outwardly they appeared to be so pious, so religious and so dedicated, while inwardly, their hearts were full of greed and self-indulgence. They put on a show for the people. Jesus used the cup and dish to illustrate their hypocrisy. They were clean on the outside and dirty on the inside. Which one of us wants to drink out of a dirty cup or eat out of a dirty dish? The outside may look sparkling clean, but if we look at the inside, and see a dirty, filthy, germ-laden residue, we will neither drink out of that cup or eat from that dish. Jesus found the hypocrisy of the Pharisees revolting.

There are some today that put on a REAL GOOD SHOW, but that is exactly what it is – only a show to convince others of their goodness. They may fool us, at least for a while, but they do not fool Jesus, because Jesus looks at our hearts. He knows exactly what we think. With the cleansing power of His love, grace and mercy, may we always keep the cups and the dishes of our heart clean on the inside as well as on the outside.

WOE TO THE PHARISEES – SIXTH OF SEVEN

"Woe to you, teachers of the law and Pharisees, you hypocrites. You are like whitewashed tombs, which look beautiful on the outside, but on the inside are full of dead men's bones and everything unclean. In the same way, you appear to be righteous, but on the inside you are full of hypocrisy and wickedness." – Matthew 23:27-28

THE WHITEWASHED TOMBS

Now, the whitewashed tombs were glowing,
So that nothing dead was showing,
But we know, that the glowing,
Was to cover death inside.
And, the Pharisees, we're knowing,
On the outside then, were glowing,
And we're knowing, that their glowing,
Covered evil thoughts inside.
For their smiling, so beguiling,
Was a cover, as they lied,
Mocking Christ, our Lord who died.

During the days of our Lord's ministry, most of the tombs of the dead had been whitewashed. It has been suggested that this practice of whitewashing the tombs was done in an effort to give the locale a neater appearance. A primary reason for whitewashing tombs was to make them more visible, especially at night, because a Jew who stepped on a grave became ceremonially unclean. Regardless of the underlying motive for the whitewashing, the inference in this scripture is that these tombs appeared to be one thing on the outside, but were something entirely different on the inside. Whereas the fifth "woe" dealt primarily with the actions of the Pharisees, this woe deals basically with their appearance. On the outside, they appeared to be beautifully righteous, but on the inside, like dead men's bones, they were in a state of decay because of hypocrisy and wickedness.

In our Christian walk we may encounter some who appear to be saints, but who have a special agenda fueled by self-interest, which is definitely not glorifying to the Lord. May we have the spiritual discernment to recognize this, and the strength of our Lord not to be swayed from the straight and narrow path of righteousness. Let us "live" on the inside, as well as on the outside, for the glory of Jesus Christ.

WOE TO THE PHARISEES – SEVENTH OF SEVEN

"Woe to you, teachers of the law and Pharisees, you hypocrites. You build tombs for the prophets and decorate the graves of the righteous, and you say, if we had lived in the days of our forefathers, we would not have taken part with them in shedding the blood of the prophets. So you testify against yourselves that you are descendants of those who murdered the prophets. Fill up, then, the measure of the sin of your forefathers." – Matthew 23:29-32

TO SEE JESUS ON THAT TREE

Though they said they'd not be willing,
Of the Prophets, to be killing,
Through conniving, they were driving,
Toward that cross on Calvary.
And for them, they did not languish,
Any thoughts of our Lord's anguish,
Only gladness, and no sadness,
To see Jesus on that tree,
So beguiling, was their smiling,
With their thoughts upon that tree,
That they lost eternity.

This seventh and final "woe" emphasizes the hypocrisy of the Pharisees. They spent time building tombs and redecorating the graves of the prophets, many of whom had been killed. They vehemently avowed that had they been living when these righteous men were killed by their forefathers, that they would have had nothing to do with it. But even as they were making this statement, they were planning the death of Jesus. Our Lord used this illustration to wrap-up His condemnation of the hypocrisy of the Pharisees. Then, in overview, He continued with a stinging, scathing personal denunciation of the Pharisees, calling them "snakes" and a "brood of vipers."

As we study these seven "woes," we grasp how insidious the Pharisees were, how subtle, how malicious, how conniving. We also clearly see how our Lord reacts to the perversion of the gospel. May we, with the Lord's help, always be so focused on Him and on the truth, that we can easily recognize error when we hear it, and with His grace, correct it, all to the glory of God.

FOR I HAVE LEARNED

"For I have learned to be content, whatever the circumstances." –
Philippians 4:11b

BE CONTENT

In a quandary, often musing, with our thinking, so confusing,
Indecision, then derision, while reflecting on the past,
Mind engaged in aimless seeking, our balloon is slowly leaking,
With a rushing, and a gushing, the deflation seems so fast,
And the sorrow of the morrow, is connecting to the past,
And our soul is sinking fast.

But our thinking of the morrow, and perception of its sorrow,
Is a wasteful, and distasteful, way to spend our time today.
Christ lay down His life to win us, let His peace reside within us,
For His living, and His giving, is what's needed for today.
Let our sadness, turn to gladness, and contentment be our way,
As we trust our Lord today.

In this scripture, Paul is thanking the Philippians for gifts that he had
received from them – apparently, money to assist him in his ministry. Though
he was expressing appreciation for the gifts, he was also teaching them, and us,
a great lesson. He said, "I have learned to be content, whatever the circumstances." Paul then proceeded to give a synopsis of his life. He had turned from
a life of plenty to a life of poverty and from being well-fed, to sometimes going
hungry. He did all this for the Lord. His point was that in whatever dire circumstance he found himself, he had learned to be content. Paul used the word
"content," not "satisfied."

In our walk with the Lord, not all of our pathways are going to be paved
and smooth. Somewhere along that path we encounter "chug holes," or obstacles in our path, or even "real deep ditches." Even in the midst of circumstances
such as these, the scriptures instruct us to be content, not satisfied. But how can
we have contentment when everything in our lives is going wrong? When we set
our minds on Him, something supernatural happens and our burdens are suddenly lifted. They are shifted from us to Him, and from that moment on, we
can have His peace, and His contentment, because we have His love, and His
mercy and His grace to sustain us, and to guide us down this pathway of life.

April 22

JOINT HEIRS WITH CHRIST

"And if children, then heirs, heirs of God, and joint heirs with Christ, if indeed we share in His suffering in order that we may share in His glory." – Romans 8:17

AN HEIR WITH CHRIST

From the God of all creation,
Came a joyful revelation,
His decision, made provision,
For a Christian family.
And we're heirs with Christ while living,
Through the Father's graceful giving,
And believing, we're receiving,
Life with Him, eternally,
For creating, or relating,
Only God, who makes a tree,
Also makes a family.

"Joint heirs with Christ in the Kingdom of God;" what an incredibly marvelous truth this is. We have already received His Spirit as a deposit, guaranteeing our inheritance (Ephesians 1:13-14). This Spirit will sustain us all the days of our life here on earth, even through death, to be with our Lord in spirit until that glorious event that we call the "Rapture" takes place. Then our spirit will be enhanced with a new, glorified body, and we will spiritually and physically be with the Lord forever, and ever, throughout all eternity. This is our inheritance, but we also find, in this scripture, another truth. We look forward to sharing in His glory, but while on this earth, as Christians, we may also share in His suffering.

In some parts of the world, even today, there are saints who are put to death because of their faith. But we are fortunate to live in a nation where we have freedom of worship. However, even so, we will suffer to some extent because of our faith. We will not be accepted by some and will be ridiculed by others. But we must look forward to that glorious day when we will meet our Lord in the air with a new, resurrected, imperishable body. From that moment forward, we will be with the Lord spiritually and physically for all eternity. That is our inheritance from the God of all creation. Only God can make a tree, but he also makes a family.

GOD DISCIPLINES HIS SONS

"Our fathers disciplined us for a little while as they thought best; but God disciplines us for our good, that we may share in His holiness." – Hebrews 12:10

THROUGH HIS CARING

Let our journey, while we're living,
Be enhanced by what He's giving,
Though it's raining, with the paining,
That His discipline has wrought.
For our good, there's no denying,
Yet we face it with a sighing,
But through caring, He is sharing,
All His holiness we sought,
And His ration, of compassion,
So enormous, for it's fraught,
With the mercy His Son bought.

None of us likes discipline. As a child, most of us discovered what it was, and we didn't like it, whether it was the rod or the taking away of privileges. But most of us, as we grew into adulthood, began to realize that our parents, to the best of their ability, had been training us for "our own good," and we respected them for their efforts. In this scripture, we are promised that if we are children of God, we will be disciplined with some type of hardship – that it will be a training process, not pleasant, but for "our good." And that when we have been trained, we will enjoy a harvest of righteousness and peace.

Most of us can get into enough trouble all by ourselves. That is one thing we don't need God's assistance for. We are quite capable of personally creating situations that result in one type of hardship or another, then when we can't get out of that particular situation; we look to God for help.

Whether we create the situation, or God puts us in a particular situation, we are trained, because we begin to realize that we are not in control. We begin to grasp the truth that "we can't do it by ourselves," and that is exactly where God wants us. Then and only then will we turn to God in meekness, through Jesus Christ, and begin to reap that harvest of righteousness and peace that only our Lord can give us. So, we know that even though His discipline seems unpleasant at the time, He is actually sharing this discipline with us, that we might reap a bumper crop of His righteousness and peace, to the glory of God.

April 24

HE MUST BECOME GREATER

"That joy is mine, and is now complete, He must become greater; I must become less." – John 3:29b-30

HE IS GREATER

Now, regardless of our gender,
He's the Giver, and the Sender,
He's the Healer, and the Sealer,
Of our soul for evermore.
So, let's sooner, and not later,
Lift Him up, for He is greater,
And we ponder, at the wonder,
That He is salvation's door.
For believing, we're receiving,
With a knock upon that door,
Life with Him for ever more.

To set the stage for this scripture, let's take a look at John the Baptist, the last Old Testament prophet. He was preaching and baptizing, and had drawn enormous crowds, with many followers. Some of his followers came to him and stated that the one John had baptized (Jesus) was drawing larger crowds than John. In fact, the words used were "everyone is going to Him." John's response displayed his personal joy that the Messiah had come. He declared that, "He must become greater, and I must become less." With this statement, we have an excellent perspective with regard to John's mindset. In the first place, he experienced joy, then, with absolutely no sense of self-pride, and with no hesitation, he put Jesus first.

In our Christian walk, do we always put Jesus first? Do we put Him first in our business community, in our office, in our home? Do we take Him home from church on Sunday and spend this week with Him, or do we drop Him off as we leave the parking lot? If He knocked on our front door today, would He be a welcomed guest, or would we just not have time for Him? Our prayer is that in all areas of our life, we will never be so busy that we can't place Jesus in an absolute primary position, there to walk with Him, and talk with Him. We plan to spend an eternity with Him. So why don't we get acquainted with Him right now? Let's put Him in first place.

April 25

MAY YOUR WILL BE DONE

"Jesus prayed, 'My Father, if it is not possible for this cup to be taken away unless I drink it, may your will be done.'" – Matthew 26:39

LET'S BE WILLING

When we feel our soul is sinking,
Let's let Him revise our thinking,
And be willing, through His filling,
To obey what God has said.
For, instruction while we're living,
Is God's Will that He is giving,
Our assistance, not resistance,
Through His love as we are led,
Eases paining, and we're gaining,
Greater grace, as we are fed,
And we do what God has said.

While on this earth, Jesus was fully deity, but He was also fully man. In fact, He often referred to Himself as the "Son of Man." He could feel, just as we can feel. Pain was no stranger to Jesus; neither was humiliation or mockery. He came into this world to go to the cross, and in agony, to shed His blood for the sins of the world. He knew what He was facing. He understood the agonizing pain in store for Him, and even more so, the pure anguish that He would suffer when, for a short time, He would become sin and be forsaken by the Father. His disciples had gone to sleep, and had temporarily forsaken Him. He was alone with His thoughts. His thoughts focused on the cross, and the fact that when He would become sin, and suffer the indignities of the cross, He would then be utterly alone. Even though His Father would also forsake Him for a time, He was obedient to His Father's will, even unto death.

How often have we arrived at a crossroad in our life when our will and the Father's will were not the same? How did we react? Were we submissive to His will or did we choose our own road to travel? Our prayer is that when we again find ourselves at the crossroad, that we let the indwelling Spirit of Christ guide us, and let His strength propel us on the road of obedience, all for the glory of God, through Jesus Christ, our Lord.

April 26

I HAVE WASHED YOUR FEET

"Now that I, your Lord and Teacher, have washed your feet, you should also wash one another's feet." – John 13:14

WASHING OTHER'S FEET

On this earth, let us not grumble,
But be Christ-like, and be humble,
Never swerving, ever serving,
As if washing other's feet.
Let compassion for our brothers,
And the love of Christ for others,
Be a sharing, and a caring,
For the ones today we meet,
And the living, and the giving,
Of our Lord, let us repeat,
As if washing other's feet.

In the days that Jesus walked this earth, the prime, and almost only mode of land transportation, was by foot. Except for camels in caravans and donkeys for special occasions, everyone walked. The shoe that they used was a mere sandal with thongs to hold it on their feet. They did not know what socks were, therefore their dirty feet needed washing after walking. This was a menial task, performed on others only by servants. In this scripture, Jesus washed His disciples' feet, putting into practice the words He had spoken Mark 10:45, in which He said, "For even the Son of Man did not come to be served, but to serve." By this very act of feet washing, He humbled Himself, and made Himself a servant and then instructed His disciples to wash one another's feet.

The instructions Jesus gave His disciples concerning the washing of feet are as applicable for us today, as they were for His disciples then. Not just in a literal sense, but in spirit and in truth. When we humble ourselves and spiritually wash someone's feet, we act as a servant of our Lord. We put the needs of other people before our own personal needs.

In our Christian walk, are we willing to serve, or do we want to be served? Do we have a humble, Christ-like spirit, or do we still have a hint of pride in our attitude? Do we truly consider the needs of others to be as important as our needs? On this dusty road of life, how many "feet" have we washed today? Do we care? He does.

116

April 27

YOU FOOLISH GALATIANS

"You foolish Galatians. Who has bewitched you? Did you receive the Spirit by observing the law, or by believing what you heard?" – Galatians 3:1-2

NOT BECAUSE WE'RE WORKING
Now, in Christ, we are believing,
So, in Christ, we are receiving,
Through His living, and His giving,
Life with Him eternally,
And, His life, we know that's lurking,
Is not ours because we're working,
But His sharing, through His caring,
Is His gift to us that's free.
And we're captured, 'til we're raptured,
Then with Him, we'll ever be,
Throughout all, eternity.

Paul was extremely upset with the Galatians. He had given them the pure gospel, then in His absence, false teachers had convinced some of them that in order to be saved, they must obey the law and work – that the gospel alone was not enough. To say that Paul was upset is an understatement; Paul was furious with the false teachers and he was not too happy with the Galatians who were listening to these false teachers. Almost the entire book of Galatians projects a scathing denunciation of works, and/or observance of the law as being even remotely akin to the gospel. In fact, the Martin Luther's study of the book of Galatians was the primary motivating factor that produced the Protestant Reformation. In Romans 11:6 we are told, "and if by grace, then it is no longer by works. If it were, grace would no longer be grace."

Legalism is a creeping plague. Just a few rules, regulations and work requirements don't seem to bother most people, especially in this country where we were taught at an early age that if we wanted something, we must earn it. This seems to be our heritage. But Jesus has already removed the only price tag attached to our salvation, and we, by simple faith, receive salvation as a free grace gift from our Lord.

Let our prayer be that if we encounter even a whiff of legalism in our walk with the Lord, we will immediately recognize it and denounce it. And that we will never be in a position of being a hindrance to anyone seeking the pure truth of the gospel, and the salvation that is there is through faith in Jesus. We can bring this creeping plague of legalism to an abrupt halt with the simple application of the grace of God, through Christ.

April 28

THAT THEY MAY HAVE LIFE

"The thief comes only to steal and kill and destroy. I am come that they may have life, and have it to the full." – John 10:10

HE WANTS THE BEST

He lived and died, then death defied,
He lives in you and me.
As we abide, secure inside,
Life's fullness we can see.
He wants the best, and all the rest,
For you and me to be.
He passed the test, to give us rest,
For all eternity.

Allegorically, Jesus had just finished identifying Himself as both "the Gate for the sheep," and "the Good Shepherd." He also identified the false prophets as "the thief" who comes only to steal, kill and destroy, and, of course, the believers are identified as "the sheep." Jesus has just made two profound statements. The first being that salvation is through Him (the gate for the sheep), and the second, that He (the Good Shepherd), will die for the believer. He then proceeds to teach the difference between the false prophets and Himself, identifying His true, sacrificial love for each one of us as opposed to the false prophet's hidden agenda that contained only love for self. In other words, Jesus puts us first, while the false prophet puts himself first.

Jesus is teaching us more than one truth in this scripture. The obvious truth is that salvation is from and through Him, and that He wants us to have an abundant, joyful life, but a secondary truth is also evident. Philippians 2:5 tells us that our attitude should be the same as that of Christ Jesus. As the Good Shepherd, the interest of Jesus was His sheep, not Himself. His attitude was that of loving servant, who does what is best for others. Is this descriptive of our attitude and actions toward others? When we help others, what is our motivation? Is it pure, or do we have a hidden agenda? Do we let the love of Christ flow through us to others, or do we just receive it, then use it all ourselves?

Lord, You want us to have an abundant life. Our prayer is that Your indwelling Spirit will give us both the direction and the strength to live life to its fullest by putting others first, and by letting Your love flow through us to others through Jesus Christ.

April 29

DO NOT WORRY

"Therefore I tell you, do not worry about your life, what you will eat or drink; or about your body, what you will wear." – Matthew 6:25

ARE WE ANXIOUS?

Are we anxious, do we worry,
Are we always in a hurry,
To fume and fret, and think aloud,
And always see that big, dark cloud.
That bridge afar, we think to cross,
But woe are we, it's all or loss.
We ride the horse before we mount,
And give the sum, before we count.
We put the horse behind the cart,
And throw the bulls-eye at the dart.
We swim before we're in the pool,
Forget about the golden rule.

Just prior to this passage of scripture, Jesus had taught that we couldn't serve two masters, God and money. In 1 Timothy 6:10, we are told that the love of money is a root of all kinds of evil. Of course, money, itself, is not evil. No, money is not evil, but excessive love for money is evil. In fact, Jesus made the point that earthly possessions and heavenly treasure cannot be laid-up by men at the same time. As husbands and fathers, we need to provide food, clothing and shelter for our family. Sometimes, as we look to tomorrow, we don't know exactly how this is going to be accomplished, and we begin to worry. In our mind we see a bridge barring our way, and that bridge represents possible failure, so what do we do? In our mind, we cross that bridge time and time again. Had we only waited, we might not have had to cross that bridge at all.

The message Jesus is giving us is that if God takes care of the birds of the air and the lilies of the field, think of how very much more importance that He attaches to us. So do not worry and don't be anxious. We need to take first things first, and get our priorities in perspective. We don't need to put the horse behind the cart or throw the bull's-eye at the dart. We don't need to look for additional bridges to cross. There will be plenty, but with God's help, through the love and grace of our Lord, Jesus Christ, if there is a bridge that we must cross, let's cross it only once.

April 30

HE HAS RISEN

"He is not here; He has risen." – Matthew 28:6

THE THIRD DAY

Now, the third day there emerging,
Was our Lord, with living surging,
And the sizing of His rising,
Was for all the world to see.
For, his Father, God, had told Him,
That no tomb would ever hold Him,
And His living, loving giving,
Was His work to set us free.
And the lightness, and the brightness,
Of that Easter morn will be,
Our key to eternity.

Throughout Christianity, three of the most precious words ever uttered were, "He has risen," for we are saved by His life (Romans 5:10). If Christ had not risen, then we, also, would not rise from the grave. But the good news is that He did rise, and, as believers, so will we.

We can just visualize that Easter morning, as the sun's rays begin to gently massage the morning dew on the grave. Then behold, we see an open tomb with the angel of the Lord completely enshrouded in brilliant white, with an appearance that is like lightening; then He turns to the women and says, "He is not here; He has risen." The promised resurrection had become a reality. Our Lord was crucified until dead, then buried, but the tomb could not, and did not hold Him. He arose. He arose to offer us His life, by simple faith in Him. We accepted, and put our faith and our trust in Him, and our reward is that we will spend a joyful eternity with our Lord. His living, and His giving, was His work to set us free, and the lightness, and the brightness of that Easter Morn will be, our key to eternity.

May 1

YIELD YOURSELF

"But yield yourselves unto God." – Romans 6:13b

IF WE'LL ONLY YIELD CONTROL

In pursuit of fame and power, we just know our strength will tower,
And prevailing, in our sailing, is our pride of pure delight,
But our ship with self-direction, sails off course, without detection,
For ensuring, there is brewing, such a magnitude of might,
And the motion, on our ocean, with a gale throughout the night,
Fills our very soul with fright.

Now, this notion of the motion, of our ship upon the ocean,
Turns to lashing, and to crashing, that relieves us of control,
And the sounding, of the pounding, lets us know our ship is grounding,
And abounding, midst the grounding, is a storm within our soul,
But prevailing, midst our wailing, is God's Son, who will take hold,
If we'll only yield control.

The good ship "Christian" is sailing over this ocean of life. Christian knows the destination. The Great Mariner has even charted the simplest, safest route to follow, but there seems to be a problem. Christian knows a shortcut. He will sail right through the South Pacific, enjoying all the exotic islands, arriving and leaving as he chooses. But Christian, in his calculation, failed to take something very important into consideration – the weather. So as our good ship Christian was happily sailing along through the exotic South Pacific, a great typhoon developed. Christian was engulfed in the spawning of a spate that caused the waves to come crashing down on the little ship. The pounding was threatening an imminent grounding. All of a sudden, Christian decided he was not as much in control as he had thought. Perhaps he should have let that Great Mariner who charted his courses be in control. But when sailing was smooth, it was so difficult to yield control. But, not now – Our little ship, Christian, with tears on his sails, turned his eyes skyward, and said, "Help, Great Mariner, Help – I YIELD CONTROL."

How many of us are like our good ship, Christian? Even though we have accepted the Lord and know our destination, we know a shortcut that will enable us to be in control. And with some of us, it takes a real bad storm in our life before we are ready and willing to completely turn over control of our life to the Lord.

May 2

FEED MY SHEEP

"Jesus said, 'Feed My sheep.'" – John 21:17b

LET'S BE FEEDING

Let's not journey here in sadness,
But, let's travel here with gladness,
For the living, Lord is giving,
Us a duty here to keep.
We're to heed what He is saying,
As we go about, obeying,
And by heeding, we'll be feeding,
All His sheep, with love so deep,
That the feeding, will be leading,
Other souls to be His sheep,
And those souls, our Lord will keep.

Peter was the rock, "petros." What a rock he had been. He had given Jesus equal status with Moses and Elijah and had rebuked the Lord when Jesus told the disciples He was going to the cross. In fear, he had denied Jesus three times; then even after receiving his marching orders for evangelism, had "gone fishing." Peter could be seen as a "rock" only in the eyes of Jesus, because thus far, he had failed miserably. But after all this, Jesus effected a reconciliation. He asked Peter three times if he loved Him. Three times Peter said, "Yes Lord, You know I love You." Then Jesus said, "Feed My sheep." And the rest of the story is that Peter became that "rock" that Jesus foresaw. From a miserable failure, he became the first great evangelist and one of the very strongest leaders in the church.

Yes, Peter became that "rock." When the Spirit of Christ indwelt Peter, he became "rock solid." Just as sheep need to be fed, so do Christians in order that they might grow in the Lord. And non-Christians need to be fed the word, in order that they might accept Jesus as their Savior. How does Jesus see us? Are we a rock, or a feather? When the wind of adversity blows, do our demeanor and actions reflect the qualities of a rock, or, like a feather, do we just drift with the breeze? Are we feeding His sheep? Are there lost sheep who need to hear the gospel? Lord, our prayer is that through Your indwelling Spirit, we might become "rock solid," and with Your strength, let us feed Your sheep, all for the glory of God, through our Lord Jesus Christ.

NOTHING EXCEPT JESUS CHRIST

"For I resolved to know nothing while I was with you except Jesus Christ, and Him crucified." – 1 Corinthians 2:2

HIS BLOOD UPON THAT TREE

To our Lord who gives salvation,
Let us turn with adoration.
Let's not languish, in His anguish,
As He died upon that tree.
But, we know, in fact, His dying,
Was the proof that He was buying,
Through the raining, of the paining,
Living life, for you and me.
For the sender, of God's splendor,
Shed His blood upon that tree,
To give us eternity.

Paul, with this admonition to the Corinthians, is explaining his position in Christ. He is also giving them an insight into the powerful driving force of the Holy Spirit, who had Paul completely dominated. He first made mention of his lack of eloquence or superior wisdom, then admitted that his preaching was not with wise or persuasive words, but with the power of the indwelling Holy Spirit. As educated as Paul was, and he certainly was well educated, having studied under the most respected teacher of that day, he made a point of telling the Corinthians that nothing was important except the message of the gospel. Paul, in his humility, wanted to get the message across that the faith of the believer rested, not on men's wisdom, but on God's power.

In our daily walk with the Lord, as we attempt to tell others of the gospel, and let Him live His life through us, are we guilty of putting too much importance on eloquence of speech, or knowledge of the Bible? Do we, because of lack of biblical knowledge, feel inadequate? Are we predisposed to timidity because of this lack of knowledge? There is a vast difference between knowledge and wisdom. Even if our knowledge is somewhat limited, I firmly believe that if we are in God's will, His indwelling Spirit will guide us into all truth and will give us an incredible amount of wisdom and power, that we might be a witness for Him. Our prayer is that He will use us in His power, all for the glory of God, through our Lord, Jesus Christ.

May 4

WHEN YOU PRAY – FIRST

"And when you pray, do not be like the hypocrites." Matthew 6:5

NO HYPOCRISY

When we pray, let us be leaning,
On the Lord, Who gives us meaning,
For by leaning, He'll be cleaning,
Our soul of, hypocrisy.
For, with Him, when we are talking,
There's no show, with others gawking,
But a leaning, that has meaning,
Through our Lord, for you and me.
And His meaning, has us leaning,
Only on that bloody tree,
Where He died, for you and me.

Before Jesus gave His disciples a model prayer, which we call the "Lord's Prayer," He gave them, and us, instructions regarding how to pray. His first instruction was how not to pray. He said, "Do not pray like the hypocrites," and this specific point of reference was to the Pharisees. The Pharisees put on a show FOR MEN TO SEE, RATHER THAN MAKING A REQUEST FOR GOD TO HEAR. Both in the synagogues, and on the street, the Pharisees would make a great show of appearing righteous before men by legalistic demonstrations, while their hearts were full of greed and self-indulgence. Simply stated, they were hypocrites. Their outward appearance did not coincide with their inner convictions. Their hearts were full of pride and lust, and completely devoid of love and mercy. Their cup looked clean on the outside, but on the inside, dirt and grime rendered it unusable. Their prayers consisted of long, eloquent phrases to impress men, but this did not impress God.

In our prayer life, the Lord is not impressed with eloquence, or length, or any show of knowledge by us. Rather, He hears and answers a sincere request from our heart, if that request is within His will. Our prayer is that when we pray, our prayer is not for others to hear, but for Him to answer, all for His glory, through our Lord, Jesus Christ.

May 5

WHEN YOU PRAY – SECOND

"But when you pray, go into your room, close the door and pray to your Father, who is unseen." – Matthew 6:6

IN PRIVACY, LET'S MEET HIM

When we pray, let's be connected,
And through Him, let's be directed,
Undetected, but directed,
With the essence of our prayer.
For, in privacy, let's meet Him,
And with tender love, let's greet Him,
No deception, just perception,
Of His love, which is so rare,
And perceiving, we're believing,
And receiving loving care.
He's the answer to our prayer.

Jesus said, when you pray, go into your room, close the door and pray to your Father, who is unseen. Let's analyze exactly what Jesus was saying, and what it means to us. First, He said, "Go into your room." Find a place, or places, where you can easily communicate with the Lord in prayer. Second, He said, "close the door." Get some privacy. Find a location, or locations, where you can pray in private, not having distractions, rather, having an atmosphere of serenity, where you can have a very private conversation with the Lord. Third, Jesus said, "Pray to your Father, who is unseen." The Father is Spirit, and we worship Him in spirit and in truth. As Jesus reminded us that the Father is unseen, is it possible that He was reminding us that we should never place ourselves in a position that the thrust of our prayer could be for men to hear, instead of for God to answer?

When we go into our room and close the door, whether in our home, office or car, the door we close eliminates distraction so that we might very privately have a conversation with the Lord. Our fellowship with the Lord through prayer is the highest form of worship we can possibly achieve while on this earth. Let's thank God, through our Lord, Jesus Christ, for this privilege.

WHEN YOU PRAY – THIRD

"And when you pray, do not keep on babbling like pagans, for they think they will be heard because of their many words. Do not be like them, for your Father knows what you need before you ask Him." – Matthew 6:7-8

HE KNOWS OUR NEEDS

When we pray, let us not scatter,
Many words, for they don't matter,
But what's needed, will be heeded,
Through our Lord, who death defied.
Not desire, but what is needful,
In His promise, to be heedful.
Let His kindness, cure our blindness,
For He knows our thoughts inside,
And His gifting, so uplifting,
Meets our needs, since we've relied,
On His walking, by our side.

This is the third, and last, instructive admonition Jesus gives His disciples regarding prayer before giving them a model prayer. He had just told them not to pray like the hypocrites pray, that is for men to see. Then He instructed them to seek privacy when they pray, so there would be no distraction. And now He admonishes them not to babble on and on, thinking that a long prayer with many words would get God's attention, because God already knows what we need before we ask.

Let's delve a little deeper into the message Jesus is giving us. First, quality is better than quantity. A simple, sincere prayer lifted up to the Lord is much better than one that goes on and on and on without apparent direction. Second, the Lord knows what our needs are before we ask. Now, this is a little scary. This means that the Lord knows exactly what our thoughts are continually, and there are times when most of us, if not all of us, are not real proud of what we are thinking. We ask then, "If the Lord, knows, why do we ask in prayer?" The answer, at least partially, is that by prayer, we acknowledge His deity, and our dependence on Him, and we have prayer as a means of having fellowship with Him. The third thing we need to understand is that God has promised to meet our "needs," not our "desires." Not all of our desires are best for us, nor are they within the will of God, but all of our needs are within His will.

BY THEIR FRUIT

"Thus, by their fruit you will know them." – Matthew 7:20

A ROTTEN TREE

When we look at others sharing,
Who, indeed, seem like they're caring,
Fruitful bearing, while they're sharing,
Shows the status of the tree.
For our Lord, who is providing,
Grows the fruit, where He's residing,
But rejection, brings detection,
That the fruit that's grown will be,
Not a ration of compassion,
But a rotten fruit to see,
For it's from a rotten tree.

A good tree gears good fruit, and a rotten tree bears rotten fruit. When we see the fruit, then, we can identify the tree. In this scripture, Jesus was pointing out that the fruit the Pharisees and other false teachers were producing proved that they were, in fact, false teachers. They produced no spiritual fruit of love, joy or peace, nor did their fruit production include patience, kindness, goodness, faithfulness, gentleness or self-control (Galatians 5:22). They were hypocritically pious, self-centered, self-serving, religious, legalistic zealots. Their tree had the appearance of being a good tree until harvest time. Then based on the rotten fruit they produced, the tree itself was proven to be rotten.

A tree is still known by the fruit it produces. However, sometimes, prior to harvest time, the tree looks good, because we have not yet seen the fruit. But eventually we will, then we can identify the tree. There are many false teachers preaching today, just as there were when Jesus walked this earth. Sometimes it is difficult to identify them. Their branches appear to be strong and straight, their leaves a glossy green, and they begin to blossom. The tree looks great now, but what about harvest time? What fruit will it produce? Our prayer is that through the strength and power of the Holy Spirit, the Lord will give us the discernment to identify the false prophet, for we know that if the fruit is rotten, so is the tree. With the Lord's help, let's live our life in such a manner that there will be absolutely no doubt what kind of tree we are, because of the fruit produced.

May 8

CHRIST IS THE SAME

"Jesus Christ is the same yesterday, today and forever." – Hebrews 13:8

ALWAYS THE SAME

Let us thank our Lord, up yonder,
For the great and glorious wonder,
Of creation, and salvation,
As upon this earth He came.
Yesterday, is like tomorrow,
With the Lord, there is no sorrow.
With His ration, of compassion,
His today, is just the same.
And forever, and forever,
As we glorify His name,
He will always be the same.

In this life, we see very little consistency, and much inconsistency. The "constant," when applied to living human beings, constitutes almost an "extinct species." We know, and are associated, with a variety of people as we attempt to live this Christian life. Some of them are passing acquaintances or business contacts, others are casual friends, but with some we have a very personal, intimate relationship. But regardless of how well we know them, or how well they know us, the fact remains that there is absolutely no guarantee that they will not disappoint us, nor that we will not disappoint them. Even though we, as Christians, are indwelt with the Spirit of Christ, we also have another nature, our old sin nature at work within us, doing battle with our spirit. Though we intend to project this Christian spirit twenty-four hours a day, there are times when we fail miserably. We are inconsistent. Our old nature keeps doing battle with our spirit. Satan continues to tempt us. Is there a solution?

To answer the question; First, Satan will continue to work through our old nature. Second, our old nature will remain with us as long as we live. Therefore, there will be a constant battle. But the good news is that by continually keeping our mind set on Jesus and spiritual things, we can help our spirit control the old nature, and the more we keep our mind set on Him. The more control our spirit will have. Jesus is the only perfect Person who ever lived, and with Him, there is absolute consistency. Other people may fail us, and we may fail other people, but our Jesus will never fail us. He is the same yesterday, today and forever.

May 9

NOT JUSTIFIED

"Know that a man is not justified by observing the law, but by faith in Jesus Christ." – Galatians 2:16a

JUSTIFIED BY FAITH

Justified by faith in Jesus,
That's the way our Father sees us,
Not by serving, nor observing,
The religious niceties.
We are righteous by believing,
And His grace we are receiving,
And forever, and forever,
Through His blood, our Father sees,
Not our sinning, but His winning,
For each saint, a set of keys,
That unlocks eternities.

The act of being "justified" by God the Father was accomplished by His Son, Jesus Christ with His shed blood on that tree at Calvary. We were accepted by God the Father when we, by faith, accepted Christ as our Savior. This cleansing took place immediately when we accepted Christ, and from that point forward, throughout all eternity, the eyes of the Father see us through the cleansing blood of Jesus. In Matthew 9:13b, Jesus said that He had not come to call the righteous, but to call sinners. The fact was, and is, that all had sinned and had fallen short of the glory of God, and were justified freely by His grace (Romans 3:23). Being justified by God means that we are judged righteous by God, not for what we have done, are doing, or will do, but because of what Jesus has done for us. Justification leads to salvation, an eternity with our Lord. It is accomplished, not by works of the law, but by faith in Jesus Christ. "For He who had no sin, became sin for us, that we might become the righteousness of God, in Him" (2 Corinthians 5:21).

In our Christian walk, we see so many people who think they must do something else in order to be saved, or to retain their salvation. They miss the exhilarating experience of having a personal relationship with Jesus Christ because they are constantly trying to "work hard enough," or "be good enough" to be entitled to salvation. We are justified and saved by simple faith in Jesus, and by His grace, we look forward to an eternity with Him.

FROM TOP TO BOTTOM

"At that moment the curtain of the temple was torn in two from top to bottom." – Matthew 27:51

THE TEARING OF THE CURTAIN

Now, no longer do we falter,
By not going to an altar.
Let our fearing, turn to hearing,
What the Bible has to say.
For, as death our Lord was bearing,
The curtain there was tearing,
So now never, nor forever,
Will an altar be the way,
But the living, Jesus giving,
Up His life for us that day,
Means He lives in us today.

There was an inner room in the Temple, also called the Holy of Holies. Everyone was denied access to this room except the high priest, and he could enter only "once a year," (Hebrews 9:7) on the "Day of Atonement." He sprinkled the blood of an innocent lamb on the altar, first to cover his sins, then to cover the sins of the people. This inner room was separated from the outer room by a curtain, or veil. When Jesus shed His blood on the cross for you and for me, the blood of the innocent Lamb of God was poured, not sprinkled, on the altar at the cross. By our believing in Him, and accepting Him as our Savior, our sins are not just covered, they are taken away in the eyes of God because of the propitiatory accomplishment of our Lord. The significance of the tearing of the curtain is twofold. First, it signified the passing of the Old Covenant and the introduction of the New Covenant. Second, the tearing from "top to bottom" indicated that this changing from old to new was done from above, that is, was done by God, not by a freak of nature.

An underlying, prevailing truth in this scripture is that we go directly into the presence of God. We no longer go through an earthly high priest who has access to God through a holy place once a year. Jesus is our High Priest, sitting at the right hand of the Father. He has continuous access to God the Father. The only holy place on this earth is where Jesus lives, and He doesn't live in buildings. Jesus lives in the hearts of believers and because of Him, we live.

May 11

WHO TAKES AWAY SIN?

"Look, the Lamb of God, who takes away the sin of the world." – John 1:29

THE LAMB OF GOD

Now, the Lamb of God is Jesus,
And it's through Him that God sees us.
He was harried, but He carried,
All our sins to Calvary.
Under law, two goats were cited,
One was slain, the other blighted,
But through Jesus, now God sees us,
Through His blood upon that tree,
And our sinning, from beginning,
Like a scapegoat's plight to be,
Carried Jesus to that tree.

In this scripture, John the Baptist was revealing to the nation Israel, that Jesus was the Messiah. He introduced Jesus as the "Lamb of God" who takes away the sins of the world. In Leviticus, chapter sixteen, the "order of business" for the Day of Atonement was specified. This was the most solemn holy day for Israel, and it was observed on the tenth day of the seventh month. On that day, two innocent male goats were selected. One was killed, and its blood was sprinkled on the altar in the Holy of Holies as a sacrifice for the sins of all the people. The remaining goat was called the "scapegoat." The high priest would, by placing both hands on the head of the goat, ceremonially place the sins of all the people on the goat. And the goat would then be taken to a solitary place, then released into the desert, there to carry the burden of all of their sins.

This Day of Atonement ceremony observed by the nation Israel, became a reality for us when Jesus went to the cross. In a sense, Jesus was both the "sacrificial lamb" and the "scapegoat" because, when He went to the cross, he carried the burden of the sin of the world on His shoulders. In fact, "He, who knew no sin became sin, in order that we might become the righteousness of God, through Him" (2 Corinthians 5:21). There is, however, a vast difference between what the Day of Atonement accomplished and the results Jesus achieved. Theirs was a temporary covering for sin, while the work of Jesus gives us, when we believe, a permanent cleansing from sin. He didn't just cover our sin. In the eyes of the Father, He took away our sin.

May 12

THE LEAST OF THESE

"The king will reply, I tell you the truth, whatever you did for one of the least of these brothers of mine, you did for me." – Matthew 25:40

LET'S SHOW KINDNESS

As we show to others, kindness,
Unto Christ, it's also kindness,
For the fineness, of His kindness,
Shows His love through you and me.
Let us have a single mindness,
As we show to others, kindness,
For in showing, we are knowing,
He is using you and me.
Let's be heedful, planting's needful,
And His seed of love will be,
Planted here, through you and me.

In our Christian walk, if our heart is right, we earnestly, very sincerely want to do something to glorify the Lord. Very frequently, we have a multitude of people telling us what we should do. They say we should go to church every time the doors are open, never miss a meeting, get down on our knees and pray, spend a designated amount of time each day in prayer, or perhaps, keep a list of our weekly contacts, the names of those we invited to church. There is nothing wrong with these activities, though, perhaps a bit of legalism is involved. But the question is, is this how we glorify the Lord? Our Lord's "great commandment" was, "Love the Lord, your God, with all your heart and with all your soul, and with all your mind," and the "second greatest commandment" was "Love your neighbor as yourself." (Matthew 22:37-39)

If we really want to glorify the Lord, why don't we do what He says, instead of what others suggest? He says, "Love God and love your neighbor." And, instead of an establishment of routine activities, why don't we first honor Him by obeying His commandments? Then, instead of routine activity, or "lip-service," we will be engaged in action. In fact, we might call it "love-action" for our Lord. He tells us that whatever we do for the least of our brothers or sisters, we do for Him. This is a clear-cut, concise road map that shows us the way to our destination, which is to glorify our Lord.

May 13

ONE BODY

"The body is a unit, though it is made up of many parts; and though all its parts are many, they form one body. So it is with Christ." – 1 Corinthians 12:12

"And He is the Head of the body, the church." – Colossians 1:18

HE'S THE HEAD

There's no if, nor but, nor whether,
We are one with Christ, together,
For believing, we're receiving,
That same Spirit from the Son.
Though to some, it is confusing
We're the body He is using,
And by sharing, and by caring,
We are working for the Son,
For His giving, gives us living,
He's the Head of everyone,
Who accepts God's Only Son.

In these scriptures, Paul is using the human body as an analogy for the church. He depicts Christ as the "Head," and the believers as the "body." Christ, or course, is the Head of the church. When He walked this earth, He used His own body to spread the gospel, but He is now seated at the right hand of God the Father, and we are the body He uses to carry on His work. In Corinthians 12:26, Paul gave us another truth when he said, "If one part suffers, every part suffers with it." We can certainly attest to that truth in our own body. For example, if we sprain an ankle, because of that weak ankle we put more weight on our other ankle. And this shift in weight can lead to a misalignment of our spine, which in turn causes us to have back problems. Throughout this ordeal, the nerves send a message to our brain, and we develop a headache.

Within our church, the admonition from Christ is not only to spread the gospel, but also to love one another and to have Christian fellowship with each other. There are times when we don't act very lovable. In fact, there are times when we are just downright grumpy. We become a weak ankle, causing others members pain. This inevitably causes that pain to go to our brain, which is in our head. In other words, by our actions we give Jesus a headache.

WHERE WOULD THE BODY BE?

"If they were all one part, where would the body be?" – 1 Corinthians 12:19

HIS PART IS FROM THE HEART

Now, the subject we're addressing,
Is God's gifting of a blessing,
And the gifting, is uplifting,
As each member does his part.
Some may think importance lacking,
But they're wrong, for God is backing,
With His caring, and His sharing,
Every small deed on the chart,
For unfolding, is God's holding,
Up the Saint, who does his part,
When his part, is from the heart.

We can't do "too little" for the Lord. Now, most of you will immediately, and perhaps very forcefully disagree with me, and tell me that we can't do too much for the Lord. We are both correct within the specific sphere of intent, because we know that we could work for Him all the days of our life and never repay Him for His mercy and grace. But the point I am making is that there is no endeavor for the Lord that is inconsequential to the Lord if that endeavor is from the heart.

As an example, in any church we can look around us and see the leaders, the pastor, the administrative staff, the teachers, the superintendents and others who are highly visible. We can see the work they do for the Lord, and in most instances, it's good work. If we compared these church members with "body members," we might name them "the eyes" or "the mouth" because these are real important in order both "to see" and "to speak." But how would the mouth know where to speak if there were no eyes? How much good would the eyes be if there was no way to communicate? How could either serve the Lord if there were no legs or feet? We sometimes have an extremely distorted view of importance. Though the function of a particular member may have "zero visibility" to most of us, that member, and his function within the body has "maximum visibility" to the Lord if his service comes from a heart filled with Christ.

PRAYER AVAILETH MUCH

"The effectual fervent prayer of a righteous man availeth much." – James 5:16b

THE POWER OF PRAYER

The power of prayer is given us,
By the One who reigns above.
The power of prayer is wondrous,
And is given through God's love.
In times of need, we seek God's grace,
And we seek His mercy, too.
Let's pray for grace, in every case,
And let's seek His mercy through
The One who died, and gave His all,
And Who walks with us each day.
He answers prayer, He hears our call,
As we humbly ask, and pray.

We, as Christians, have received a special gift from God, and that gift is being able to communicate directly with God. This scripture deals with the prayers of a righteous man. Do we really think that in and of ourselves, we have enough righteousness to be rewarded with answered prayer? The answer, of course, is an emphatic "NO." But we, as believers, have something much greater than personal righteousness. We have the righteousness of Christ imputed to us, and this places us in the position of being able to communicate directly with God the Father through Jesus Christ. This scripture also tells us that the prayer of a righteous man "availeth much." In other words, if our prayer is within God's will; we will have an affirmative response. In all instances, our prayer will be answered. Sometimes the answer is "yes;" sometimes "no," and sometimes "wait." Of course, the most difficult answer to deal with is "wait."

Let's analyze our prayer. What is our agenda? Is it a selfish prayer, or is it a selfless prayer? Is our concern for others, or for ourselves? Are we looking for personal gratification, or will the answer we desire glorify God? Do we have a hidden agenda? May our prayer this day be, "Lord, help us by Your grace, that our prayers will be prayed in Your strength, and in Your power, and that the answer we desire will be all for Your glory, through Jesus Christ."

May 16

TO PREPARE A PLACE FOR YOU

"I am going there to prepare a place for you." – John 14:2b

AT THE END OF LIFE'S GAME

Each hour and each minute, we ponder our limit,
As we stand on the threshold of time.
A struggle within us, but grace there to win us,
And love that's so great, it's sublime.
We fall down and recover, as grace we discover,
God's gift to those who believe.
His kindness and virtue, a faith that we nurture,
His life, that is ours to receive.
Neither pain nor hardship, can cancel His Lordship,
For those who believe on His name.
Though life may be fleeting, we've scheduled a meeting,
With Christ, at the end of life's game.

Just prior to this scripture, Jesus told His disciples, and is telling us today, that in His Father's house there are many mansions. And the great news is that He was going there, and now has gone, to prepare a place for us.

As we proceed down the pathway of life, we encounter pain and hardship, and then we discover grace through His Lordship. Our pathway is not always smooth. We encounter barriers along the way. There are some potholes here and there, and the ditches on both sides are real deep. As we walk along this pathway of life, we seem to be continually stumping our toes on the ruts, or stepping into some pothole, or falling into one of those real deep ditches. But those are the times we really discover His grace and His mercy and His love. We are currently engaged in the game of life here on earth, but as Christians, we have all of this to look forward to, for we know that:

Neither pain nor hardship, can cancel His Lordship,
For those who believe on His name, and . . .
Though Life may be fleeting, we've scheduled a meeting,
With Christ, at the end of life's game.

May 17

ALL WHO ARE WEARY

"Come to Me, all you who are weary and burdened, and I will give you rest." – Matthew 11:28

LORD, GIVE US REST

Lord, our very souls to you we bare.
We're weary, we're so tired, we need care.
Our spirit's low, we're burdened out there.
Sometimes, we're prone to just look and stare,
And at times, we seem to be aware,
That love for You is so rare, out there,
But Lord, please help us that we might dare,
Rest completely, in Your loving care.

There appears to be a multiplicity of absolutes in this statement by Jesus. Rest is essential to the human body. In fact, we are built in such a way that sleep "recharges our battery." Sleep is so vital that without it we would die. But that was not the primary thrust of this teaching by Jesus. His main and fundamental concern was for those who were weary because of the burden of sin. He was concerned for everyone, because "all have sinned and fallen short of the glory of God." Jesus was also concerned about the legalistic burden the Pharisees were placing on the people with their manmade laws, but the main thrust of His message was that they could, and we can, come to Him for rest.

We can exercise strenuously, be extremely physically tired, then rest, and it is amazing how quickly we recuperate. But there is a difference between being tired and weary because of physical exertion and being burdened down by either sin or legalistic requirements. All of us carried that heavy load of sin on our shoulders until we came to Jesus. Then with love, grace and mercy, He gently removed it. He set us free, free to love Him, love each other and have the freedom to enjoy the grace He extended us, but some of us were not satisfied. We wanted a checklist to be sure everyone could be graded, and with this legalistic approach we tossed aside our freedom, and replaced it with a heavy burden of guilt, and doubt and pride. Our eyes were no longer on the Lord, but on ourselves. And this burden became heavier and heavier.

Lord, our prayer to you this day is that through Your love, mercy and grace, that you give us the strength, direction and determination to say, "Dear Lord, please help us that we might dare, rest completely in Your loving care."

WE HAVE HIS GRACE

"Through whom we have gained access by faith into this grace in which we now stand." – Romans 5:2a

IT'S IN THE BANK

We know our Lord, He set us free,
He gave His life, for you and me.
He rose again, that we might be,
With Him throughout, eternity.
His grace for us, is in His bank,
His mercy too, and Him we thank.
Our checks endorsed, by One with rank,
But we must draw them on His bank.

When we receive Christ into our heart, we receive, not only salvation, but God has favored us with an inexhaustible supply of grace, and mercy and peace. We are not promised that there will be no trouble in our life, but we are promised that "His grace is sufficient" (2 Corinthians 12:9). For the purpose of illustration, let's draw an analogy for this inexhaustible supply of God's favors.

Someone who is extremely wealthy opens a bank account for us with an inexhaustible supply of funds. The only restriction on this account is that the Chairman of the Board of this bank must endorse each check that we write. This Chairman of the Board then favors us by pre-endorsing all of our checks. Then, all we have to do to secure an unlimited amount of funds, is to draw those pre-endorsed checks on the bank. This is an analogy of the position we have in Jesus. God, the Father, has favored us with an unlimited amount of His love, grace, mercy and peace. He has deposited these favors in the bank owned by His Son, and Jesus has pre-endorsed our checks. All we have to do is use them.

As Christians, we have access to all of God's favors through His Son, Jesus Christ. But there is a great sadness in the fact that so many of us try to rely on what we can do, instead of what Jesus can do, and will do for us, if we will only ask. Our prayer is that by the grace of God, we decrease self-reliance and self-awareness, and increasingly expand Christ-reliance and Christ-awareness. Let's use those pre-endorsed checks. Let's draw them on His bank, and receive that inexhaustible supply of His favors, all for the glory of God.

May 19

LIVING WATER

"Jesus answered, 'Everyone who drinks this water will be thirsty again, but whoever drinks the water I give him will never thirst.'" – John 4:13-14a

THE QUENCHING OF OUR THIRSTING

If it's not the well that's living,
Then it's not the well that's giving,
Us the living, loving, giving,
Of His life to you and me.
And for quenching of our thirsting,
Our Lord's Spirit will be bursting,
With no ration, of compassion,
In the hearts of you and me.
He will render, love so tender,
And give grace, that we might see,
He is our eternity.

Jesus is using an analogy of a well to differentiate between water drawn there that never permanently quenches one's thirst, and "living water." By way of analogy, He tells her that water from any other source, that is, any other form of worship, will not quench the thirst and give eternal life. He continues by telling the woman that God is Spirit, and Him His worshipers must worship in spirit and in truth. He is the Truth. He tells her that when she drinks the water He gives her, she will never thirst again.

Those of us who are Christians have permanently quenched our thirst for salvation by drinking the living water Jesus has provided. But even though we look forward to an eternity with Him, as we travel down life's highway, how often do we stop to drink from another well? The "well of self achievement" is attractive. It tantalizes our senses, but it's shallow, and soon the well runs dry. The "well of knowledge" fascinates us at times, but without the wisdom of Christ to purify it, the water becomes stagnant. The "well of ambition" holds certain allure for us, but without Christ, our egos will contaminate it. There are many wells on the side of life's highway, and we may be tempted to drink from some of them, but without Christ, we had better check the water because without Jesus, there is no peace.

May 20

LIKE A LITTLE CHILD

"Therefore, whoever humbles himself like this child is the greatest in the Kingdom of Heaven." – Matthew 18:4

LIKE A CHILD

Like a child, He wants us listening,
To His voice, with Spirit glistening,
'Til our caring, and our sharing,
Like a child is full of grace.
Let's be humble while we're living,
And like children, keep on giving,
His projection, love-connection,
Like a portrait of His face,
To our brothers, and to others,
As like servants, we embrace,
All the glory of His grace.

This passage of scripture should convey a message to each one of us. As that child, with all humility, stood and looked up into the eyes of Jesus, we can almost visualize how those trusting little eyes sought the face of our Savior. Jesus said, that whoever humbles himself like this child would be the greatest in the Kingdom of Heaven. This is a remarkable statement. Obviously this child knew nothing about doctrine and apparently was not old enough to have reached the age of accountability. Thus, he was certainly not a teacher or a leader, but the child had something, that to Jesus, was more important. That was humility, and trust.

Even as Christians, in fact, especially as Christians, on the road to maturity there are numerous ditches that we can fall into. One of them is named "knowledge." Now, there is absolutely nothing wrong with knowledge, except and unless we think that knowledge is the same thing as wisdom. Knowledge comes from our study, but wisdom comes from God. Another ditch we can fall into is named "good works." Again, there is certainly nothing wrong with good works, except and unless that while in the process of doing good works, we look around to see how we are doing in comparison with others, then we tumble headlong into the deepest ditch of all. It's called "pride," and this ditch is far removed from the trust and humility exhibited by the child that looked up into the face of Jesus.

BUT, STAY IN THE CITY UNTIL

"But stay in the city until you have been clothed with power from on high." – Luke 24:49b

NOT TOO FAST – NOT TOO SLOW

Lord, not too fast, and not too slow,
Please show us, the way to go,
That we may work, and do Your will,
And be Your child, and work until,
You take us home, to be with You,
But while we're here, please, Lord imbue,
Us with Your grace, Your power, too,
That we may work, and work for you.

In this scripture, Jesus was giving final instructions to His disciples before His ascension. He told them to teach and preach the gospel. But first, He said, "wait." He told them to "stay in the city" until they were clothed with power. They were soon to be equipped with the Holy Spirit who would give them directions.

What does God want me to do? What work does He have for me to do? Shall I "put out the fleece" as Gideon did, or plunge headlong into some type of work for Him? The answer to this question is not simple, but we do have the answer in the scriptures. Jesus said to wait until you are "clothed with power." The disciples waited for the indwelling Holy Spirit who clothed them with power for their ministry. We, as Christians, already have the Spirit of Christ indwelling us, so we are equipped, but the question is for a specific work, are we clothed with His power? Regarding the work we choose to do, there is a test we might give ourselves. Is it for self, or is it for God? Is it to receive accolades from others, or is to glorify God? Do we have a hidden agenda, or do we put God first? When our spirit is synchronized with God's Spirit, we can almost literally feel a surge of power, God's power through Christ, which propels us into our work for Him. Our prayer is:

Lord, let us "wait in the city" until your indwelling Spirit gives us directions. Then clothe us with such a surge of Your power that we know with all certainty that the work we do is according to Your will, and all for Your glory, through Jesus Christ.

May 22

HE TOUCHED HER HAND

"He touched her hand and the fever left her, and she got up and began to wait on Him." – Matthew 8:15

BUT, WE FEEL HIS TOUCH

A touch is not a touch, until one feels it.
A cure is not a cure, until one heals it,
But, we feel His touch, and we know He lives,
And we're healed by Him, and the love He gives,
So we live this lie, and we run this race,
For we know by faith, that we're His by grace.

This scripture records the physical healing of Peter's mother-in-law by Jesus. First, Jesus touched the woman, and she was healed. Second, she then began to wait on Him. Third, that evening, Jesus ministered to many who were in need. By the inference in this scripture, let's move forward in time two thousand years and determine what this means to us today.

First, Jesus has the power to heal, physically, emotionally and spiritually. A specific physical healing that we pray for may, or may not, be in God's will. But Jesus has the power of healing in His touch. In fact, there are times when, if we are in His will, we can almost literally feel His touch in our lives, a supernatural transposition of His healing power to us, and subsequently, His peace that surpasses all understanding. Second, just as the woman in the scripture began to wait on Jesus out of gratitude, we, as Christians, should serve Him, never because of fear or adherence to rules and regulations, but because of sheer gratitude for what He has done for us. It's because of His love, mercy and grace that we have our peace in Him. Third, just as this woman, out of gratitude and love for Jesus, served Him. His ministry was continued that evening. When we serve Him out of love and gratitude, we contribute to His ministry. Whether ours is a menial task in the background, or one more conspicuous, each service done for Jesus is important and meaningful. Jesus uses each one of us to carry on His ministry. Our prayer is that He will touch us in such a way that we not only feel His healing power that gives us peace, but that through His power and strength, might serve Him in whatever capacity He chooses – all for the glory of God.

DON'T CONFORM

"Do not conform any longer to the pattern of this world, but be transformed by the renewing of your mind." – Romans 12:2

BE TRANSFORMED

Now, we need to be reviewing,
What this mind of ours is doing,
Not conforming, but transforming,
As His Spirit shows the way.
And as we do our reviewing,
Let our mind, on God, be viewing,
And His caring, and His sharing,
Will instruct us what to say.
From conforming, to transforming,
Let our mind, through Christ, today,
Be a mind that will obey.

Instead of conforming to the pattern of this world, we can be transformed by the renewing of our mind. We are Christians, and our desire is to live the Christian life. But there are so many distractions out there. The world does not know Christ, and the world's god seems to be either dishonesty, money, power or immorality, with a total disdain for spiritual things. In this world, there are times when we seem to be on a very tiny island, completely engulfed by torrential winds and rain, that threaten to sweep us into a turbulent sea. We need to hang-on. The good news is, we have Someone to hang onto, and that is Christ Jesus. In this particular scripture, we are given instructions regarding how to resist the worldly gods and be transformed into the person that Christ wants us to be.

Even with our salvation assured, we still have choices with regard to how we live this Christian life, and these choices are triggered by our mindset. We can set our mind on the world instead of on Christ, or on ourselves instead of others, and we will live a miserable life. Or we can do what the Lord has told us to do, and that is set our mind on spiritual things. And in some supernatural way, our actions will follow that mindset and we will enjoy the peace that only our Lord can give us.

May 24

I AM THE DOOR

"I am the door; if anyone enters through Me, he shall be saved, and shall go in and out, and find pasture." – John 10:9

WE KNOCKED UPON HIS DOOR

We were saved as were finding,
Jesus Christ, whose love is binding,
For believing, we're receiving,
Life with him forevermore.
He was God from the beginning,
And we're saved from all our sinning,
And He told us, He would mold us,
But we had to find that door,
Gently tapping, then by rapping,
As we knocked upon His door,
He gave "life" for evermore.

So much of the teaching of Jesus was either by parables or by analogy. In this scripture, Jesus is teaching by pastoral analogy. Most of the people understood the relationship of the shepherd to his sheep. The shepherd would lead them to green pastures and water during the day, but would lead them to a safe place each evening. He would also continually protect them day and night.

The primary teaching of Jesus in this scripture is that He is the Messiah, the long awaited Savior of the world, and, like a door, He is the entranceway into the Kingdom of God. Those who would be saved must enter through Him. In fact, John 14:6 tells us that no one comes to the Father, except through Him. Another truth that is evident in this scripture is that as we live our lives on this earth, go out to pasture and engage in whatever our life's work may be, the Good Shepherd knows us and loves us. And when the day is done, when our life on this earth is over, our Good Shepherd has provided us a safe place, not just for an evening, but for an eternity. We knocked upon His door, and He gave us life forevermore.

NOT WORLDLY WISDOM

"Not with words of human wisdom, lest the cross of Christ be emptied of its power." – 1 Corinthians 1:17b

NO POWER IN HUMAN WISDOM

Now, the human wisdom showing,
Is a sign of worldly knowing,
And no tower, of our power,
Can provide eternity.
But, our Lord, who lived with vision,
At the cross, made His provision,
And the tower, of His power,
Through His love for you and me,
Is indwelling, and is welling,
While His Spirit sets us free,
With His strength, eternally.

There is no power in human wisdom to produce salvation, in fact, human wisdom, though it can be helpful in many instances, usually has an adverse effect on the one who possesses it. Human wisdom is the child of "worldly" knowledge, and the one who possesses this wisdom has a tendency to be proud of his or her accomplishments. Pride and humility cannot live in the same house. Without humility, we can never have spiritual wisdom.

The One who died on the cross is our only source of salvation and lasting peace. He arose that we might have life in His name, and with His indwelling Spirit, we also receive His love, grace, mercy and strength. The power in human wisdom will never sustain us, but the strength of His indwelling Spirit will sustain us with an unbelievable amount of power if we will but keep our eyes and our minds set on Him. Our prayer is, "Lord, give us a sufficient amount of Your grace to enable us, with all humility, to rely on the power of Your indwelling Spirit, all for the glory of God, through Jesus Christ."

May 26

BUT SEEK FIRST

"But seek first His kingdom, and His righteousness, and all these things will be given to you." – Matthew 6:33

GIVE US THE FAITH

We know in truth, the pain You bore,
The anguish there, the love, and more,
You had for us, and had before,
We entered through, that special door.
Please Lord, give us, the faith we need,
In times of stress, in thought, in deed.
Please plant in us, the grace we need,
To have the faith, to let you lead.
We have Your love, You know our need,
And with the faith, to let you lead,
Please help us see, what others need,
And spread Your love, by word and deed.

In our Christian walk, one of the most difficult things for most of us to do is to divorce our mind from worry. Jesus clearly instructed us not to worry, not to be anxious, and he assured us that we would be supplied all of our needs. But He also said to seek first His kingdom, and His righteousness.

As we live this Christian life, we not only have a burning desire to provide for our family, we have a moral and spiritual obligation to do so. Though at times we may fail miserably, Jesus will honor our efforts, if those efforts are within His will. Jesus didn't say, "don't work," He said "don't worry." He also did not say He would provide for all of our "wants." He said He would provide for all of our "needs." There is a difference.

Some may view this teaching of Jesus as a deterrent to our pursuit of excellence in whatever endeavor we may undertake, but that is not the case. What Jesus is teaching us is to get our priorities in order, and to first seek Him and His righteousness. If we reside within His will, our needs will be taken care of. Our highest priority is to let Him live His live through us, and by both word and deed, pass His love on to others. Our prayer is that we keep our priorities in order, and that with our every endeavor, we first seek Him, and His righteousness, all for the glory of God.

BE PREPARED

"Preach the word; be prepared in season and out of season." – 2 Timothy 4:2

LORD, PLEASE USE US

Lord, please use us, as you will,
Our hearts with love please fill,
We're yours forever more,
We knocked upon that door,
But now, midst all the strife,
Please use us in this life.
Lord, please use us, as you will,
We pray, let us be still,
So we can hear Your voice,
And know for sure Your choice,
Of how we serve You here,
We know You're always near.

We are admonished to spread the gospel, and to be prepared whenever the opportunity presents itself. Not all of us are preachers, and not all of us are teachers, but all of us who are members of the body of Christ have an obligation to tell others about the saving grace of Jesus Christ. The members of the body are the means by which the Lord both spreads the gospel to non-Christians and gives comfort and encouragement to fellow Christians.

Since there is no designated season for doing the Lord's work, we are to be prepared at all times to preach, teach and spread His word. As a teacher, there have been times, numerous times, when I was personally disappointed with the lesson I taught. There had been no eloquence; I really had not felt like teaching and I was not on a "spiritual high" when I taught. I really felt like I failed, and I did. But God did not fail, because it has been amazing how often I thought the lesson I taught was inferior, yet it touched someone. We must remember, it's not our words that are important. It's God's word that's important. In whatever capacity we work for the Lord, if we will make ourselves available, God will make us capable. Our prayer is, "Lord, please use us as you will, and give us the grace to be ready when You say "go," and leave the results to You, all for the glory of God, through our Lord, Jesus Christ."

ETERNAL LIFE

"Whoever believes in the Son has eternal life." – John 3:36

HE LIVES WITH US FOREVER

Now, He lives with us forever,
Once we take that final step,
And it's not by our endeavor,
But by faith, when we accept,

His life, His death and His rising,
When He walked upon this earth,
And He, we are recognizing,
Gives to all the saints, His worth.

For the essence of His story,
When by faith we do believe,
Is to give each saint His glory,
And His life, we do receive.

When we by faith receive Christ, we are promised eternal life with Him. Most of us think of eternal life as beginning at that point in time when our body dies, and our spirit departs to be with the Lord. Or at the Rapture, whichever occurs first. But the truth is, our eternal life began immediately when we placed our trust in Christ, and Christ alone. This saving faith was God's requirement for us to immediately receive the Holy Spirit. Revelation 5:12 tells us, "worthy is the Lamb," and the Lamb of God is our Lord, Jesus Christ. We have His Spirit, His very life, within us. Our "soulish, sinning nature" is not acceptable to God, but when we yield and let the Spirit of Christ lead us and guide us, we become worthy through Him. The worth of Christ is actually imputed to us by the grace of God.

As we attempt to live the Christian life, we often put ourselves down because we know we are not worthy, but we must remember that God has equipped us for service with the indwelling Spirit of Christ. We must have no pride in self, but instead, have humility. When we yield to God, we are equipped for service by the strength and power of the indwelling Holy Spirit. This makes us worthy through Christ. Our eternal life with Christ has begun, and will continue throughout all eternity.

A GOOD MAN BRINGETH FORTH

"A good man out of the good treasure of the heart bringeth forth good things; and an evil man out of the evil treasure bringeth forth evil things." – Matthew 12:35

THE ONLY WAY

From the heart of man abounding,
Comes a good or evil sounding,
His reaction, has impaction,
On the world we know today.
We can go about arranging,
How the world should now be changing,
But true changing, is arranging,
That the heart must first obey,
And this changing, and arranging,
Is through Christ, the only way,
That our world will change today.

There is a great truth in this passage of scripture that we need to recognize. Our deeds represent the ultimate fruition of the condition of our heart. Good fruit comes from a good tree, and rotten fruit comes from a rotten tree. By nature, our heart is evil unless we are abiding in the Lord. We look out on this world we live in, and we see so many changes that need to be made. Slavery, in one form or another, is still rampant in some parts of the world. Abortion is in "full bloom" right here in our own country. Both slavery and abortion have to be an abomination to the Lord. There are Christian organizations that are diligently working to change the laws and to abolish abortion. These organizations, if working within our legal system, should certainly have our support. But this scripture gives us a great insight into the ultimate solution of stamping out evil. The hearts of men and women must be changed before the evil in this world will subside. Evil acts spring from an evil heart.

As Christians, we have a tremendous challenge facing us. The only permanent solution for evil is the Lord. We have not only a God-given opportunity, but also an obligation to spread the gospel while we are here on this earth. As we tell others about Jesus, and, as they accept Him, "heart by heart" evil is being stamped-out. Jesus and evil cannot live in the same heart. Good fruit and rotten fruit cannot come from the same tree.

TURN THE OTHER CHEEK

"If someone strikes you on the right cheek, turn to him the other cheek."
– Matthew 5:39

STRIKE ME HERE

When our right cheek they are striking,
It is never to our liking,
And we're burning, with a yearning,
To strike back, and make them pay.
But the Lord within us dwelling,
Is instructing us by telling,
That His ration, of compassion,
Is enough for us today,
So be learning, to be turning,
The left cheek, as if to say,
Strike me here, I will obey.

In our normal, human state of secularity, when someone does us an injustice, our immediate state of mind demands that we strike back, that we get even, that we retaliate. In fact, we really don't want a tooth for a tooth; we want two or three teeth for our one tooth. If we are a man, we call this being "manly." Yet our Lord has told us that if someone strikes us on one cheek, to turn the other also; that if someone does us an injustice, we are to be submissive instead of being belligerent. We are to love instead of hate. How can we accomplish this? We can't, but He can.

As Christians, we have the Spirit of Christ indwelling us, giving us the potential and the capacity to turn the other cheek. We also have our soulish nature to contend with, and that nature tells us to get even. In order to be obedient to this command of our Lord, we must set our minds on Jesus, and let His Spirit override our soulish nature. When we do this, we are actually promoting His kingdom here on earth, because the world sees Jesus through us. We are His ambassadors here on earth. Our prayer is, "Lord, give us Your strength and Your grace, so that we are prepared today; that we're learning, even yearning to be turning the other cheek, all for the glory of God, through our Lord, Jesus Christ."

GO THE SECOND MILE

"If someone forces you to go one mile, go with him two miles." – Matthew 5:41

HE IS GUIDING, WE'RE ABIDING

In our daily life connection,
If we're forced to change direction,
Let's be walking, and not balking,
And let's walk that extra mile.
For, though we may feel rejection,
Through our Lord, we have connection,
That connection, means direction,
For He's with us all the while,
He is guiding, we're abiding,
And at first we walk a mile,
Then we walk that extra mile. . .

During the days our Lord walked this earth, Rome ruled the known world and Roman soldiers were dispersed throughout the Roman Empire. There was a law that provided for a Roman soldier, at his discretion, to force a citizen of an occupied country to carry his heavy equipment one mile. That person was not required to carry it any farther, just one mile, but the person doing the carrying was usually not exactly thrilled about the first mile. This was forced labor, and was resented, but Jesus said, go the extra mile.

This teaching by Jesus is very similar to His teaching of turn the other cheek. But with this admonition, Jesus is placing us in the position of being forced to do something against our will. But that action that we are forced into, will, perhaps, help someone else. So Jesus tells us to exceed their demands with good works.

There are times when we feel that we are being forced to do something that we just don't want to do, and our old, natural, secular self just puffs up with resentment. But regardless of the motive of the one applying pressure, if our action will help someone, we should, with love in our heart, swallow pride, set our eyes on the Lord and go the extra mile. Our prayer is that since we know He is with us all the while, let's let Him do the guiding. And let us do the abiding, and give us the grace, after we have walked the first mile, to walk that second mile, all for the glory of God.

JUSTIFIED THROUGH FAITH

"Therefore, since we have been justified through faith, we have peace with God through our Lord Jesus Christ." – Romans 5:1

IN GOD'S EYES, WE'RE PURE

God makes us His ward, through Jesus, our Lord,
He extended an invitation,
To all who believe, that they might receive,
And by faith, we made application.

Salvation's a gift, our souls He will lift,
And there is no modification,
For we must believe, before we receive,
From the Lord, our justification.

Then we will find peace, a joyful release,
We no longer face condemnation.
In God's eyes, for sure, we're clean, and we're pure,
We're grateful for purification.

Since the fall of Adam, sin has reigned in the world. Mankind has been separated from God because of sin. God sent His only Son to this earth to pay the sin debt owed by all of us. That debt was paid at the cross by the blood of Jesus, and when we put our faith and our trust in Him, we received salvation because we were justified (declared righteous) by God the Father. Through our faith and by God's grace, we have been imputed the righteousness of Christ. For the purpose of salvation, our sins have been, not just covered, but takenaway (John 1:29). The sacrificial offering in the Jewish temple of the blood of sheep and goats was but a foreshadowing of the cross. That ritual would give temporary covering for sin, but the blood of Jesus does not just cover, it permanently erases our sin.

When God the Father, looks at us, He looks at us through the blood of Jesus. Hence, our salvation is assured because the blood of Jesus cleansed us. This assurance of salvation because of our justification should give us a great sense of peace, a peace that the world does not have nor understand. It is a supernatural gift given by God. Regardless of the problems and anxieties that we may face, we don't face them alone. We have the Lord. For this, we are eternally grateful.

June 2

STREAMS OF LIVING WATER

"Whoever believes in Me, as the scripture has said, streams of living water will flow from within him." – John 7:38

LIVING WATER

When, in Christ we are believing,
Then His Spirit we're receiving,
Always flowing, ever showing,
What our life through Him should be.
Let us live this life by sowing,
Seeds of love, where 'ere we're going,
For we're knowing, that the sowing,
Is His will for you and me.
Streams of water, living water,
Will flow out from you and me,
To pass on, eternity.

In this scripture, Jesus is promising His disciples, and all believers, that His Spirit will indwell in each one of us after He is glorified. Today, His Spirit indwells each and every believer, and this Spirit is an enabling Spirit, given to direct our lives. Through this Spirit, we have the potential to let the power of Christ change our lives. But we must continually adapt our attitude to His will in order for that potential to be completely realized.

His Spirit will comfort and direct us, but will never force us. We can live a miserable life as a Christian unless we yield to Him, and follow His directions. Conversely, we can experience a supernatural peace, and an abundance of His grace, mercy and power, if we will only yield our spirit to His Spirit. Then "streams of living water" will flow out from us, as we pass His love and the gospel on to others. Our prayer is, "Lord give us a sufficient amount of Your grace and Your power, that we might yield completely to Your will, so that streams of living water might flow through us to others, all for the glory of God."

June 3

BUT I PRESS ON

"But I press on to take hold of that for which Christ Jesus took hold of me." – Philippians 3:12b

PRESSING ON

Pressing on should be our answer,
To the Lord, our great Enhancer,
With the caring and the sharing,
He designed for you and me.
Through His Spirit He is giving,
Us the strength within for living,
His anointing, now is pointing,
Out His way for you and me.
Let's not mumble, neither stumble,
But press on that we might be,
Living proof of Calvary.

Our salvation was bought and paid for at the cross by Jesus. Although we participated by having faith in Him, He furnished us the grace for our faith. In this scripture, we are told to take hold of, or to act upon, that which Jesus has planned for us. We are chosen by God to work for Him through Jesus Christ. We may think that we can occasionally volunteer to do a little work for the Lord, and that's all He expects of us, but if we think that, we have missed the point altogether. We are told to press on, as if we are running a race, and to understand and act upon the full realization of what Jesus has done for each one of us.

There is a vast difference between deciding to do a little work for the Lord and actually having been taken hold of by the Lord. When He takes hold of us, there is a supernatural desire deep within us, a burning, yearning desire to work for Him. We can hardly wait to arise each morning. There are not enough hours in the day for us to work for the Lord. We are not doing the driving – we are being driven by the Lord. Our prayer is, "Lord, reveal to each one of us what Your will is for our lives. Then give us a burning, yearning desire to press on and take hold of that for which you have already taken hold of us, all for the glory of God."

June 4

YOU HAVE HIDDEN THESE THINGS

"I praise you, Father, Lord of Heaven and earth, because You have hidden these things from the wise and learned, and revealed them to little children." – Matthew 11:25

AS CHILDREN WE INHERIT

God, through Christ, let us inherit,
And completely without merit,
By believing, we're receiving,
Life with Him eternally.
Like a child, our spirit kneeling,
Let His Spirit be revealing,
But perception, is deception,
By the "wise," for they don't see.
Their direction, is rejection,
But as children, we can be,
With our Lord, eternally.

There is a great truth in this passage of scripture. A little child looks to his father with faith and trust in the father's judgment and ability. You might even say that is almost a blind faith. But a wise or learned man so often has his faith and trust placed in self – in his knowledge, college degrees, ability and self-sufficiency. As Jesus is speaking of the wise and the learned, He is describing the "worldly wise." He is not describing the wisdom that comes from God, for God's wisdom leads us into the discovery that only Christ is sufficient. God gives us His love, mercy, grace and peace in addition to salvation. But in order to receive the full blessings of God, we must have a mindset like that of a little child. We must have faith, trust and full confidence in the Lord.

It is almost impossible for the Lord to use us, and certainly not to the fullest, until and unless our attitude has not a trace of self-sufficiency left. A humble attitude, together with a trusting heart, blend to form a catalyst that promotes our spiritual oneness with our Lord, thereby giving us the opportunity to experience God's fullest blessings. Our prayer is that through Your grace, our hearts will be trusting, yet humble in all areas of our life, like a small child looking into the eyes of a loving Father, all for your glory, through our Lord, Jesus Christ.

THINK ABOUT SUCH THINGS

"Finally, brothers, whatever is true, whatever is noble, whatever is right, whatever is pure, whatever is lovely whatever is admirable – if anything is excellent or praise worthy – think about such things." – Philippians 4:8

CHRIST DIRECTED

May our thoughts be all directed,
And through Christ, be all connected,
Christ connected, and directed,
To what's noble, right and true,
As we're given wont to ponder,
Let us turn our eyes up yonder,
To the Tower, with the power.
Thoughts precede the things we do.
If connected, we're directed,
By our Lord, the One who's true,
Who will guide what 'ere we do.

In this scripture, these admonitions given by Paul to the Philippians are certainly applicable to all Christians. He admonishes them, and us, to have our mind set on things that are true, and noble and right – things that are pure, lovely and admirable.

Thoughts give birth to attitude, and attitude determines what we will, or will not, do with the time we are apportioned here on this earth. We have choices. We can either think about ourselves, how we have either failed or succeeded, the problems we face and all the bad things that can happen to us and live a miserable Christian life, with absolutely no peace. Or, we can set our minds on spiritual things, things that are pure, true and noble – how we can help others and how we can serve our Lord, and we will be rewarded with a peace of mind that utterly surpasses all understanding. If our thoughts are Christ-connected, our attitude will be Christ-directed. Our prayer is that the Lord will give us a sufficient amount of His grace that we will not only be Christ-connected and Christ-directed, but will also be Christ-effective, all for the glory of God, through Jesus Christ.

I PASS JUDGMENT ON NO ONE

"You judge by human standards: I pass judgment on no one." – John 8:15

NOT TO JUDGE, BUT TO SAVE

Not to judge us, but to save us,
Was His kindness that He gave us,
All His tender, loving splendor,
And the right to bear His name.
He's our Savior, and our brother,
God's the Father, there's no other.
Neither stigma, nor enigma,
Can attach to smear His name,
And through sorrow, or the morrow,
He will always be the same,
Saving us, is why He came.

There is a great truth in this scripture that we need to understand. Christ came into this world, not to judge it, but to save it. We are taught, and it's absolutely true, that God loves the sinner but hates sin. Being an unchangeable, just God, His position regarding sin was then, is now and will always be, that a penalty must be paid. That penalty is death. Being a loving God, He provided the penalty payment for our sin with the blood of His only Son upon the cross. When we, by faith, accept this payment for our sin, we become a member of the family of God for all eternity. So when Jesus said that He passed judgment on no one, the truth was that all had sinned, and were already standing under condemnation. Jesus had come into this world to pay our penalty of death, to offer Himself as a blood sacrifice for our sins. By exercising saving faith in Him, our sin debt is paid, and God's justice prevails.

Even though Jesus came into this world, not to judge, but to save, there will be a point in time when He will return and execute the orders of God the Father. At that time, even though God is a loving God, the wrath of God will be inflicted on all that have not accepted His Son. Our prayer is that while we are yet on this earth, that our particular ministry, whatever it might be, will help promote the saving grace of the gospel, all for the glory of God, through Jesus Christ.

June 7

LET US PUT UP THREE SHELTERS

"Peter said to Jesus, 'Master, it is good for us to be here, let us put us three shelters – one for You, one for Moses and one for Elijah.'" – Luke 9:33

IMPORTANCE OF THE SON

One the mount where He was staying,
Came two men while Christ was praying.
Then the greeter, Simon Peter,
Told our Lord what should be done.
Though he saw the revelation,
Peter chose no elevation,
For his thinking, was then linking,
All the three, the same as one.
And his thinking, was not linking,
The importance of the Son,
With the souls, that would be won.

As usual, unrestrained, impulsive Peter spoke before he thought. A shelter was temporary structure constructed to prolong the visit of an important person, a place where he could rest, but Jesus had already told His disciples that He had work to do those last few days. He had no time for rest.

In this scripture, we clearly see the difference between the way people think, and the truth that God speaks. In all probability, Peter thought he was being very magnanimous as he elevated Jesus to a position equal to that of Moses and Elijah. He was according Jesus the same importance that he believed should be given both Moses and Elijah. He, not only spoke before thinking, he clearly did not know what he was talking about. Regardless of the importance of Moses, the lawgiver, and Elijah, the prophet, their importance paled into oblivion when compared to the importance of Jesus Christ, the Son of God and Savior of the world. Peter clearly had his priorities confused, to say the least.

As we live this Christian life, how often do we have our priorities confused? How often do we attempt to "build a shelter" for someone or something, and elevate that person or that thing to a position equal to or superior to the Lord? Our prayer is, "Lord, give us the grace and determination to continually prioritize our thoughts and our actions, so that you will always occupy the very highest elevation in all areas of our life, all for the glory of God."

158

June 8

LIVING WATER

"Whoever believes in Me, as the scripture has said, streams of living water will flow from within him." – John 7:38

LIVING WATER

Now, His Spirit, outward going,
Is like water, downhill flowing,
Ever rushing, with a gushing,
If we'll only let it go.
As He wills, let's not be shirking,
But through us let Him be working,
Spirit flowing, ever going,
As His seed of love we show,
A full ration, of compassion,
Whether mate, or friend, or foe,
Let His "Living Water" flow.

The living water that Jesus refers to is the Holy Spirit living in the heart of each believer. This Spirit assures us of eternal life, satisfies our need for God and gives us direction and empowerment. Jesus, in this scripture, is telling us that the outpouring of this Spirit through each one of us will be a blessing to others, as well as to ourselves. We must take note at this time that we are merely the vessel through which this blessing passes, not the source. The source is Jesus Christ.

As we live this Christian life, it is God's plan that our mind and our Spirit be in unison with His will, thereby enabling Christ, through His indwelling Spirit, to live His life through us. We have nothing to do with the actual flow of this living water as it goes out from us, but we have everything to do with stopping that flow. The Lord will use each one of us, to the extent of His will for our lives and our obedience to His will. Our prayer is, "Lord, give us the grace and the determination to personally step aside in order that we might be used as a vessel, through which streams of living water will flow, all for the glory of God, through Jesus Christ, our Lord."

WHAT WILL HAPPEN TOMORROW?

"Why, you do not even know what will happen tomorrow. What is your life? You are a mist that appears for a little while and then vanishes." – James 4:14

WE HAVE JUST TODAY

There is no tomorrow, we have just today,
For gladness or sorrow, for work, or for play.
We stammer and stutter; we start out the day,
And often we mutter, each step of the way,
But we should be smiling, with joy in our heart,
Not fear the beguiling, the world does impart.
Let's let His love reach us, without so much fuss,
His grace there to teach us, His joy is for us.
There is no tomorrow, we have just today,
Please help us let Jesus, just show us the way.

"Speculation" breeds "anticipation" and, whether positive or negative, anticipation takes us out of today and places us into tomorrow. Positive anticipation certainly has merit, whereas negative anticipation can destroy whatever peace and joy we might have. But anticipation to the exclusion of a full understanding of our current position in Christ will rob us of a multitude of blessings.

As Christians, we have salvation, TODAY. The Lord has also allotted us a certain amount of time on this earth. None of us know how much time we have, but even as Christians, we seem to have a propensity for speculation. That leads to anticipation of what will happen tomorrow, and most of the time our anticipation is immersed in anxiety.

God's will for our lives is to have a loving relationship with the Father, and with all others, through Jesus Christ. These relationships are not for tomorrow, but for today, hour by hour, minute by minute and second by second. There are twenty-four hours in each day, and we can either use them or waste them, but we can't save them. Lord, our prayer is, "Give us the grace to take our eyes off tomorrow long enough to enable us to enjoy a loving Christian relationship with You, our spouse, our family and our friends today, all for the glory of God, through our Lord Jesus Christ."

THAT THEY MAY BE ONE

"I have given them the glory that they may be one as We are one." – John 17:22

WE'RE ONE WITH THE FATHER

God, the Father, had a vision,
And through Jesus, made provision,
Love abounding, grace surrounding,
To be one, with you and me.
For His Spirit's in us dwelling,
And His goodness now is welling,
And this lifting, is His gifting,
Through His love, for you and me,
And His caring, has us sharing,
With our Lord, who set us free,
An entire, eternity.

In this chapter, Jesus is offering a prayer to the Father, first for Himself, then for His disciples, then for all believers. In this section, His prayer is that we be one with the Father, just as He is one with the Father. He also states that He has given us the glory necessary to be one with the Father. The glory He has given each one of us is His indwelling Holy Spirit.

As a young man or woman, we thought that an eternity with our Lord would begin at some far distant point in time. As we progressed in age, most of us probably altered our view of time as we removed the "far distant" portion. But the truth is that ever since we put our complete trust in Jesus Christ, we have been in an eternal relationship with God, through Christ, which was made possible by the indwelling Holy Spirit. When we set our minds and our hearts on spiritual things, through the power of the Spirit, that eternal relationship becomes a glorious walk with Christ down this pathway of life. We become one with the Father, through the Son. We are capable of having His character through the power of the indwelling Spirit. Our prayer is, "Lord, give us the grace to have and to exhibit your character in our daily walk, that we might have a oneness with you, all for Your glory, through Jesus Christ."

June 11

PEACE BE WITH YOU

"Again Jesus said, 'Peace be with you.'" – John 20:21

THAT GIFT OF PEACE

Though in our heart, we know we're saved,
And all our sins, through Christ are waived,
As we walk down, this road of life,
Our peace seems lost, midst all the strife.
But if we keep, our eyes on Christ,
The One whose love, has all sufficed,
Through grace alone, he will impart,
That gift of peace, within our heart,
So, with this peace, within our hearts,
This gift of peace, our Lord imparts,
Let's live each day, with eyes not dim,
But realign our eyes on Him.

In this scripture, Jesus speaks to His disciples and tells them, "peace be with you." John 14:27 identifies what this peace is, for in that verse Jesus says, "My peace I give you." So those of us who are believers actually possess the capacity to experience the same peace that Jesus had. That peace is a supernatural gift that is beyond human comprehension. As Christians, we experience this peace, but it seems to be rather elusive, for we can have it one minute, and completely lose it the next. What is our problem? And, perhaps a more pressing question would be, what is the solution?

We don't live in a perfect world, and the only perfection we have is in Christ. During our daily schedule, whether that be with family, with friends, or with business acquaintances, we experience perplexing pressures, problems and disappointments. Our circumstances are out of control. Our expectations are shattered. We begin to focus our eyes and our minds on circumstances instead of on Christ. We let negative circumstances control our thinking, or we feel enough pressure in some aspect of our daily life, that we let it affect our attitude. When this happens, we invariably set our eyes on self instead of others, and on circumstances instead of Christ. The solution is to realign our eyes and our mind, and focus on Jesus, and what He means to use, then count our blessings, and supernaturally, that peace that surpasses all understanding will return to us. We thank God for this gift of peace that is ours.

HE IS FAITHFUL

"For He who promised is faithful." – Hebrews 10:23b

WE'RE RELYING

When by faith we are believing,
Through our Lord, we are receiving,
For believing, we're receiving,
Life eternal, through the Son,
Through our Lord, we are assessing,
This great promise of His blessing
God prevailing, love unfailing,
He is faithful, victory's won.
We're relying, 'til we're dying,
As on earth, our race is run,
On His promise, through His Son.

This scripture makes a simple statement concerning a great truth. God is faithful. Whatever promises He makes, He will keep. This is simply His nature. He is also a just God, and He hates sin, but love prevailing, He provided the propitiation for our sin with the sacrifice of His only Son on the cross. This satisfied His just nature and opened the door for each one of us to bask in the radiance of His love, mercy and grace. By simply believing in, and relying on His Son, we, by faith, become a member of the family of God. This entitles us to receive every blessing God has promised us through Christ, and there is absolutely no doubt whatsoever regarding the validity of His promises. They are like money in the bank, waiting for us to write a check on them. There is, in fact, a "heavenly bank," full of God's inexhaustible spiritual blessings with our name on the account, just waiting for us to withdraw and use day, by day, by day.

In this world we live in, there are very few constants. We think we know people and then we are disappointed. They think they know us and then we disappoint them. There are very few things on this earth that are for sure. But the one, absolutely sure constant, is that God is faithful, and He will fulfill His promises to each one of us. What a glorious position that each of us who are Christians occupies through Jesus Christ. God is faithful, and victory is won, for we're relying on God's only Son.

June 13

WE ALWAYS THANK GOD

"We always thank God, the Father of our Lord Jesus Christ, when we pray for you." – Colossians 1:3

LORD, PLEASE JUST FIX IT

Our prayer to God, please don't nix it,
But Lord, we ask, please just fix it,
As we languish, in our anguish,
Over things we think we need.
Though our sagging spirit's sinking,
Let us realign our thinking,
And be kneeling, for God's healing,
For He wills the best, indeed.
Him, we're thanking, and we're banking,
On His knowledge of our need,
Thanking Him, by word and deed.

Do we revert to prayer only when our circumstances are completely out of control, when we realize that we have completely lost control of a situation? So many of our prayers are, "Lord, please fix it. We've really messed it up, but we know You can take care of it, so Lord, please fix it." First, when we pray, are we coming to God with "our will" in mind, or with "His will" in mind? Second, do we have "prayer fellowship" with the Lord on a continuing basis, or do we go to the Lord in prayer, only when we realize we can't handle a situation by ourselves.

God knows our needs, and has promised to take care of them. In this scripture, Paul both begins and ends his prayer by thanking God. In the sixth chapter of Matthew, Jesus tells us to pray to the Father that His will be done. What is our attitude when we pray? Is it a selfish prayer, to think only of "our needs within our will" or does it glorify God because we pray according to "His will," lifting the needs of others up to Him? To address the second question, Paul, in Colossians 1:9 writes, "We have not stopped praying for you." The Lord wants to have prayer fellowship with us on a continuing basis. When we pray sporadically, or pray only in an emergency, we are relegating the Lord to an inferior position in our lives. It is as if we are saying, "Lord, we will use you as a substitute only when we lose control." Our Lord is not a substitute. He is a "full time player," and in this game of life, as we run with the ball, if we will let Him do the blocking every down, and follow Him, we will score touchdown, after touchdown, after touchdown.

June 14

HE SAT DOWN

"But when this Priest had offered for all time, one sacrifice for sins, He sat down at the right hand of God." – Hebrews 10:12

WE DON'T TAKE ANOTHER TEST

The Lord's living, and His dying,
And His act of death – defying,
Is the story, of His glory,
Then He sat down for a rest.
In the Gospel, He was casting,
He has cleaned us everlasting,
So forever, and forever,
We don't take another test.
First He saved us, then engraved us,
In God's book, eternal rest,
From our Lord, who gives His best.

In this scripture, the Priest referred to is Christ. We are told that he offered one sacrifice for sins, for all times, then He sat down. Now, what is the significance of His sitting down after His sacrifice?

The writer of Hebrews was writing principally to Jewish people. They were very familiar with the duties of the priests. They continually offered sacrifices for themselves and for the people because the blood of animals was a symbolic, temporary covering for their sins.

Their job was never finished because the blood of bulls and goats would never take away sin. Theirs was an outward, ceremonial cleansing only, and had to be performed time after time after time. Their work was never finished, but Jesus offered one sacrifice for all sin, for all time with His own blood, and this sacrifice would never have to be offered again. His work was finished, and we are told that He then sat down at the "right hand of the Father." His "sitting down" after He sacrificed Himself on the cross is a clear indication that He was truly finished. His work was done, and He returned to the Father.

Hebrews 9:22b tells us that without the shedding of blood, there is no forgiveness, and we had to be forgiven our sin in order to be cleansed and accepted by God. When we exercise faith in Jesus, our sins are immediately washed away by His blood. What a glorious gift this is, for we are placed in the family of God forever.

THE GIFT OF GOD

"If you knew the gift of God and Who it is that asks you for a drink, you would have asked Him and He would have given you living water." –John 4:10

LET US TURN TO THE GIFT

If ever we fear, this world so near,
With its greed, its sin and its strife,
Let us turn to the gift, to the one who will lift,
Each saint to eternal life.

Though troubled our days, and weary our ways,
We cling to the grace from above,
With our hearts open wide, and Christ Jesus inside,
Let us turn to the gift of God's love.

With grace thus abounding, and trumpets resounding,
With joy, we shall see, face to face,
His crowning of glory, the end of the story.
Let us turn to the gift of God's grace.

The Greek word "dorea" is used in John's gospel only in this verse. The word denotes a "free gift," stressing its gratuitous character, and in the New Testament it always denotes a supernatural or spiritual gift. The gift referred to in this scripture is eternal life, and is subsequently referred to as the life-giving Holy Spirit, or Spirit of Christ that indwells each believer.

In this scripture, Jesus was giving the Samaritan woman a preview of God's saving grace (eternal life) through Him. He called it "living water." This eternal life is a gift, a free gift from God through His Son.

Even though we, as Christians, understand and realize that salvation is a free gift from God, how often we seem to forget, and begin to believe that we must do something else to earn our salvation. This gift is free to us, though it cost our Lord the anguish of the cross. The work we do for the Lord, we do, not to earn our salvation, or justification, or righteousness, but with loving thankfulness, and in appreciation for what He has already done for us. We simply accept this gift by faith in Christ, then we receive His life-giving Spirit that enables us to serve Him in love, and let Him live His life through us.

June 16

ON EAGLES' WINGS

"You yourselves have seen what I did to Egypt, and how I carried you on eagles' wings, and brought you to Myself." – Exodus 19:4

ON WINGS OF EAGLES

When we start to let our thinking,
Bereft of pride, just keep sinking,
And we feel our soul is shattered,
And we know our body's battered,
Let our eyes toward Christ be turning,
And our hearts through Him be learning,
For through Christ, and His connection,
God has given us direction,
And like wings of eagles gliding,
With our Lord to do the guiding,
We are lifted from our failing,
With the grace of God prevailing.

Pride in self is such a dreadful sin, that when we realize its total implication, we desperately want to be removed from any association with it. We, through the grace of the power of our Lord, replace pride with humility. This is exactly what our Lord wants us to do. And He empowers us to do it through our dependence is on Him and not on self. But, at this time, let us be sure we understand exactly what it means to have humility. Being humble before God means that we acknowledge that we can't do it, but He can. And we thankfully accept what He does. At that point, there might be a tendency for the Christian to "get down on himself or herself," a tendency to think about, and perhaps brood about his or her lack of self worth, a feeling of total inadequacy. But this is not what being humble before God means.

When we replace pride with humility, we actually activate an unbelievable source of power and strength through Jesus Christ. His indwelling Spirit can "break out" through that broken shell of pride, and can be used by us. With humility, we don't just lose pride in self but we replace it with pride in Jesus. And from that point forward, we may not have much self-power, but we have an inexhaustible amount of Christ-power at our disposal. Our prayer is that we use this Christ-power wisely, and with prudence, all for the glory of God, through Jesus Christ.

June 17

THE LOVE OF MONEY

"For the love of money is a root of all kinds of evil." – 1 Timothy 6:10

CONTENTMENT IS OUR PRAYER

Love of money has connection,
With an evil root direction,
For the striving, and the driving,
Are for selfish gains out there.
Through our Lord, let us be driving,
With a Christ-like holy striving,
To be living, and be giving,
Of His love, and grace, and care.
Let's be resting, in His nesting,
With contentment as our prayer,
For we're in His loving care.

The Bible does not teach that money is evil, but that the love of money is a root of all kinds of evil. In Matthew, the sixth chapter, Jesus teaches that we cannot serve two masters, we cannot serve both God and money. When someone loves money enough, it will become his or her master. It will, in fact, almost become a god to be worshipped.

With money comes a sense of power. With power comes a sense of self-sufficiency. With this sense of self-sufficiency, we plunge headlong into the sin of pride. Money, itself, is not responsible for this condition, but the "love of money" is. We can look around us in today's world and see two distinct types of wealthy people. One type avoids the limelight, loves God, and gives of his or her wealth to worthy causes, and quite often anonymously. The other type seeks the spotlight, and loves, not God, but the power that money buys, and sees to it that any of his or her money spent should bring back a profitable return. One type is dependent upon God, the other upon money. One agonizing truth that will be revealed at some point in time to persons within the second group, is that God outlasts money. For just a season, the earthly power that one has because of wealth will be evident, but that season soon passes and we will face eternity. We will face this eternity either with, or without, our Lord. Our prayer is "Lord, help us that we might be content in whatever circumstances we might be in, and give us the grace to keep our eyes and hearts focused on You alone, all for Your glory."

June 18

PETER WALKED ON WATER

"'Come,' He said. Then Peter got down out of the boat, walked on the water and came toward Jesus. But when he saw the wind, he was afraid and, beginning to sink, cried out, 'Lord, save me.'" – Matthew 13:29-30

OUR FAITH

We have faith in our Lord's teaching,
He says "come," and we start reaching,
But when walking, we start balking,
Midst the windstorm and the rain.
For, by faith, we do the striving,
But a wind will stop the thriving,
And from meekness, we find weakness,
As our faith begins to wane.
Let's let weakness, turn to meekness,
For through Christ, it's not in vain,
And our faith through Him we gain.

This scripture depicts, too well, the reaction some of us as Christians have to adversity. Just as He said to Peter, "come," walk on water, He also beckons us to "come" live for Him, with perhaps a special assignment. Just as Peter began his walk, we begin our work for the Lord. At first, we are so enthusiastic; there are just not enough hours in the day for us to serve the Lord. Then something happens. We face some type of adversity, the storm clouds gather, and just as Peter did, we can almost see the wind. At that point, our minds focus on self, our faith begins to wane and our immediate response is a huge call for help. The Lord responds with love, mercy and grace; our faith is renewed, and, in fact, in many instances, increased.

This scripture embodies a very special truth for each and every Christian who is trying to live the Christian life. As long as Peter kept his eyes on Jesus, he walked. The moment he saw the wind, he sank. As long as we keep our eyes and our hearts focused on the Lord, He will give us the faith and the strength to do what He wants us to do. The moment we begin looking at the wind, we set our eyes and our hearts on self instead of on Jesus. Our prayer is, "Lord, by Your grace, give us the direction and the durability to remain focused on Jesus, instead of self, then give us the strength to do Your will, all for Your glory, through our Lord, Jesus Christ."

LET THE DEAD BURY THE DEAD

"Another disciple said to him, 'Lord, first let me go bury my father.' But Jesus told him, 'Follow Me, and let the dead bury the dead.'" – Matthew 8:21-22

NOT DELAYING, BUT OBEYING

Now, our Lord has our clock wound-up,
It will tick until the round-up,
But from wound-up, to the round-up,
The last tick, we just don't know.
So, the time we have for living,
Is the time we have for giving,
A full ration, of compassion,
As along our path we go,
Not delaying, but obeying,
Our dear Lord, who loves us so,
Spreading love, where 'ere we go.

On the surface, as we read this scripture, it would appear that Jesus is denying this disciple his right, and in fact, his obligation to bury his own father. But let's take a close look at what the scripture says. Jesus wants each one of us to follow Him, and to do His work here on earth, as our time permits. This disciple indicated he wanted to follow Jesus, but not then. This verse does not indicate that this man's father had died, only that he wanted to delay following Jesus until some point in time when he would need to bury his father. He was making excuses in order to delay working for Jesus today. For him, there were other things more important than Jesus. Jesus knew his heart, and his reply was to let the spiritually dead bury their own dead. These verses show the deep contrast between the response of this disciple, who was not ready to follow Jesus, and the response of Matthew, the tax collector, who "immediately" got up and followed our Lord.

When Jesus calls us, what is our response as Christians? Do we check our schedule to see if we can possibly fit Him into our daily routine, or do we give Him priority? He doesn't want excuses and delays. He wants "loving action" from each one of us. Now the Lord has our clock "wound-up," and it will "tick" until the "round-up," but Lord give us the grace, the purpose and the direction to do Your will while our clock is still ticking, then we will join You at the "round-up" for all eternity. What a blessed "round-up" that will be.

HE HAS RISEN

"'Don't be alarmed,' he said. 'You are looking for Jesus the Nazarene, who was crucified. He has risen.'" – Mark 16:6

LIVING LIFE

Now, our Jesus did the buying,
Of our freedom, by His dying,
Death defying, after dying,
He arose for you and me.
So our thankful recollection,
Is His glorious resurrection,
For He's guiding, while residing,
In the hearts of you and me,
And believing, we're receiving,
Living life that sets us free,
Throughout all eternity.

The most glorious and important three words in Christianity are "He has risen." Had He not risen, there would be no Christianity. Jesus came to this earth as a babe then as a man, with but one destination, the cross. He defeated Satan at the cross when He sacrificed Himself for the sins of all mankind. He actually bought our freedom with His blood, then, as we believed, He gave us life at that instant, a life that will be ours for all eternity. We have an ongoing, personal relationship with God, through Jesus Christ our Lord.

As we progress through life, people may fail us, and we may fail people. Even our brothers and sisters in Christ may fail us at times, and we may fail them. But there is one absolute constant, our Jesus will never fail us. Jesus is the same yesterday, today and forever. (Hebrews 13:8). We look forward to an eternity with Him where there is no sickness, pain or sorrow. He bought our freedom, then set us free. He gave us His life, eternal life, and He walks with us every day of our life here on earth. What a glorious gift this is.

June 21

GOUGE IT OUT

"If your right eye causes you to sin, gouge it out and throw it away." Matthew 5:29

LET'S STOP LOOKING

With our eye, if sin we're booking,
Through our Lord, let us stop looking,
For in sinning, there's no winning,
Just a slap, in our Lord's face.
Let us live with His direction,
As we make our own projection,
For the living, and the giving,
Of His mercy, love and grace,
To our brothers, and to others,
As we run this earthly race,
Let's serve Him, with love and grace.

In this scripture, Jesus is obviously using hyperbole to illustrate the deadliness of sin when he says, "If our right eye causes us to sin, gouge it out and throw it away." If not a hyperbole, there would be a great multitude of one-eyed Christians on earth. But there is absolute truth in this statement as He connects it to the following verse in which He says, "It is better for us to lose one part of our body, than for our whole body to be thrown into Hell." However, the truth that Jesus is teaching in this scripture is twofold. First, if there is anything in our life that would keep us from exercising saving faith in Him, we had better gouge it out and throw it away, or we can, indeed, look forward to an eternity in Hell. But to those of us who are Christians, who have His salvation, He is giving us instructions and issuing us a command for our own good.

Jesus wants the very best for each one of us, and he knows that when we focus our eyes on people or things other than Himself, we begin enlarging self and diminishing Jesus. In this particular scripture, Jesus was dealing with the sin of adultery, but His teaching applies to any sin. If we have anything in our life that hinders a loving, personal relationship with our Lord, we need to gouge it out and throw it away. Our prayer is that the Lord will give us a sufficient amount of His grace, so that our propensity to sin in any area of our life might be identified, then gouged out and thrown away. We pray that we will stop looking at any and all distractions and refocus our eyes and our hearts on Him.

IT IS CALLED TODAY

"But encourage one another daily, as long as it is called today." – Hebrews 3:13

TODAY

Now, today, let's not be waiting,
For our time is fast abating.
Let's not ponder, think and wonder,
But, let's get it done today.
The Good Lord, who's in us living,
Sets the time for us He's giving.
Too much ponder, makes us squander,
Precious time along the way.
Let our sharing, and our caring,
For the Saints, begin today,
And continue, day by day.

We are admonished to encourage one another, and, of course, this admonishment is given to each one of us throughout the epistles. But, in this scripture, there is urgency involved. We are told to encourage each other daily, then, as if to reemphasize, the writer of Hebrews adds, "as long as it is called today." The word, "tomorrow," is not in his vocabulary. He is stressing today.

In the process of understanding this urgency, with regard to salvation, the adage, "The road to Hell is paved with good intentions," certainly has validity. The one who intends to accept Christ as his or her personal Savior, but intends to do it tomorrow, has absolutely no guarantee that tomorrow will ever come. Salvation can be lost because of procrastination. We, as Christians, even though our eternity is guaranteed, also face the same dilemma regarding the work we intend to do for the Lord. We have a headache or pressing business matters to attend to. We have some kind of "ox in the ditch." Just as soon as we get it out, probably "some time tomorrow," then we will do the work our Lord wants us to do. We can't today, but we will tomorrow. He has given us a certain amount of time to live and work for Him, and He alone knows how much time we have. Our prayer is, "Lord, help us that we might not procrastinate, but give us the grace to have the urgency to work for You today, not tomorrow, and if we work for You each day, tomorrow will take care of itself."

THE WHOLE MEASURE

"And become mature, attaining to the whole measure of the fullness of Christ." – Ephesians 4:13

CHRIST THE TREASURE

When we're "one" with Christ we measure,
And we measure with the Treasure,
Christ the treasure, is our measure,
As we're striving to obey.
Through His death, and resurrection,
He exemplified perfection.
As we're growing, let's be sowing,
Seeds of love, along the way.
Our connecting, Christ perfecting,
As we work, and love and pray,
Helps us measure, day by day.

There is a great truth in this scripture. Just as Paul was instructing the Ephesians, he is also instructing us to strive to measure up, not to what others may be, but to the fullness of which Christ is, and what He exemplifies. This would first entail a firm conviction that Jesus is our Lord and Savior, then a determination to obey His commandments. Any teaching that is not congruent with the gospel of Christ should never sway us. Likewise, we should never compare or measure ourselves with others (2 Corinthians 10:12). Conversely, we should always measure ourselves with Jesus. This, of course, places us in a position where we never measure up. But Paul's admonition to us is to keep trying, become more mature spiritually, not become discouraged and love the brethren. Of course, before we can have any success with this course of action, we must first, not only believe that He is our Lord and our Savior, but have a very personal relationship with Him. Then, as we mature in Christ, we are given the grace necessary to become more like Him.

Christ is, indeed, our treasure. As we continue to try to measure up, let's let His "perfection" be our "connection" and guide. And may His grace propel us into action to be continually striving for the "whole measure" of His fullness, all for the glory of God.

GOD RAISED US UP

"And God raised us up with Christ and seated us with Him in the heavenly realms, in Christ Jesus." – Ephesians 2:6

LET'S PLANT THE SEED

Through our Lord, we're realizing,
God, Himself, has caused our rising,
So it's fitting, that we're sitting,
In a place so high, indeed.
But let us be so discerning,
For it's not a seat we're earning,
But the gifting, of the lifting,
Was by grace, and not by deed.
Through God's giving, let's be living,
So the world, so much in need,
Will find Christ; let's plant the seed.

We, as Christians, often become so strenuously involved in things of this world that we tend to forget what God has actually done for us. He has raised us, elevated us spiritually and seated us with Christ. He, not only has given us an eternal family with Christ as the Head, but he has also given us the Holy Spirit to guide and direct us as we attempt to live this Christian life.

As Paul continues his dissertation, we are taught that this gift was given us, not for any work or personal endeavor, but only by God's grace, expressed in His kindness to us in Christ Jesus. We are currently temporary residents, wherever our home may be, because our permanent home is in Heaven with Jesus. Awaiting us is an inheritance that is imperishable and undefiled, one that will not fade away, reserved for us in Heaven. This is our sure hope of salvation.

We not only have this to look forward to, but we are equipped with His Spirit to live this Christian life. Through God's grace, if we will let His Spirit prevail, we are ably equipped to face any adverse circumstance. Our prayer is, "Lord, let us keep our eyes and our hearts focused on You. And by Your grace, and through the power of Your indwelling Spirit, direct and strengthen us that we might live in such a manner that we plant the seed of salvation for a world in need, all for Your glory."

June 25

HE IS ABLE TO HELP

"Because He Himself suffered when He was tempted, He is able to help those who are being tempted." – Hebrews 2:18

HE WILL HELP US

As on earth we walk this highway,
Leading up to Heaven's skyway,
The sensation, of temptation,
Is a thing we face today.
But our Lord, His Spirit bracing,
Gives us strength, what 'ere we're facing.
His connection, gives direction,
As we walk along the way.
From our highway, to the skyway,
As we travel day by day,
He will help us to obey.

We, as Christians, possess two distinct "natures." One is our old sinful nature, while the other is the indwelling Spirit of Christ. As we travel down life's highway, we face every kind of temptation. The word "temptation" denotes a "trial" or a "test" that we are confronted with. To be tempted in itself is not a sin, however, if our response to temptation is made with our sinful nature in control, our response is sin. The sinful nature is a nature of lust, greed and immediate personal gratification, with the prevailing thought process being centered on self. This is the only nature a non-Christian has when confronted with temptation. A non-Christian might possibly be very intent about having a proper response to temptation, but, in truth, he is not equipped for a proper response.

Conversely, we as Christians have the very Spirit of Christ indwelling us, so we are equipped for a proper response to temptation if we will only let His Spirit break through our sinful nature and control our thoughts and our actions. When we sin, there is a very simple explanation for our sinning. We are thinking of self.

There is not a single sin of the flesh, soul or spirit that does not focus on self. Our prayer is, "Lord, in all areas of our life, let us be focused on You, instead of self. And give us the grace for a proper response, a Christ-like response to any and all temptation, all for Your glory as we walk this earth's highway, day after day, after day."

June 26

HE MADE HIM TO BE SIN

"He made Him who knew no sin, to be sin on our behalf, that we might become the righteousness of God in Him." – 2 Corinthians 5:21

THROUGH HIS CLEANSING

For our Lord, who knew no sinning,
Who was pure from the beginning,
Let us languish, in His anguish,
As he died upon that tree.
But indeed, His pain and sadness,
Gave to us, His gift of gladness,
For abounding, and resounding,
Was His love for you and me.
And forever, and forever,
Through His cleansing on that tree,
He gives us, eternity.

A righteous, loving God, came to this earth in the person of Jesus Christ. He made Himself to be sin on our behalf, shed His blood on the cross to pay for our sin debt, that we might become the righteousness of God in Christ Jesus. This was our righteous God's supreme and final judgment on sin. He paid the price for the sins of the world, thus enabling the entire human race to again have fellowship with God through Jesus Christ. By simple faith in Christ, we are cleansed of our sin, and stand pure and righteous in the eyes of God, thus enabling us to have loving fellowship with God, beginning the moment we believed, and extending throughout all eternity.

It is true that we are saved by His life, and not by His death (Romans 5:10), but we must never relegate the cross to an inferior position. Had it not been for the cross, the blood of Christ, which enabled us to be reconciled to God, would not have cleansed us. Without redemption, there is no reconciliation, and without reconciliation there is no salvation. But God, through the work of Jesus on the cross, made complete provisions for our eternity when we, in simple faith, accept Christ. This is a gift. We can't buy it, and we can't work for it. We can only thankfully accept it. Our prayer is that we might live our life in such a manner that God knows how thankful we are, and to God be the glory.

THROUGH HIS SON

"God has given us eternal life, and this life is in His Son. He who has the Son has life; he who does not have the Son of God does not have life." – 1 John 5:11

LIVING – LIFE ETERNALLY

Through the Lord, let's help each other,
Let us comfort one another,
For God's vision, made provision,
For each Saint's eternity.
Through His love, the Father gave us,
Jesus Christ, the one who'll save us,
And His giving, is a living,
Life He gives to you and me,
For believing, we're receiving,
Living-Life eternally,
As we face eternity.

God has given us eternal life and this life is in His Son. Eternal life begins for the believer the moment Jesus Christ is accepted by faith, and continues throughout all eternity. We are promised by the Father that if we have the Son, that is, believe on Him, we have life. But we are also warned that if we do not have the Son, that is, do not believe on Him, we do not have life. What a glorious promise this is for the believer. However, with this extension of God's grace, we also inherit an obligation.

Our obligation to God is to help and comfort one another, and to spread this gospel to unbelievers. We, who are believers, have the indwelling Spirit of Christ to help us in all areas of our life, and to direct our work for the Lord. How many of us want to face the Lord on judgment day and try to explain why we failed to tell some lost soul about God's plan for salvation? Do the unbelievers see Christ in us? As we depart from church each Sunday, does Christ stay with us the remainder of the week, or do we drop Him off at the convenience store as we leave church, and pick Him up again the following Sunday? If the unbeliever is moved by God's Spirit, but rejects Jesus, is there anything we, either could have done, or would have done differently, to have helped alter his decision? When the unbeliever views the membership of a Christian church, does he see saints or hypocrites? Are we living up to our obligation and responsibility to do what God wants us to do, and to be who God wants us to be?

WITH THE LORD FOREVER

"And so we will be with the Lord forever." – 1 Thessalonians 4:17b

AND THE FUN HAS JUST BEGUN

When our life is done, we breathe our last,
And they lay us down to rest,
Then our joy's complete, not like the past,
For at last we have his best,
AND THE FUN HAS JUST BEGUN.
For at last we see, His shining face,
His radiance all aglow,
And we now see the fullness of His grace,
And we're there, and not below,
AND THE FUN HAS JUST BEGUN.
For, with Christ our soul will soar and soar,
And our joy intensify,
And forevermore, and more, and more,
We reside with Him on high,
AND THE FUN HAS JUST BEGUN.

This simple statement truth found in the fourth chapter of 1 Thessalonians, "And so, we will be with the Lord forever," sums up the sure hope of every believer. On television, I saw Billy Graham being interviewed, and the one conducting the interview was obviously attempting to "trip-up" Mr. Graham. The question asked was, "Exactly where is Heaven?" Billy Graham's answer may or may not have been original, but it was "classic." His answer was, "Heaven is wherever Jesus is." There is such a great truth in that statement. No one knows for sure the exact location of Heaven, but we know for sure who will be there. And we are promised in 1 Corinthians chapter two, that "No eye has seen, no ear has heard, no mind has conceived what God has prepared for those who love Him."

When we think of Heaven, we think of love, peace and joy, and the fact that there is no sickness and sorrow there, and we are reunited with our loved ones. This is absolutely true. But to put our expectations into a real earthy expression, "We will have fun in Heaven," and when we get there, whether we have been there 10 minutes, or 10,000 years or 10 million years, THE FUN HAS JUST BEGUN.

YOU OF LITTLE FAITH

"You of little faith, why are you so afraid?" – Matthew 8:26a

GIVE US FAITH

Though in this life, the pain we bear,
May seem so great, our soul to wear,
Please let us have, the faith to dare,
Place all our needs, within Your care.

We pray You give, this faith we need,
In times of stress, in thought, in deed.
Direct our life, and take the lead.
We know Your love, You know our need.

Just as these disciples of Jesus looked out and beheld a furious storm beginning to engulf them, we as Christians will face many storms in our lives. We look out and see the huge waves descending upon us, and our reaction will depend entirely upon the degree of faith we have in Jesus. When the storm becomes furious, we certainly call upon the Lord, but are we calling upon Him in fear or in faith? There is a difference.

If our relationship with the Lord is a "Sunday only" affair, we may be like these disciples. We may turn to Him in fear instead of faith. If we have a personal relationship with the Lord – day by day, hour by hour, minute by minute – there is no way that we can turn to Him in fear. That's because we have already established the fact that He knows our needs, and that He will protect us and take care of us. This does not mean that we should do nothing to avoid the storm, but it does mean that we know Jesus is our "unsinkable lifeboat." Thus we have no reason to fear because our faith is in Him, and this gives us a peace that the world does not understand.

Our prayer is, "Lord, let our relationship with You be such that by Your grace we will never turn to You in fear, but always in faith, and to God be the glory.

June 30

CHRIST HAS SET US FREE

"It is for freedom that Christ has set us free. Stand firm, then and do not let yourselves be burdened by a yoke of slavery." – Galatians 5:1

WITH THE FREEDOM OF HIS GRACE

For our Lord, let us be reaching,
Other Saints, with freedom's teaching,
For it's awful, to be lawful,
Teaching works, instead of grace.
For, our Jesus is the answer,
He's our Lord, the great Enhancer,
And by caring, and by sharing,
We are free to run this race,
His love showing, His grace glowing,
As we toil in His embrace,
With the freedom of His Grace.

One of the most calamitous things that can happen to a Christian, especially a new Christian is to be involved in a church that places more emphasis on tradition than it does on Christ. There is nothing wrong with tradition if it is used properly. But from tradition springs a spirit of mandatory selectivity regarding how we worship, and what rules and regulations we must adhere to, and exactly what we must believe. Some of these things look and sound great from afar, but when we examine them closely, just like some kinds of cheese, they simply "don't smell good." They have an odor, and that odor is called "legalism." Jesus, during His entire ministry on this earth, denounced legalism. In fact, the proponents of legalism, the Pharisees, were the ones who demanded that he be crucified. Legalism robs us of our freedom in Christ. Legalism is a religion, with its own set of specific rules, regulations and traditions that are almost mandatory within each legalist church – and the rules and regulations vary from church to church. Christianity is not a religion – it is a personal relationship with Jesus Christ. Through His empowering Spirit, we can pass His love on to others, working in the freedom we have by His grace. What a glorious gift this is.

BUT WE PREACH CHRIST CRUCIFIED

"But we preach Christ crucified, a stumbling block to Jews and foolishness to Gentiles." – 1 Corinthians 1:23

GOD'S DIRECTION IS THE CROSS

The religious have direction,
And the scholars have selection,
But reflection, on election,
Is the cross, where Jesus died.
For the Jews, with their objection,
And the Greeks with their rejection,
Lost connection, with election,
And our Lord, they both defied,
God's connection, and direction,
That the Jews and Greeks defied,
Is that cross, where our Lord died.

In this scripture, Paul is describing why both the Jews and the Greeks were rejecting the gospel. To the Jews, the cross was a stumbling block, and to the Greeks, it was foolishness. Of all people, the Jews, who were God's "chosen people" should have accepted the gospel. But their original faith had diminished until all that was left was self-centered works. So intent were they on the adherence to minute details regarding their rules and regulations that they had no capacity left for God's grace. Their god was a self-centered "works-righteousness." Consequently, they rejected both Christ and the gospel.

The Greeks had a somewhat different mindset. They were simply "too smart" to accept the gospel. They had many brilliant philosophers among them, and the wisdom of the world was at their disposal. Their god was self-centered worldly wisdom. Consequently, they rejected the gospel.

Today, as we see the gospel rejected, we see a correlation between the reasons then, and the reasons now. All rejection has to do with self and self-centeredness. We are either "too smart" with worldly wisdom, or we are "too intent" with self-centered works to recognize and accept the wisdom of God. God's wisdom gave us the cross to be central to salvation, beginning with justification, advanced by sanctification and climaxed by glorification. Our prayer is that the Lord might use us in some small way to spread the gospel, and that through God's grace, others will become believers, all for God's glory through Jesus Christ.

July 2

AT GOD'S COMMAND

"By faith we understand that the universe was formed at God's command, so that what is seen was not made out of what was visible." – Hebrews 11:3

GOD SPOKE INTO EXISTENCE

Stretching eons in the distance,
Our Lord spoke into existence,
No resistance, or assistance,
And the universe was made.
For, by faith, God's truth we're seeking,
He created by His speaking,
He's the lightness, and the brightness,
And His light will never fade,
And His brilliance, gives resilience,
For through Christ, our debt was paid,
And eternal life conveyed.

One of the most difficult things for me to comprehend is how anyone could possibly believe there is no God. The so-called "atheist," who measures everything by logic, has to be utterly illogical to explain the existence of creation without direction from a "Director." If we regressed to the point of eliminating faith, and measured creation by "pure logic" only, how could anyone believe that this universe, containing billions and billions of galaxies, accidentally came into existence? We hear that there was a "Big Bang," and then everything, without a Director, fell into place in perfect order. By logic alone, this is the most illogical hypothesis imaginable. They assume matter already existed. By logic alone, we must ask, "How did this matter originate?" And then, without direction, "How did it fall into place in perfect order?" By logic alone, we know that there has to be a supreme Architect of the universe, a Creator and Director, and we call this supreme Being, God.

Our God is not only the Creator, but He is a loving God, who manifested Himself in the flesh on this earth as Jesus Christ, died on the cross for our transgressions, and rose from the grave to give us life in His name. We, as Christians, have faith, not only in His original creation, but His life-giving Spirit, Who guarantees us an eternity with Him. Our God is "far removed" from some cold, calculating scientific hypothesis regarding an accidental "Big Bang."

July 3

DO YOU TRULY LOVE ME?

"Again Jesus said, 'Simon, son of John, do you truly love me?'" – John 21:16

DO WE TRULY, TRULY CARE?

Is our love for Christ a notion?
Do we just go through the motion?
Is emotion, our devotion?
Do we truly, truly care?
Is our love an extra caring,
Or a special love of sharing?
With compassion, do we fashion,
Any special deeds out there?
To our brothers, and to others,
Is His love passed on out there?
Do we truly, truly care?

The renderings of the word "love" that we find in the New Testament are most frequently from the Greek root words "agape" or "phileo." The word "phileo" denotes tender affection or brotherly love, and our emotions produce this love, whereas the word "agape" refers to the entire personality, where, not only our emotions, but our very "will" is involved. In others words, "agape-love" extends above and beyond "phileo-love." It is a Christ-like unconditional love that expects nothing in return. In this passage of scripture, Jesus is asking Peter, and He is asking us, "Do you agape me?" Do you "truly love" me?

In this modern era, the meaning for the word "love" has many connotations. We have so cheapened the word that we even say, we just "love" meat and potatoes, or we just "love" that song. This meaning is far removed from the simple question that Jesus is asking us. Do we truly "love" Him? Are the works we do for Jesus over and beyond obligation? In addition to emotion, are our mind and our will involved in our decisions for Him? Do we work because we "want to" or because we think we "have to?" Do we work because of fear, or do we work because of love? 1 John 4:18 tells us that "there is no fear in love, but perfect love drives out fear." Fear and love cannot be occupants in the same house at the same time. Our prayer is, "Lord, give us Your grace, that we might realize the difference between obligation and loving inspiration. Let us use our will in loving extension of Your love, all for the glory of God, through our Lord Jesus Christ."

July 4

GOD BLESS OUR NATION

"The light shines in the darkness, but the darkness has not understood it."
– John 1:5

MAY GOD BLESS OUR NATION

May our nation, not tomorrow, be a Sodom and Gomorrah,
For that horror of tomorrow, is a thing we see today.
With our morals sharply swerving, in a downward spiral curving,
And our nation's, limitations, are increased by sin's decay,
And the harming is alarming, so alarming is today,
For our nation, LET US PRAY.

May the God of all creation, in His mercy, BLESS OUR NATION.
May His gifting, so uplifting, when we face eternity,
Cause within our hearts reaction, that will spur us into action,
And may action, have impaction, through our Lord's morality.
May the urgence, cause resurgence, as he works through you and me,
THAT OUR NATION MIGHT BE FREE.

As we pause to celebrate our nation's independence, we observe the decadence, moral decay and the falling away from God's values currently so rampant in our nation. We read the daily newspaper, or we watch television, and the preponderance of abject immorality is overwhelming. Truly, though "THE LIGHT SHINES IN THE DARKNESS, THE DARKNESS HAS NOT UNDERSTOOD IT." We do not want this nation to become a Sodom and Gomorrah. We can take a page out of history and reflect on the fall of the Roman Empire. Immorality became a way of life, and the empire fell.

We understand that there is only so much we can do to change the direction our nation seems to be heading in, but the thing we can do is let God use us to spread the gospel. Only God can change the hearts of men and women, but He can use us to spread the GOOD NEWS. Our prayer on this Fourth of July, as we celebrate our independence, is that the God of all creation will look with favor on our nation, and that in some small way He will use us to spread the gospel. We are currently blessed with freedom in this nation, a freedom that very few nations enjoy. We pray that God will use us, so that the light that shines in the darkness will be understood. MAY GOD BLESS OUR NATION.

July 5

EVIL IS RIGHT THERE WITH ME

"So I find this law at work: When I want to do good, evil is right there with me." – Romans 7:21

SELECTING HIS DIRECTING

Though His Spirit is indwelling,
In us, evil is rebelling,
So selection, of direction,
Is a choice for you and me.
Let "our will" as we're selecting,
Be "His Will" with Christ directing,
His injection, of direction,
Will give us serenity,
Thus selecting, His directing,
So we're all that we can be,
Is a "must" for you and me.

In the latter part of Romans, chapter 7, Paul presents a truth that is a problem, then gives the solution to the problem in chapters 7 and 8. That truth is that even though we are Christians, and have the very Spirit of Christ indwelling us, we also are living with a "sin nature," and that is the problem. Mankind, since the fall of Adam and Eve has possessed a sin nature. Jesus came into this world to pay our sin debt, thus enabling us to have, not only salvation, but also fellowship with God, through our Lord Jesus Christ. As believers, through His indwelling Spirit, we possess His very nature. But we also have a sin nature to deal with. As believers, our conscience reflects His nature. But in order for His nature to prevail in our lives, we must focus on Him and on spiritual things instead of on self and on selfish things. This is the solution to the problem. This focus on Christ is an assertion of our will. Prior to becoming Christians, this solution was impossible. We existed in our sin nature only, but now we are equipped with the indwelling Spirit of Christ, which gives us, not only direction in our lives, but the strength and power to overcome this sin nature.

Our prayer is, "Lord, we know You give us choices. We pray for Your grace, that our selection of direction in our lives may continually be the same as Your selection of direction, and that through Your indwelling Spirit, we might exhibit Your love and Your grace to others, all for Your glory, through our Lord, Jesus Christ."

July 6

OUR FOUNDATION

"For no one can lay any foundation other than the one already laid, which is Jesus Christ." – 1 Corinthians 3:11

CHRIST ALONE

As we search for information,
Christ alone is our foundation.
Our projection, has connection,
With our Lord at Calvary.
He's the basis for believing,
He's the life we are receiving,
His foundation, gives elation,
Christ, our Lord, is Deity.
So enthralling, is His calling,
For He died upon that tree,
To give life to you and me.

Whether we are pastors, teachers or lay people, as believers, our primary mission on this earth is to honor God. This involves, not only living our lives in such a manner that others can see Christ in us, but taking advantage of every opportunity we have to pass on to others the gospel of Jesus Christ. Congruent with this opportunity is an obligation to be absolutely sure the gospel we spread is the pure, unadulterated truth of the grace gospel. The only foundation for this gospel is Jesus Christ, with the focal point being the cross. Christ died for our sins, cleansed us with His blood, arose to give us His life, and this free grace gift is ours when we are truly sorry for our sins, and place our trust completely in Him. This is the pure gospel of grace. There is no other.

Today, as in the days of Paul's ministry, there are many that distort the gospel, some out of ignorance, and some deliberately, in order to control others. Some of the most prevalent distortions are either adding to gospel, subtracting from the gospel or teaching a different Jesus than the one we know. As Christians, we have a very personal relationship with the Lord. Jesus Christ alone is our foundation and we thank God for Him. There is no other foundation.

July 7

WE KNOW HIM

"We know that we have come to know Him if we obey His commands."
– 1 John 2:3

WE OBEY IN LOVE, NOT FEAR

Down life's pathway, as we're going,
Are we really, truly knowing,
His great ration, of compassion,
That He has for you and me?
He commands, and we are hearing,
We respond, but not by fearing,
Our obeying, we are saying,
Is response to "Love" we see,
For His living, loving, giving,
He extends to you and me,
Is for all eternity.

This verse does not mean that a Christian never disobeys the commandments of Christ, but it does refer to those Christians who live a life generally within the perimeters of obedience to Christ. If we never disobeyed Christ, we would never sin. We actually have the necessary equipment, His indwelling Holy Spirit, to accomplish a sinless life. But in this process of sanctification, our sinful nature rears its ugly head, and perfection will never be accomplished until our will is completely synchronized with His will.

Our obedience to the commands of Christ should always be because of our love and respect for Him, never because we fear Him. If we fear Him, we are really not that well acquainted with Him. We obey His commands because we know Him, not because we would like to know Him. The word "fear" should not even be in the Christian's vocabulary. We have nothing to fear if we know Jesus, and He knows us. 1 John 4:18 tells us, "There is no fear in love, but perfect love drives our fear." And "the one who fears is not made perfect in love."

As believers, let us continually strive for obedience to Christ in all areas of our lives. And may we never obey in fear, but always in faith, as we, by God's grace, focus our minds and our hearts on the love, grace and mercy of God through our Lord Jesus Christ.

July 8

ABOLISHING THE LAW

"By abolishing in His flesh the Law with its commandments and regulations. His purpose was to create one new man out of two." – Ephesians 2:15

EQUAL RATING

Now, the purpose of His dying,
Then His act of death-defying,
Was His changing, by arranging,
That the law no longer sting.
With God's morals still applying,
But the sting removed by dying,
His creating, equal rating,
Through His Grace in everything,
Is His living, loving, giving,
Of His Son, to whom we cling,
In our Lord, we're everything.

This passage of scripture could very early be misinterpreted if taken out of context from other scriptures. In Matthew 5:17, Jesus tells us that He came, not to abolish "the law and the prophets," but to fulfill them. In 1 Corinthians 15:56, we are told that "the sting of death is sin, and the power of sin is the law." Jesus did not abolish God's moral law – He fulfilled it. In His flesh, as He lived a perfect sinless life and then gave Himself up on that cross, He fulfilled God's moral requirements. What He abolished was the "sting of death" in sin, that was the penalty for disobedience under the law. Consequently, He abolished our penalty of sin under the law, by shedding His blood to pay our sin debt.

This scripture also tells us God's purpose was to create one new man out of two. The Jews had been God's chosen people, but with a few exceptions, they had been disobedient. The birth, life, death and resurrection of Jesus brought a New Covenant from God, not only to the Jews, but also to all that would believe. Thus, since Jesus had filled the requirements of the old Law, all mankind was placed under a new Law, the law of grace through faith in Christ. All who accept Jesus as their personal Savior have "equal rating," and this rating guarantees us an eternity with Jesus. What a glorious, gracious gift this is.

July 9

GET SOME REST

"Come with Me to a quiet place and get some rest." – Mark 6:31

JESUS, LOUD AND CLEAR

As we work for Christ by action,
Efforts will have more impaction,
As we're tested, if we're rested,
Then our focus will be clear.
For our Lord, there's not much gaining,
If our spirit's tired and waning.
Let's be heedful, planting's needful,
And the seed we plant down here,
We are knowing, will be growing.
Let's be sure while we're down here,
We teach Jesus, loud and clear.

In this age of the automobile, we all know what it is to have a low battery in our car. If our battery is low enough, our car will not start, and if we get it started, we know we have a limited amount of time before the same thing happens again. The solution is to recharge our battery so our automobile will operate as it was designed to operate.

In this scripture, the apostles had just returned from a third preaching tour in Galilee. Apparently, their tour had been successful, but they were tired. They were tired physically, mentally and spiritually, and at that point, their batteries were low. Jesus recognized this and gave them instructions. He said, "Come with me, by yourselves, to a quiet place, and get some rest." He was telling them, and telling us, that there is a point at which we become utterly exhausted physically, and perhaps mentally and spiritually as well. At that point, we need to recharge our battery. As he instructed His apostles, He is also instructing us, We need to GO TO A QUIET PLACE WITH HIM AND REST. We need, at least temporarily, to shut out the rest of the world, rest our body and communicate with Jesus in prayer. This recharges our battery. Then we are ready to resume our work for the Lord with renewed vigor, a clear mind and uplifted spirit.

Our prayer is, "Lord, give us the grace to recognize when our battery is low. Let us get it recharged, then with renewed energy, a clear mind and an uplifted spirit, let us resume our work for You, and teach and preach Jesus LOUD AND CLEAR, all for Your glory, through our Lord Jesus Christ."

THE BODY OF CHRIST

"On the contrary, those parts of the body that seem to be weaker are indispensable." – 1 Corinthians 12:23

I'M A TOE

I'm a toe, so if not working,
And the foot and knee are jerking,
Is there shirking, therein lurking,
When my toe will just not go?
As the body parts are working,
Let there be no smirking, lurking,
And no shirking, while we're working,
The whole body needs the toe.
So, while working, let no jerking,
Interfere with where I go.
Let me function as a toe.

Many truths in the Bible are conveyed to us by analogy. As believers, we are called "the body of Christ." When Jesus walked this earth, He used His own body. Now, we are "His body." Some of us are eyes, some hands, some feet, and yes, some of us are even toes. If we are a toe, and we look at the eyes, the hands and the feet, our natural thought process jumps to the conclusion that our function in the body is really rather insignificant. We would prefer being an eye, or a hand or a foot. Conversely, the eye, the hand or the foot may look down upon the toe as a part of the body that really has no major function. But I pose this question, "Have you ever had a REAL SORE TOE?" I HAVE. The pain begins in the toe, works its way up the leg and torso and almost literally "explodes" in the brain. When this happens, we understand real fast how important our toe is.

God gave each member of the body at least one gift. These gifts were not haphazardly distributed, but were carefully apportioned according to the perfect will of God. They are to be used by each member of the body as God intended. If we are a toe, we should, with all humility, perform our function and thank God for the eyes, hands and feet. If we are an eye, hand or foot, we should, with all humility, perform our function and thank God that we don't have a SORE TOE.

"Lord, if I'm an eye, a hand or a foot, let me function as such. If I'm a toe, let me function as a toe, all for Your glory through our Lord Jesus Christ."

July 11

BARNABAS TOOK MARK

"They had such a sharp disagreement that they parted company. Barnabas took Mark and sailed for Cyprus." – Acts 15:39

LET'S LIFT UP SOMEONE TODAY

Let's encourage as we're sowing,
Seeds of Love for Christ-like growing.
Let the caring, and the sharing,
Of our Lord, begin today.
By His grace, let us be knowing
As we honor Christ by showing,
That our brothers, and the others,
Need our help, along the way.
May our sighting, be His lighting,
As we're striving to obey.
Let's lift up someone today.

The very name "Barnabas" means "one who consoles," or "one who exhorts." Barnabas was an encourager. God used him to convince the "pillar" apostles that the converted Saul, now Paul, was sincere. Barnabas, along with his cousin, John Mark, and Paul embarked on the first missionary journey. As they departed, Barnabas was the leader. When they finished, Paul was the leader. John Mark had deserted them in the middle of their first journey, and now at the beginning of the second, Barnabas wanted Mark to accompany them, but Paul refused, so Barnabas took Mark, and sailed for Cyprus. There is absolutely no evidence of disrespect or animosity between Paul and Barnabas, just a difference of opinion. Paul wanted nothing to hamper or interfere with the preaching of the gospel and neither did Barnabas, but the difference between the two was that Barnabas saw the potential in John Mark, and Paul did not. New Testament history proved Barnabas to be right. In 2 Timothy chapter four records that when Paul knew His days were numbered on this earth, He asked Timothy to come to him quickly, and to bring Mark because Mark was helpful to Paul in his ministry. Mark was the only one other than Timothy who Paul asked for and of course, this is the same Mark who gave us the second of the synoptic gospels. Barnabas encouraged him, and God used him.

In our Christian walk, may we never become so focused on what we are attempting to do for the Lord, that we neglect encouraging one another.

July 12

ACCEPT ONE ANOTHER

"Accept one another, then, just as Christ accepted you, in order to bring praise to God." – Romans 15:7

WITH WARTS SHOWING

Let our love for one another,
For a sister, or a brother,
All sustaining, never waning,
Be a Christ-like love within.
Though our soul is sometimes glowing,
There are times when it's not showing,
And affecting, our accepting,
Is a nature wrought with sin.
With "warts" showing, we are knowing,
That the answer for all men,
Is "His Love" that dwells within.

As we walk this Christian walk, we look around at our brothers and sisters in Christ and see "warts." These warts may merely be "quirks" in their personality, or an occasional scowl instead of a continuous smile, or an attitude that we don't like, or any number of things that we don't approve of. They may not even realize they have these warts, but we know they have them, because we see them. With our "soulish nature" we have 20/20 vision when looking at the faults of others. Our problem is, when we look within our own lives, sometimes we are almost completely blind. We can't see our own warts, but others can.

In the seventh chapter of Matthew, Jesus tells us not to judge others. He uses the analogy of our seeing a speck of sawdust in our brother's eye, while we pay no attention to the plank in our own eye.

In today's scripture, with Paul's admonition to "accept one another," if we don't completely accept our brothers and sisters in Christ, we are in direct disobedience to our Lord's command. Who are we to be more discerning than our Lord is? Our prayer is that God might give us the grace and strength to let the indwelling Spirit of Christ break through the sin nature in all areas of our lives. And may we might use a "wart remover" on ourselves, and not be so concerned about the warts of others, all for God's glory, through our Lord Jesus Christ.

PRIDE – BEFORE A FALL

"Pride goes before destruction, and a haughty spirit before a fall." – Proverbs 16:18

THE VALLEY SO NEAR

A mountaintop perch, so lofty, it seems,
So safe and secure, so regal, it teems,
With pride in our heart, for all we have done,
Our wisdom so great, the battles we've won.
We sit on our perch, and see others fall,
And swell up with pride, that we know it all,
A faith in ourselves, our knowledge so dear,
Our eyes don't detect, the storm clouds so near.
Then lightening begins, the thunder clouds roll,
The force of the gale, will soon take its toll.
Our mountaintop perch, we thought so secure,
Will tumble and shake; the storm grows mature.
An avalanche shakes, we start our descent,
Our life's in shambles, no clue, and no hint,
Of the why or how, just buried with fear,
We look down below, the valley, so near.

"Pride goes before destruction, and a haughty spirit before a fall." This adage is as true today as it was when it was written, which was probably sometime in the tenth century BC.

Pride is probably the primary reason that sinners reject the Lord. If we don't think we have a problem, we don't look for a solution. But most of us who know the Lord still have a pride problem.

In whatever endeavor we undertake, most of us have some degree of success if we work hard enough and smart enough. But then, as we begin to be successful, our soulish nature begins to sell us on the idea of how smart we are, and we buy it. We almost literally swell up with pride because we're so smart. We are on a mountaintop safe and secure, because we know it all. But, about that time, we detect some storm clouds, and those clouds "spawn a spate" of such magnitude that we are swept off our mountaintop perch and hurled downward toward the valley below. We are not quite as smart as we thought we were. Fear rears its ugly head as we plunge downward toward that valley, so near. We need some help, and we need it real fast.

July 14

I WALK THROUGH THE VALLEY

"Even though I walk through the valley of the shadow of death, I will fear no evil. For You are with me. Your rod and Your staff, they comfort me." – Psalm 23:4

LET'S THANK HIM FOR THE VALLEYS

We come to a stop, the valley below,
Not knowing God's plan, His seed there to sow.
His love for the saints, His mercy for all,
With faith in His Son, who answer His call.
His grace we receive, His joy we can feel,
As upward we look, and humbly we kneel.
God's mercy and love, His plan for each one,
Who truly depend, on God's only son.
A mountaintop perch, so lofty, it seems,
We swell up with pride, and trust in our dreams.
But valleys below, God gives us to find,
His Grace and His Love, and our peace of mind.
Thank God for valleys, the valleys below,
Valleys we're placed in, our soul there to grow,
Love so abundant, in times of distress,
Hearts over-flowing, the joy of God's rest.

From our mountaintop perch, with our prideful self-reliance, we have been flung downward into this valley of doubt, fear and frustration. We crash-landed so hard we are no longer standing; we are on our knees, and that is exactly where our Lord wants us. Whether or not "we spawned this spate" in our lives, or God let it happen, or God "caused it." As we address the problem and seek the solution, we are being taught two great truths. Prideful self-sufficiency should not even be in our vocabulary, and should be replaced with humility. And, God's unconditional love, mercy and grace through Jesus Christ is more than sufficient for all of our needs.

With humility, we become teachable, and with the power of the indwelling Spirit of Christ, we trade doubt, fear and frustration for God's love, mercy and peace. The joy of our fellowship with the Lord is so great that it is absolutely indescribable. Let's thank God for the valleys.

July 15

LIFE MORE ABUNDANTLY

"I am come that they may have life, and that they might have it more abundantly." – John 10:10

LET'S LOOK UP INSTEAD OF DOWN

As we're waking down life's highway,
On the road to Heaven's skyway,
Let's be living, what He's giving,
With a smile, and not a frown,
For abundance is His gifting,
That our spirit might be lifting.
Let no looming, glooming, dooming,
In our attitude be found.
But with smiling, so beguiling,
Let the joy of Christ be found.
Let's look up, instead of down.

The picture of a Christian that the world, and at times some other Christians paint, depicts a man walking down the street prim and proper, straight laced, with a somewhat haughty, "I'm better than you," attitude. He looks neither left nor right, but straight ahead, his stiff neck suggesting that perhaps his collar is too tight, and with a slight scowl on his face that would suggest he ate something that didn't agree with him. This image of a Christian that the world has is caused by the world's perception of who we are. And the world's identification of who we are is perceived only by what they see. When they look at you, and look at me, what do they see? Do they see doom and gloom, or do they see a radiant smile that permeates our very being, and radiates outward to others, depicting the explicit joy of Christ in our lives?

Our Lord told us that He came that we might have life, and have it more abundantly. When He was on this earth, He gave us a pattern for living. He enjoyed people. He enjoyed parties. In fact, from scripture, we could easily draw the conclusion that He was the life of the party. There was no scowl of doom and gloom on His face, except perhaps when He thought of all of those lost souls whom would reject Him. As Christians, we have His very life. Our prayer is that when others see us, they see Christ in us. Let our smiling be so beguiling, for in Christ our joy is found. LET'S LOOK UP, INSTEAD OF DOWN.

July 16

TO THE LEAST OF THESE

"And the king will reply, 'I tell you the truth, whatever you did for one of the least of these brothers of mine, you did for Me.'" – Matthew 25:40

TO THE LEAST

To the least of these with kindness,
Do unto with Christ-like mindness,
Be concerning, not discerning,
With no thought of self in mind.
For through Christ, our grace connection,
Let's let Him show us direction,
No detection, of rejection,
Should we ever bring to mind,
But in caring, and in sharing,
Through our Lord, let us be kind,
To the least, as Christ defined.

This passage of scripture has some eschatological significance. But without delving into that complex subject, let us consider this teaching of Jesus as it pertains to each one of us in our daily Christian walk.

The key word in this scripture is the word "least," and it denotes a person who is, in our estimation, the "very least." We can compare that person to one we see who might have the "very least" education, position, manners, morals or money – a person who has absolutely "no influence." So what does this suggest to us? Jesus is telling us to love unconditionally and perform our acts of kindness with absolutely no thought of reward. In other words, the Lord is telling us to remove ourselves from our foremost thoughts, and to replace self-interest with kindness to others.

Even as Christians, we have a tendency to categorize people. These people are "real important" because they have money, power, prestige or position; but these other people are "not real important" because they have neither money, power, prestige nor position. These are certainly not the only criterion for our tendency to categorize people. They may seem to us to be just plain unlovable, but we must remember that at times we're not so lovable ourselves, but Jesus loves us regardless.

"Lord, we pray that You give us the grace to love others unconditionally, and to treat each one as if we were personally performing a service for You."

TRUST NOT IN OURSELVES

"But we had the sentence of death in ourselves, that we should not trust in ourselves, but in God who raises the dead." – 1 Corinthians 1:9

TRUST IN GOD

In a deep, dark hole, with no way out,
That's what our nature, is all about,
We can't see the light, our head is down,
But that's where the grace, of God is found.
We put aside self, while on our knees,
As we trust in Him, our spirit sees,
That the darkness now, begins to fade,
As it turns to light, the light God made.
Let's focus on Christ, the one who died,
Then arose again, and death defied.
As we run today, this earthly race,
Let's trust in God, and in His grace.

In this scripture, Paul admonishes the Corinthians, and each one of us, to trust in God and rely on His grace through our Lord, Jesus Christ, not just for salvation, but in all circumstances.

As we walk down this pathway of life, circumstances are not always to our liking. There are times when our spirit is sagging, our energy lagging, our feet are dragging, and it seems that we have fallen into a deep, dark hole with no way out. Along this pathway of life, there are many such holes to fall into. And as though they were not plentiful enough, we dig a few ourselves. We tumble headlong into these deep, dark spiritual holes and we can't get out. We can't seem to see the light for the darkness. What has happened to us, and what is the solution?

We are not promised a trouble free life when we become believers, but we are promised that His grace is sufficient. As we walk along life's pathway and find these deep, dark holes, whether man-made, God-made or self-made, the only way we go crashing down to the bottom is to have our mind and our eyes focused on self, and self alone. The obvious solution is to focus on Christ instead of on self, because where Christ is, there is no darkness. But it's our choice. We can focus on self and be miserable, or we can focus on Christ and find peace and joy through His grace. But we must make this choice. We must have "willful perspiration" before we can enjoy "spiritual inspiration."

July 18

WE WERE CHOSEN

"Just as He chose us in Him before the foundation of the world, that we should be holy and blameless before Him." – Ephesians 1:4

IN CHRIST

Now, before the world's foundation,
We were chosen for salvation,
And believing, we're receiving,
Life with Christ forever more.
But, the key words for receiving,
Are "In Him" that we're believing,
For selection, of election,
Is through Christ, who died before,
Our foundation, for salvation.
On that cross, our sins He bore,
He's the one, and only door.

This is one of the scriptures in the Bible that can easily be misinterpreted, and has been, to the detriment of evangelism. It is true that this scripture tells us that God chose us before the foundation of the world. And this statement alone, when taken out of context, lends credibility to "sure election" and predestination. But if we look carefully at the scripture, we will see that the key words are "In Him," that is, "in Christ." God chose those of us who "believe on" and "put our trust in" His only Son. Christ was the firstborn of many brothers and sisters (Romans 8:29). It is absolutely true that we are "elected" by God, and are "predestined" by God to spend an eternity with Him, but only through our Lord Jesus Christ. There is no other way. Even though God is omniscient, that is, "all knowing," and He knows whether or not we will become a member of His family, He gives us a choice. We either believe, or don't believe. That choice alone determines where we will spend eternity.

The ones who teach "sure election" and predestination without our having a choice, promote disobedience to that great evangelical proclamation of our Lord, who in Mark 16:15 said, "Go into all the world and preach the gospel to all creation." If choice were not involved, there would be no need for evangelism.

Our prayer is, "Lord, use us as You will, and give us the grace and determination to spread the gospel whenever and wherever we have the opportunity, all for Your glory, through our Lord Jesus Christ."

July 19

HE GAVE POWER

"But you will receive power when the Holy Spirit comes to you." – Acts 1:8

THE TOWER OF ALL POWER

God's gift to us, for believing,
Is His Power, we're receiving,
For believing, we're receiving,
His great strength, to run this race,
But we must have recognition,
That we start with the ignition,
Then we're thriving, as we're driving,
For our Lord has set the pace.
May the Tower, of all Power,
Give us strength in His embrace,
As we run this earthly race.

Having believed in Christ, we were "marked" in Him with a seal, the promised Holy Spirit (Ephesians 1:13b). This indwelling Spirit of Christ gives us comfort, guidance, gives us peace and last, but not least, gives us power – Christ-power. In fact, the power of the Spirit is what gives us comfort, guidance and peace. As Christians, we have this supernatural power at our disposal twenty-four hours every day, but some of us never use it. We forgot how to "turn-on" the ignition.

July 20

RESIST HIM

"Be self-controlled and alert. Your enemy the devil prowls around like a roaring lion looking for someone to devour. Resist him." – 1 Peter 5:8-9a

LOUD AND CLEAR

He's a roaring lion that's growling,
But with stealth induced when prowling,
Let his growling, and his prowling,
Be resisted loud and clear.
For, we know he was depleted,
And, in fact, he was defeated,
So his growling, and his prowling,
Should not cause us any fear.
Our resistance, is insistence,
That our Lord is always near,
And His Grace is loud and clear.

The devil is real, and he has multiplicity of demons just "straining at the leash" to help him. This scripture tells us that he prowls around like a roaring lion, looking for someone to devour. At times, with his scheming, he is pleasantly devious. But in his roaring onslaught, he is ferocious and fearsome. There are times when it seems impossible to escape the consequences of his attacks, and in our own strength we can't. But we must remember that as Christians, we possess the one and only weapon that can defeat him. That weapon is our Lord Jesus Christ. We not only possess this weapon, but it is immediately available in the form of the Spirit of Christ who indwells each believer. Jesus defeated Satan at the cross.

In the scriptures, we are told that because of Satan, we will be tempted and we will suffer. There are various forms of temptation and suffering. With regard to suffering, some saints lost their very lives for the Lord, or were tortured unmercifully. By comparison, the abuse we suffer at times because of our faith seems almost inconsequential. But regardless of how we suffer, or what temptations we face, we have the weapon that will overcome, and that weapon is Christ. We invoke the name of our Lord, and the roaring lion is "de-toothed." He can prowl and he can roar, but he can't eat us. He can chew on us a little, but he can't devour us. He can be bothersome, but because of our Lord, he can't destroy us. We thank God that our Lord is always near and that His grace is loud and clear.

July 21

THE WELL IS DEEP

"'Sir,' the woman said, 'You have nothing to draw with, and the well is deep. Where can You get this living water?'" – John 4:11

NO WELL IS TOO DEEP FOR JESUS

No well is too deep for Jesus,
And through loving eyes, He sees us,
Let no thinking, stop our drinking,
From His well of love and grace.
When our soul is tired and thirsting,
From His well of love is bursting,
Such abounding, grace resounding,
As we run this earthly race.
He's the nearest, and the dearest.
We can almost see His face,
As we lie in His embrace.

     This Samaritan woman not only did not understand what this "living water" was, but whatever it was, she doubted that Jesus could produce it. She saw nothing in the hands of Jesus with which to draw this water, and besides that, the well was too deep.

     Those of us who are Christians know what this living water is it's an eternity with our Lord, beginning when we put our faith in Jesus. We are trusting Jesus with our eternity, but as we run this earthly race, and our circumstances get out of control, so often, instead of turning to Him in faith, we initially turn to ourselves in despair. We know He has given us an eternity with Him. But somehow, with our warped thinking, we don't believe He can solve this immediate crisis in our life. The well is just too deep for Jesus, so we go about with our finite minds looking elsewhere for the solution. We may even find a well or two without Jesus, but they are either very shallow, or all dried-up. As despair settles in, desperation rears its ugly head. But this is good, because at that point, the only one we have to turn to is Jesus. And when we turn to Him, He lifts our burden from us and with His love, mercy and grace, He gives us comfort and peace. It is absolutely incredible how He solves our problems. Then at last, with our trust and hope in Him, we finally realize and understand that no well is too deep for Jesus. May we never forget.

July 22

THE WORK GOD REQUIRES

"Jesus answered, 'The work of God is this: To believe in the One He has sent.'"– John 6:29

BELIEVE ON HIS SON

God gives us this information,
Work requirement for salvation,
And it's clearly, merely, dearly,
To believe upon His Son.
It's the gospel's pure foundation,
We don't work for our salvation.
It's God's gifting, and His lifting,
When we trust His only Son,
Then believing, we're receiving,
Life eternal with the Son.
Our salvation then is won.

Christianity is not a religion. It's a personal relationship with our Lord Jesus Christ. In all religions, work is required; in fact, work is the basis upon which each person is graded. In this scripture, Jesus is responding to this question, "What must we do to do the works God requires?" We can immediately identify the mindset of those asking the question. In their mind, they already "knew" they had to work for their salvation. They were simply asking Jesus to tell them which works God required. How astonished they must have been by His answer. Salvation was available to them, not by works, but by simple faith in Jesus, the Son of God. This was far beyond the comprehension and acceptance of most of His listeners. This was a free gift, and they thought that nothing of any value in this life could be free. We should note, that when asking Jesus the question, they wanted to know "only" what was "required," not what God desired.

In this, the end of the twentieth century, the mindset of most people parallels the same mindset indicated in this scripture. "I know I have to work for my salvation, but exactly 'what' do I have to do? Just tell me what I have to do to EARN it. A free grace gift through belief in Christ seems entirely 'too easy.'"

In truth, salvation is a free grace gift, given by a loving Father when we believe in His only Son. Our prayer is that God may use us in some small way to proclaim the truth of the gospel.

July 23

TRUST ALSO IN ME

"Do not let your hearts be troubled. Trust in God, trust also in Me." – John 14:1

OUR TRUST IS IN JESUS

Now, our trust is placed in Jesus,
For, through Him, is how God sees us.
He's the dawning, of the spawning,
That gives us eternity,
And, this Holy Admonition,
By our Lord, is our position,
His injection, of affection,
Through His love, for you and me,
Shows His caring, and His sharing,
From that cross at Calvary,
Throughout all eternity.

The disciples were depressed. In fact, they were completely bewildered. Jesus had told them that He was going to die, that one of them was a traitor and that Peter would deny Him three times. Their hearts were troubled. In this scripture, and in the scripture following, Jesus is giving them, and us, reassurance. His message to us is "Don't let your hearts be troubled. Trust in God, and also in Me." The key word here is "trust." Have faith. Believe. Trust in God, through Christ, is the antidote for a troubled heart.

As believers, most of us don't have a problem trusting Jesus for our eternity. We have already made the most important decision we could ever make in our lifetime. We are secure in Him for our eternity. Our "trust problem" seems to revolve around the "little things," even though to us, at the time, these "little things" magnify into "big things." Jesus knows we will have trouble in our Christian walk (John 16:33), but He also assures us that He has overcome the world, and His grace is sufficient (2 Corinthians 12:5). This is only one of many promises we have from our Lord. Isn't it incredible that we would ever have even the slightest doubt that our Lord is capable, willing and ready to extend us His grace when we have a troubled heart? How can we ever doubt the proficiency or the qualification of the One who spoke the universe into existence and gives us eternal life?

July 24

I ALWAYS THANK GOD FOR YOU

"I always thank God for you because of His grace given you in Jesus. For in Him you have been enriched in every way – in all your speaking and in all your knowledge." – 1 Corinthians 1:4-5

LET'S ENCOURAGE

Let us thank God for the others,
For our sisters, and our brothers.
Let's encourage, not discourage,
Those we meet along the way.
Let the love of God be showing,
And the grace of Christ be glowing.
Let's be feeding, what they're needing,
Let's give comfort, day by day,
And with passion, show compassion.
Let us be, a sunshine ray,
In another's life today.

Sanctification is a life long process. The Spirit of Christ works in us mightily through our spirit to change us into the kind of person God wants us to be. His Spirit is a Comforter, constant Companion, and a Dynamo of power that indwells each and every believer. But He is not a dictator nor does He force us to do anything. To mature in Christ, we must, by our own will, surrender our individuality to Christ in order to possess His Christ-power. As we walk down this pathway of life toward spiritual maturity, there are many sharp turns, a number of detours and a few dead ends. We become disillusioned, downhearted and discouraged. We need all the help we can get.

In this passage of scripture Paul, by demonstration, is showing us an additional method that God uses to help believers attain a great degree of spiritual maturity. He is "building them up," not "tearing them down." He is actually bragging, not so much on them, but on the fact that they had let God enrich their lives through Christ Jesus, and that this enrichment through God's grace was evident in both their speech and their knowledge. God was using Paul to encourage them and build them up in Christ Jesus. Paul was helping our Lord guide them down the pathway of life to spiritual maturity. He was putting a "little ray of sunshine" in their lives.

July 25

HIDDEN WITH CHRIST

"For you died and your life is now hidden with Christ in God." – Colossians 3:3

WITHOUT A BLEMISH

When our earthly tour, we finish,
God sees us without a blemish,
There's no blemish, at the finish,
For our Lord has made us pure.
Jesus Christ, the one God gave us,
Is the one God sent to save us,
Guaranteeing, that we're seeing,
An eternity that's sure.
His connection, gives direction,
As we make this earthly tour,
And our future is secure.

We know God is omnipotent (all-powerful), omniscient (all-knowing) and omnipresent (present everywhere), so we ask, "How is our life 'hidden' with Christ in God?" How does our all-knowing heavenly Father not see all of our imperfections? The answer is because He has chosen to see us through the purifying blood of His Son because we have responded to the gospel, and placed our trust in Jesus. Our position with God the Father is determined by our position in Christ. When we believed in, and accepted Jesus as our Savior, we became a member of the family of God, and positionally, our imperfections were erased and replaced with the perfection of Jesus. This does not mean that we have attained perfection. Far from it. But it does mean that our eternity is secure in Jesus because, as this earthly tour we finish, God will see us without blemish. He has chosen to see us through the purifying blood of Jesus. Our lives are hidden with Christ in God. What an exhilarating truth this is. With this free grace gift from God, through our Lord Jesus Christ, we should spend every waking minute in thankful obedience.

Our prayer is, "Lord, since You have chosen to see us without a blemish at the finish, give us the grace, the direction and the determination to do all we can do. And with Your help, let us rid ourselves of imperfections and live a life of obedience to Your will, all for Your glory through our Lord Jesus Christ."

July 26

THE REASON FOR OUR PRIDE

"Therefore show these men the proof of your love and the reason for our pride in you, so that the church can see it." – 2 Corinthians 8:24

OUR PRIDE IS IN THE SON

Now, the pride that we're expressing,
Is a pride that is a blessing,
And the blessing, we're addressing,
Is the work our Lord has done.
There is never an occasion,
To put "self" in the equation,
For we're knowing, that the glowing,
Grace of God, is through His Son.
He's the tower, of all power,
He's the one, and only one,
And our "Pride" is in the Son.

When we see or hear the word "pride," as Christians, our immediate connotation suggests an implication of boastfulness or self-aggrandizement. We all know about the fall of Adam and Eve because of pride – and the fall of Lucifer for the same reason. But pride in it's pure form does not have to be negative. It can be positive. This classification is determined completely on what the object of our pride is. Anytime we let self be the object of our pride, our "sin-o-meter" almost self-destructs with a resounding warning. Pride of self, or pride in self will lead to destruction, but pride in Jesus, pride in the gospel and pride in what the Lord is doing through others is not only healthy, it is a blessing.

In this scripture, Paul was taking pride in what the Lord was doing in the hearts and lives of believers in Corinth. He was also proud of these believing Corinthians for obeying the Lord and passing His love on to their brothers and sisters in Christ. This is healthy pride. This kind of pride is a blessing, because self is nowhere to be found. This pride is focused on the Lord and on others.

Our prayer is, "Lord, as we live this Christian life, by Your grace, let us never have self as the object of our pride, rather, let our pride and boasting be in Jesus Christ."

FIRST BE RECONCILED

"First, go and be reconciled to your brother; then come and offer your gift." – Matthew 5:24b

LET US RIGHT THAT WRONG

If we have wronged a brother,
Or a sister, or another,
Let's not worry, but just hurry,
And be reconciled today.
For, God's Spirit that's indwelling,
Through our conscience, now telling,
Us to fashion, our compassion,
And immediately obey.
Let's be showing, Christ-like glowing,
And proceed without delay.
Let us right that wrong today.

When we become Christians, we immediately receive the Spirit of Christ into our very being. Even though we still possess a "soulish" nature, this indwelling Spirit works in us in matters of right and wrong. This Spirit directs us through our conscience. Our understanding of right and wrong is given to us through the Bible and by direction from the Spirit of God. We know right from wrong. If we have wronged someone, this Spirit, working through our conscience, convicts and convinces us of our guilt. The one who is engulfed in this "guilt" state-of-being, is often described as having a guilty conscience. Just as fear cannot live in the same house as perfect love (1 John 4:18), neither can guilt be an occupant in the same house with effective worship and evangelism. We cannot be Christ-effective if we are guilt-defective. Before we can come to the altar of God (our Lord Jesus Christ) and present our gifts (offer our services), we must first have a clear conscience. In this scripture, the directive of Jesus is to go to the one we have wronged and reconcile our differences without delay.

Our prayer is, "Lord, if we have wronged another, give us the grace to immediately go to that person and right that wrong and be reconciled into a loving, Christian relationship with that person, then, with a conscience cleansed of guilt, offer our services to You."

July 28

AND YOU WILL BE MY WITNESSES

"And you will be my witnesses in Jerusalem, and in all Judea and Samaria, and to the ends of the earth." – Acts 1:8b

LET OUR WITNESS BE TODAY

Let God's very Spirit seize us,
As we witness for our Jesus,
And connect us, and direct us,
As we're striving to obey.
Whether driving on the highways,
Or diverting to the byways,
His selection, of direction,
Is the place we're in today.
Let compassion, be our passion,
For the ones along our way.
Let our witness be today.

As Christians, we are all missionaries for Jesus. In this scripture, Jesus is telling His disciples, and us, to "witness" for Him. He is literally sending each one of us out into the world to proclaim the gospel. Most of us do not consider ourselves to be missionaries. When we think of a missionary, we think of someone going to darkest Africa, the Far East or perhaps even into the slums of a large city. Most of us really don't think of a missionary in terms of service for Jesus in our everyday profession, or in our numerous business contacts. Jesus gave specific instructions to His disciples concerning where to minister. He told them to be His witnesses in Jerusalem, Judea and Samaria, but He also told them to go to "the ends of the earth."

When we think of the ends of the earth, we probably envision some foreign country where there is great need for the gospel of Jesus Christ – and these places certainly exist. But in reality, one of the ends of the earth is located right here where we live. And our ministry for Jesus is right here, right now. I believe the Lord has a purpose for our lives, and instead of daydreaming about some place way over yonder where we could really be missionaries, we should look at where we are. We are where we are for a purpose. And that purpose is to, in some way, glorify the Lord.

July 29

A SPRING OF WATER

"…indeed, the water I give will become in him a spring of water, welling up to eternal life." – John 4:14b

LET US LISTEN AND OBEY

Like pure water from a fountain,
Springing forth upon a mountain,
Is God's Spirit, we can hear it,
If we listen and obey.
Life forever is His giving,
He sustains us while we're living,
He's indwelling, and He's welling,
Up with grace for us today.
Never slowing, always flowing,
Getting stronger, day by day.
Let us listen, and obey.

In this scripture, Jesus is using an analogy to describe what the Holy Spirit does for the believer. We know we receive His Spirit immediately when we believe, and that it is a deposit guaranteeing our inheritance, which is eternal life (Ephesians 1:14). As Jesus analogically equates His Spirit with water (He describes it as "living water" in John 4:10), He tells us that this water is "welling up" to eternal life. The words, "welling up," are derived from the Greek word "anatello," which means "arising" or "springing up." The connotation is that His Spirit is not only "out-pouring," but is like a musical crescendo, in that it gradually and continually increases as it builds-up to eternal life. Because of His love, mercy and grace, God has given His Spirit to each and every believer. This Spirit supernaturally gives us, not only guidance, but also an ever-increasing source of power. The more we listen and obey, the greater the magnitude of power we receive, power to do God's will, power to have God's peace and power to live this Christian life to the utmost.

Our prayer is, "Lord, as we thank You for Your gift of eternal life, give us a sufficient amount of Your grace to listen and obey, that Your Spirit might literally well-up to overflowing in our hearts. Give us the power to do Your will in all things as we attempt to live the Christian life, all for Your glory through our Lord Jesus Christ."

July 30

I NEVER KNEW YOU

"Then I will tell them plainly, I never knew you." – Matthew 7:23

THE ONLY WAY

After dying, the rejection,
Of our Lord, has no correction,
For the giving, to the living,
Is the Gospel's only way,
There are those who would be showing,
That they have a lot of knowing,
But in knowing, they are throwing,
All the Grace of God away.
Their selection, of direction,
Is rejection, and decay,
For our Lord's the only way.

In this scripture, Jesus was probably talking about the religious leaders of that day. So many of them had so much knowledge about religion. They were founded and well versed in the Jewish faith, and some of them spoke glowingly about the Messiah. They did many good works in the name of God and the Messiah, but they completely missed the mark. They rejected the one and only Messiah, our Lord Jesus Christ. There were others also who were false prophets, who even prophesied in His name, but with a hidden agenda. They had no personal relationship with our Lord Jesus Christ.

It is entirely possible for someone to know all about Jesus, and still not "know" Jesus. We must have the Spirit of Christ indwelling us in order to be saved. There are some that are great scholars, and their knowledge of doctrine is tremendous, but this is not the criterion by which we are judged. We are judged solely by our relationship to Jesus Christ. We have either accepted Him personally as our Savior and Lord, or we have rejected Him. There is no other road to salvation.

Our prayer is, "Lord, use us as You will, and give us the grace to tell others about the gospel, that they also might experience Your saving grace, and begin a very personal relationship with You, all for the glory of God, through our Lord Jesus Christ."

July 31

COMPLETELY CALM

"'You of little faith, why are you so afraid?' Then He got up and rebuked the winds and the waves, and it was completely calm." – Matthew 8:26

HE WILL CALM OUR STORMY SEA

With our mind on this ensuing,
In our soul, a storm is brewing,
Then it batters, and it shatters,
Like a roaring storm at sea.
Then, with fear, as our soul totters,
Jesus stills the raging waters,
Then the raining, of the paining,
In our soul, will cease to be,
For His ration, of compassion,
Is so great for you and me,
He will calm, our stormy sea.

This account of the authority Jesus had, even over nature, is also recorded in Mark 4:35-41 and Luke 8:22-25. The Sea of Galilee was notorious for its sudden storms. A furious storm suddenly engulfed the boat that He and His disciples were using to cross this sea. The disciples were terrified. In fearful desperation, they awakened Jesus. Then with a gentle admonishment to the disciples for lack of faith, He rebuked the winds and the waves and it became completely calm. They had a problem and Jesus was the solution.

In our own lives, we so often see a storm cloud looming on the horizon, then it seems to suddenly engulf our very soul with its turbulence. We feel helpless. The roaring winds, and the turbulent waves of circumstances are so great that we are floundering and, in our own mind, in danger of sinking. We have lost control. We have a problem. What is the solution?

As Jesus pointed out in this scripture, the fear and anxiety we experience when we have a storm raging in our life is because of lack of faith in Him. He who created the universe and controls nature is certainly powerful enough to take care of any minor inconvenience in our life. He loves us and has promised to take care of our needs. He has told us that His grace is sufficient. So, our problem is lack of faith, and the solution is simply faith in Jesus, for His ration of compassion is so great for you and for me, that, if we ask, He will completely calm our stormy sea.

WORK OUT YOUR SALVATION

"Continue to work out your salvation with fear and trembling." – Philippians 2:12b

LET'S WORK OUT THE WAY WE LIVE

Now, salvation is through Jesus,
For through Him is how God sees us,
But God frees us, then through Jesus,
To work out the way we live.
With a reverence that is showing,
Let's work out the way we're going.
An attitude, of gratitude,
Should be ours each day we live.

This is a scripture that can be, and has been, misinterpreted in many instances. Salvation is by the grace of God through our Lord Jesus Christ when we believe on Jesus and accept Him as our Savior. Therefore, the state of "being saved" is not an issue in this scripture, rather, how we choose to live is the issue. We are told to work it out with "fear and trembling." This, in no way, indicates doubt, anxiety or terror, rather, this reference concerns an "active reverence" on our part, and a "one-dimensional" mindset of purpose in response to God's grace.

There are no limitations regarding what God can do, but there are limitations on what He will do. Just as God alone, through Jesus, offered us salvation but required us to have faith in order to receive it, He also instructs us regarding how to live. But in order to live a purposeful Christian life, we must take the initiative. We have the indwelling Spirit to guide us, but He will not force us. We, alone, make the final decisions. In 2 Peter 1:5, the scripture says, "add to your faith, virtue." Just as morality, or a lack thereof, is an extension of our will, so are habits and character traits. If we have bad habits or character flaws, it is not something God has done. He's not to blame – we are. Even though we have His indwelling Spirit to guide us, we must exercise our will correctly in order to live the abundant life and receive His strength and power through the Spirit.

Our prayer is, "Lord, by Your grace, give us the strength and determination to continually work out the way we live in such a manner that our will always exactly coincide with Your will, all for Your glory through our Lord Jesus Christ."

HE WILL LIFT YOU UP

"Humble yourself before the Lord, and He will lift you up." – James 4:10

HE WILL LIFT US UP

If we humbly make connection,
With the Lord, He gives direction.
Ever caring, always sharing,
He will lift us up today.
Let's be humble, and His gifting,
Is indeed, a graceful lifting,
For His gifting, is the lifting,
Of our spirit every day,
And His ration, of compassion,
Is so great, there's no delay.
He will guide us, day by day.

As we walk this pathway of life, things and circumstances are not always the way we want them. We get discouraged. We become despondent. Our circumstances are "out of control." Metaphorically speaking, our spirit, instead of soaring like an eagle, is slowly creeping and crawling on the ground, and from that vantage point, we lose direction and, sometimes, even purpose in and for our lives. This passage of scripture gives us the solution for that problem.

In geometry, we learned that the shortest distance between two points is a straight line. Our spirit is low, and it needs to rise. Geometrically speaking, we should look up. But this scripture is teaching us that they way up, is down, that is we must humble ourselves before the Lord, then "He will lift us up." True humility before the Lord erases all traces of pride in self. It focuses our mind and our spirit on Him and not on us. When this happens, supernaturally, we feel our spirit being lifted. We are the recipients of His mercy, grace, peace and, yes, even His power. Our true humility is the catalyst that triggers this response from the Lord. James 4:6 tells us that, "God opposes the proud, but gives grace to the humble."

Our prayer is, "Lord, regardless of our circumstances, give us a sufficient amount of Your grace that we might humble ourselves before You, erasing all traces of pride in self, trusting You and You alone to lift us up for Your glory, through our Lord Jesus Christ."

TO PREPARE GOD'S PEOPLE

"…to prepare God's people for works of service, so that the body of Christ may be built up." – Ephesians 4:12

LET'S BE BODY BUILDERS

We are told, and we are knowing,
That the Body must be growing,
Christ-connected, and directed,
Let us do our part today.
For, the teaching of the teachers,
And the preaching of the preachers,
Is a preaching, and a teaching,
That prepares us to obey.
Let that preaching, and that teaching,
Spur us on, without delay.
Let us "Body-Build" today.

"Grace has been given to each believer as Christ apportioned it" (Ephesians 4:7), so we know that some are given the gift of preaching or teaching, while others possess different gifts. The scripture today tells us that the purpose for gifts of teaching and preaching is that those so endowed with those gifts will prepare God's people for works of service, that the body of Christ may be built up. There very possibly could be a dual meaning in the words "built up." First, we know that the Lord wants each one of us to work within the body to build up one another in love, using whatever spiritual gift or gifts we might possess in this edifying process. With each body part working properly, the entire body of Christ will become a mature, living, loving and functional entity, glorifying our Lord, individually and collectively, day by day.

There is also a second meaning that could be interpreted in this admonition to build up the body of Christ, and that is to build up the body numerically. We, quite frequently, depend on the pastors alone to spread the gospel. But we also share the burden of telling lost men and women about the saving grace of Jesus Christ.

Whatever spiritual gift, or gifts, we might possess, our prayer is that the Lord will use us both within and without the body of Christ, and that we will become dedicated "body builders," all for the glory of God, through Jesus Christ, our Lord.

August 4

YOU KNOW ME

"Yes you know Me, and you know where I am from." – John 7:28

DO WE KNOW HIM?

As our view in life is vaster,
Do we know our Lord and Master?
If we're knowing, are we showing,
That we're willing to obey?
Do we need a small disaster,
To obey our Lord and Master?
Does disaster, bring us faster,
To our knees, along the way?
Let's be showing, that we're growing,
And trust Him without delay,
Let Him lead us, day by day.

Do we really know Jesus Christ? Do we fully comprehend the magnitude of His love, mercy and grace? Do we have a personal, loving relationship with Him day by day, or must we encounter some disaster along the way that almost literally brings us to our knees in order to experience that peace that surpasses all worldly understanding? We completely trust Him for our eternity. Why can't we trust Him completely day, by day, by day?

Even though we are Christians, it seems that our very nature, with our finite thinking, pictures God as a remote God far removed from this world – a God too busy to notice what is happening in our lives. Nothing could be farther from the truth. Our God is a loving Father who has given us Jesus Christ, whose Spirit indwells us, loving us, directing us and comforting us. We just need to get better acquainted with Him. Some of us treat Him like an absolute stranger until something happens in our life that we view as a disaster, then we become reacquainted real fast. This is not the way our Lord wants us to live. He wants to have a living, loving, personal relationship with each one of us day, by day, by day.

Our prayer is that by God's grace, we don't wait until we have a disaster in our life to get reacquainted with the Lord, but that we maintain a loving, caring relationship with Jesus every day of our life, all for the glory of God, through our Lord Jesus Christ.

August 5

DO NOT CONDEMN

"Do not condemn, and you will not be condemned." – Luke 6:37b

LET CONDEMNING CEASE TO BE

Now, there is no condemnation,
For we have our Lord's salvation,
With a mindness, for His kindness,
Let's condemn no one we see.
For, if I condemn a brother,
He, in turn, condemns another,
And that brother, that's another,
Just so happens to be me.
Let's be sharing, and be caring,
And condemn no one we see.
Let condemning cease to be.

In this scripture, Jesus is very politely telling us to mind our own business. He also is explaining the consequences if we condemn the actions of another, a sister or a brother. This directive of Jesus is preceded by His admonition to judge no one, and followed by His commandment to forgive one another.

In this directive, Jesus is not relieving believers of their need for discernment regarding what is right and what is wrong, rather, He is warning believers against the hypocritical judging and condemning of others. The Golden Rule is a very positive, "Do unto others as you would have them do unto you." This scripture, in which Jesus is instructing us to neither judge nor condemn hypocritically, also validates the results of our actions should we choose to disobey Him. We, in turn, will be judged and condemned by others.

Jesus never intended that His church be comprised of legalistic, hypocritical, "better than thou" members. There were enough of those in the religious world during His ministry. Rather, He wants the members of His body to love one another and minister to the needs of each other.

Our prayer is that the Lord will give us a sufficient amount of grace that we might mind our own business and get the "log" out of our eye instead of looking for the "speck" in our brother's eye, all for the glory of God, through our Lord Jesus Christ.

BY THEIR FRUITS

"So then, you will know them by their fruits." Matthew 7:20

LET OUR WALKING DO THE TALKING

On life's pathway, as we're going,
By our fruits, they will be knowing,
Not our talking, but our walking,
What we do, not what we say.
So, as we, in Christ, are growing,
Let His love, through us be showing,
Let our walking, do the talking,
As we go along life's way.
Let's be knowing, Christ is showing,
By our deeds, not what we say.
Let us honor Him today.

In His teaching, Jesus very frequently used either a parable or an analogy so that those He was teaching might better understand. Just prior to this scripture, Jesus had equated false prophets with wolves in sheep's clothing. Then He used the analogy of the good and bad fruit trees to give us a better understanding, and a keener discernment, of who is teaching and living the truth and who is teaching error. He has just said that a good tree produces good fruit and a bad tree produces bad fruit, and then He follows up with, "you will know them by their fruits."

One specific truth from this scripture that seems to just leap forward is that "actions speak louder than words." Jesus looks on the inside, not on the outside. He knows where our heart is. Anyone can give Jesus lip service, but the true test is the fruit produced. Jesus (the Vine) produces the good fruit through believers (the branches). Jesus does not produce bad fruit, so if we see bad fruit we know that it comes from some other source.

In the modern vernacular, we might attempt to explain the meaning of this teaching as, "Beware, there are those who 'talk the talk,' but don't 'walk the walk.'" Or further still, "Some talk a good game, but can't play." Not everyone, who says, "Lord, Lord" really knows Him (see Matthew 7:22). Some are wolves in sheep's clothing, and they teach just enough truth so that the error they teach may be more readily accepted.

Our prayer is, "Lord, give us Your grace that we might be spiritually discerning, separating truth from error, recognizing whether the fruit is good or bad."

August 7

ON HIM WE HAVE SET OUR HOPE

"On Him we have set our hope that He will continue to deliver us." – 2 Corinthians 1:10b

OUR TROUBLES TURN TO BUBBLES

From the Lord, we're ever living,
And we thank Him for the giving,
For our living, is His giving,
Through the cross where our Lord died.
On this earth as we're progressing,
Jesus gives another blessing,
And this blessing, we're confessing,
His Sure Hope when we abide,
For our troubles, turn to bubbles,
When our Lord is at our side,
And He's always there to guide.

The word "hope" is translated from the Greek word "elpizo," and is sometimes translated as "trust." In this scripture, the word "hope" has a completely different meaning than in today's vernacular. It propounds a favorable and confident expectation, a "sure hope," and this directive is not to the subject of, but to the author of our hope. Romans 15:13 tells us that God is the Author of hope. Paul is explaining to the Corinthians, and to us, that the One who is loving enough and powerful enough to deliver us from eternal death to eternal life will continue to deliver us from the anxieties and adverse circumstances that we face in this life. And, we should confidently have this sure hope in Him for deliverance.

However adverse our circumstances become in this life, our supreme confidence, confident expectation and sure hope must be in Jesus. He has given us eternal life, and He will take care of us in this life. What do we really have to fear? Our eternity is secure. He has promised that His grace is sufficient, but He wants us to trust Him, call on His name and set our sure hope completely on Him.

There are times when our circumstances will produce troubles. And we get so burdened with anxiety that those troubles, like stones in a stagnant pool, seem to sink us lower and lower. But if we call on His name and trust in Him – if our sure hope is completely in Him – He will turn that stagnant pool into a living spring. Our troubles will be lifted and turned into bubbles that burst forth through the living water of our Lord, and we will enjoy the peace that only Jesus can give.

August 8

YES IN CHRIST

"For no matter how many promises God has made, they are 'yes' in Christ." – 2 Corinthians 1:20

WE CAN FEEL HIS SPIRIT FLOW

In Christ Jesus we're receiving,
Living life as we're believing,
In addition, our position,
Is enhanced by Whom we know.
For what ere on earth our mission,
We're enhanced in our position,
By His glowing, Spirit flowing,
Showing us the way to go.
If selected, we're directed.
By His Grace, Our soul will glow,
We can feel His Spirit flow.

If we truly love the Lord, do we have a burning desire to do something to please Him? Is this exhibited by our interaction with other Christians? Do we dream about doing something special for Him, to be used by Him in some special project, but we just don't measure up? Our education is lacking, our vision is blurred, our free time is taken and our ability is limited. We just don't have the equipment necessary to fulfill that desire. No, regardless of our education, our vision and our ability, the equipment we personally possess is not sufficient. This scripture for today's study is teaching about better equipment.

God has made many promises to us through Jesus, and in this scripture, we are told that God's promises are "yes" through Him. We are told in Philippians 4:13 that we can do all things through Him who strengthens us. He gives us the strength and the power to do what He wants us to do through the indwelling Holy Spirit. Though our natural abilities and capacity may reflect equipment that is grossly under-powered for the task at hand, His indwelling Spirit projects a dynamo of spiritual power through the ones who are working within His will. We should never measure our spiritual ability by our natural ability, because our spiritual ability is provided by better equipment.

Our prayer is that we never let the fact that we just don't measure up naturally, keep us from knowing that if we are in the will of God, we very definitely measure up spiritually.

NOT LIKE MOSES

"We are not like Moses, who would put a veil over his face to keep the Israelites from gazing at it while the radiance was fading away." – 2 Corinthians 3:13

HIS GLORY WON'T DEPART

On our face, the Gospel story,
Is reflected by God's Glory,
The unveiling, is prevailing,
For His Glory won't depart.
Not like Moses with deception,
But through Christ, Who's God's conception,
With a living, loving giving,
Of His Spirit in our heart.
His connection, gives reflection,
Life eternal in our heart,
For His glory won't depart.

When Moses came down from Mount Sinai, his face reflected the glory of God. But Moses put a veil over his face so the Israelites could not see that under the Old Covenant the glory of God was fading away. Paul then tells us that to this day, when Moses is read, a veil will cover their hearts, and only in Christ is that veil taken away. The Old Covenant had its glory because God was involved, but it was not only surpassed by, but also completely replaced by, the glory of the New Covenant. Now those of us who are in Christ are endowed with the eternal, never-ending, unsurpassable glory of God. This glory, which will never fade away, should be reflected on the face of every believer. And it should never diminish, but should, as we grow in Christ, continue to be brighter and brighter and brighter, attaining to the full radiance of His glory when we at last see Jesus face-to-face.

Our prayer is, "Lord, let the full radiance of Your glory and Your grace be reflected by each believer, and that by our actions and our words, others will be brought into this living, loving relationship with Jesus, all for Your glory through our Lord Jesus Christ."

AMBASSADORS FOR CHRIST

"We are therefore Christ's ambassadors, as though God were making His appeal through us." – 2 Corinthians 5:20a

DAY BY DAY BY DAY

Now, the Lord is through us reaching,
And the Lord is through us teaching,
He's a tower, of great power,
And He tells us what to say.
For, there is no self-importance,
Just our will in God's accordance,
His selection, and direction,
Through His Spirit is the way.
Let's be knowing, Grace is showing,
Through our efforts to obey.
Let Him use us day by day.

As Christians, we are ambassadors for Christ. Our permanent citizenship is in the heavenly realm. In fact, in 1 Peter 2:11, we are referred to as "aliens and strangers" in this world. But while on this earth, each one of us is an ambassador for Christ. We are commanded by our Lord to spread the gospel (Mark 15:16). In 1 Corinthians 2:4, Paul gives us further instructions regarding how to spread the gospel – not with wise and persuasive words, but with a demonstration of the Spirit's power. Having studied under the greatest teacher of that day, Gamaliel, Paul was not only a scholar but also an orator. But He realized that the message is more important than the messenger. Human wisdom and eloquence of speech will not enhance the presentation of the gospel. In fact, it sometimes demeans and degrades it. The ones hearing the gospel must not be focused on the one proclaiming it, but on the gospel itself. Then, and only then, will the power of God touch their hearts and convict them of the truth of the gospel.

Our prayer is, "Lord, as Your ambassadors here on earth, let us, with all humility, present Your pure gospel of grace whenever we have the opportunity, and to whomever You will, never basking in any attainment of eloquence, but always depending on Your power to change the hearts of unbelievers. Let us never forget that the message is what is important, not the messenger. Please use us day, by day, by day, all for Your glory through our Lord Jesus Christ."

August 11

THE EYE IS THE LAMP

"The eye is the lamp of the body. If your eyes are good, your whole body will be full of light. But if your eyes are bad, your whole body will be full of darkness." – Matthew 6:22-23

LET US FOCUS

Let us focus while we're living,
On the "Gift" that God is giving,
Then the lightness, and the brightness
Of our Lord will others see.
Let our lamp be bright and glowing,
Let His grace be always showing,
Let's be knowing, that we're growing,
In the Lord, that we might be,
Christ-Connected, and directed,
With a fervor others see,
Let's be all that we can be.

To set the stage for this passage of scripture, we must first understand the problem Jesus was addressing. The Pharisees believed that God always materially blessed those He loves. Therefore, they were intent on building great treasures here on earth. They became slaves to the master of greed. Their spiritual eyes were diseased because they were focused on self; thus, they were in spiritual darkness. As Jesus continued, He told them, and us, that we couldn't serve two masters.

The lesson for us in this scripture is simple and complex; simple, in that the message is clear, but complex because we too often measure success in terms of either wealth or achievement instead of spirituality. In our race for success, we develop a spiritual eye problem. With our diseased eye, we focus on the wrong things. We become embroiled with all kinds of personal, selfish desires. When we take our eyes off the Lord, as we lose our focus, we almost immediately also lose our peace. There is no peace in the Lord when we are focused on self.

Our prayer is that the Lord will give us the grace, in all areas of our life, to always keep our eyes focused on Jesus, not on self. We pray that we might always be Christ-connected and directed with a fervor others can see, all for the glory of God, through our Lord Jesus Christ.

August 12

THE WORK OF GOD

"The work of God is this: To believe in the One He has sent." – John 6:29

JESUS ONLY

Jesus only, we're believing,
For through Him are we receiving,
Our connection, for election,
That gives us eternity.
In His Grace let us be growing,
Let His work through us be showing,
But our Savior, not behavior
Saves the soul of you and me,
Through His giving, let's be living,
For the One who set us free,
On that cross at Calvary.

In this scripture, Jesus is responding to the question, "What must we do to do the works God requires?" This question gives us insight into the thinking that was prevalent among those questioning Jesus. They just knew that they had to work for salvation, and their question was, "What works should they do?" What was God's requirement? The answer Jesus gave was too simple for them. The only requirement God had was for them to believe in Jesus. This simple answer defied their logic because, to them, they believed that they should receive a sign from God before believing. They would first see and then they would believe. Jesus was telling them that they should believe and then they would see.

Today, so many people continue to believe that they must do good works in order to earn salvation, but God demands that we recognize our inability to save ourselves and rely completely on His free gift through Jesus. He still wants to see good works from each one of us, but in gratitude for, not in pursuit of, salvation.

Our prayer is that the Lord will use us, regardless of the circumstances, to pass this truth on to others, that in some small way we might participate in the building of God's kingdom, all for His glory through our Lord Jesus Christ.

August 13

LIVE BY FAITH

"The righteous will live by faith." – Romans 1:17

THE VALLEY BELOW

A mountaintop perch, so lofty, so dear,
Our eyes don't detect, the storm clouds, so near.
An avalanche starts; we're buried with fear,
We look down below, the valley, so near.

We come to a stop, the valley below,
Not knowing God's plan, His seed there to sow,
His love for the Saints, His mercy for all,
With faith in His Son, who answer His call.

Thank God for valleys, the valleys below,
Valleys we're placed in, our faith there to grow.
God's love abundant, He gives us His best,
Valleys that teach us, the Joy of God's Rest.

In this scripture, "the righteous" refers to those of us who, by faith, have accepted Christ as our Savior and look forward to an eternity with Him. When we accept Christ, God declares us righteous because we are given His righteousness. In this passage of scripture, we are also instructed to live by faith, faith in our Lord, Jesus Christ.

Even though this admonition is clear-cut and simple, many of us seem to be slow learners. The faith that God wants us to experience in every day living has to be cultivated. Too often, our faith is in our ability, in self. We seem to be on a mountaintop with everything going our way. On that mountaintop the growth of our faith in the Lord is stunted, but God gives us a helping hand. He either permits or causes us to tumble down into the valley below. And in that valley we suddenly realize what God's love, mercy and grace really mean. At that point we begin to grow spiritually and live by faith in our Lord, so we thank God for valleys, the valleys below, the valleys we're placed in, our faith there to grow.

August 14

CHRIST ONLY

"See to it that no one takes you captive through hollow and deceptive philosophy, which depends on human traditions and the basic principles of this world rather than on Christ." – Colossians 2:8

NO DECEIVING – JUST BELIEVING

Let our life reflect a capture,
Not a worldly kind of rapture,
Let our Jesus, as He sees us,
Live His life through you and me.
Through our Jesus we're depending,
That our life is never-ending,
No deceiving, just believing,
That He died for you and me,
And the story, of his Glory,
Is He came to set us free,
To enjoy eternity.

Philosophy is the study, and love of wisdom. In this verse, Paul is telling us that wisdom is good, but not the worldly wisdom that employs hollow and deceptive philosophy that depends on human tradition rather than on Christ. In this exhortation, Paul was condemning the Colossian heresy taught by false teachers. This false teaching was accomplished in various ways, but the one common denominator was either the absence of Christ, the rejection of Christ or teaching that denied the deity of Jesus. The teaching was based on worldly wisdom, not on Jesus. If Jesus was included in their teaching at all, they were not teaching the same Jesus we know.

Today, we are literally besieged with false teaching. Just as in the days of Paul, many modern day teachers are teaching a worldly wisdom with either an outright rejection of Christ, or with no basis in Christ, or a wisdom that might accept Christ to some degree, but not the Jesus we know. They depend, not on the power of Jesus, but on self-power or natural human knowledge to produce this wisdom.

We not only reject this worldly wisdom without Christ, but it is our prayer that the Lord will use us to refute this false teaching. And, that in some small way, our life can be a testament to the saving grace of our Lord Jesus Christ, and to the fact that He, and He alone, reflects true wisdom. With Jesus, there is "no deceiving, just believing."

August 15

IF ANYONE COMES TO ME

"If anyone comes to Me and does not hate his father and mother, his wife and children, his brothers and sisters, yes, even his own life, he cannot be My disciple." – Luke 14:26

HE IS FIRST

Let us understand His teaching,
For the Lord is surely reaching,
He is reaching, and beseeching,
He's instructing you and me,
To prioritize our living,
With the code that He is giving,
Not to wonder, and to ponder,
But accept His Deity,
And be growing, in the knowing,
That He's first with you and me,
Let's be all that we can be.

This passage of scripture, if taken out of context, would seem to contradict the teaching of Jesus. But not so. Jesus is using the word "hate" as a resplendent hyperbole to clarify the priorities of one who would be His disciple. His message was that a disciple of His must put Jesus first, to the exclusion of family members, or even self.

During His ministry, those who would follow Jesus were often denounced and even ostracized by their families. The Pharisees who were plotting His death were delivering the true hate message. Many who followed Jesus did so at great risk and with much sacrifice.

Today, in this country, we enjoy the freedom to worship without fear, the risk and the sacrifice that was prevalent in those days, however, this message from Jesus to us remains constant. We must put Him first, ahead of family and self, if we are to be a true disciple. Our prayer is that in all areas of our life we will continue to be growing in His grace, knowing that we put Him first, giving us the opportunity to be all that we can be, for Him, all for the glory of God through our Lord Jesus Christ.

August 16

ON HIM

"On Him we have set our hope." – 2 Corinthians 1:10

OUR SURE HOPE

When our woes seem to abound us,
Let the love of God surround us,
Then we're growing, in the glowing,
Of His mercy, love and grace,
Then the darkness we are fearing,
Fades away with His appearing,
And His spawning, of the dawning,
As we run this earthly race,
Gives connection, and direction,
As we rest in His embrace.
Our sure hope is in His Grace.

The word "hope" in our contemporary vocabulary indicates a wishing for something that probably will not come to fruition. Not so in this scripture. This is the Greek word "elpizo" which indicates an absolute trust in, an absolute sure hope for, whatever or whoever is the object of this verb. In other words, "elpizo" expresses a "confident expectation." In this scripture, Paul is telling us to put our sure hope, our confident expectation, in the Lord. For He is not only the object of our hope, but He is the Author of hope, and it is on Him that we have set our hope.

As we struggle in this life, so often the darkness seems to blot out the light. We look at our circumstances and don't like what we see. We have a tendency to take our eyes off the Lord and focus on self. We seem to forget, at least temporarily, that our sure hope, not only for eternity, but also for inner peace as we run this earthly race, is in the Lord. When we have His connection, we go in His direction. As we surrender prideful self, the darkness of the night seems to suddenly be blotted out and replaced with God's spawning of a dawning, bursting forth with the brilliant brightness of His Son, our Lord Jesus Christ. Let us never forget that our trust, our sure hope is a reality only because of the grace of God, through our Lord Jesus Christ. As Christians, let's be growing in the glowing of His mercy, His love and His grace.

August 17

NOT AS I WILL

"Yet, not as I will, but as You will." – Matthew 26:39

OUR MISSION – SUBMISSION

Though our Lord was facing dying,
Yet in Him was no defying,
For His mission, was submission,
On a cross, our sins to pay.
As we travel down life's highway,
Leading up to Heaven's skyway,
Let our mission, be submission,
To the Will of God each day.
Let's be growing, in the knowing,
That His will for us today,
We will honor and obey.

In this scripture, as in so many others, we have recorded another confirmation of the dependence and complete submission of Jesus to His Father. In this instance, His complete submission included a painful, agonizing death on a Roman cross. His body would be wracked with physical pain, but even more painful to Jesus was the fact that as He gave His life's blood for our sins, He would, become sin on our behalf, thereby becoming temporarily alienated from the Father. This spiritual alienation was far more agonizing to Jesus than the physical pain.

In our walk with the Lord, it is not always immediately apparent what His will for us is in every circumstance. However, in due time, any cloud of doubt seems to be whiffed away if we keep our eyes on Him and assume an attitude of submission to His will. Through His teaching, and by example, Jesus taught us to be submissive to the will of God in all areas of our life. Our prayer is that by the grace of God, we assume an attitude of submission to the will of God, all for the glory of God, through our Lord Jesus Christ. Let our mission in life be submission to His will day, after day, after day.

GOD'S LOVE POURED OUT

"God has poured out His love into our hearts by the Holy Spirit, whom He has given us." – Romans 5:5

HE CONNECTS AND DIRECTS

By the Grace of God concerning,
Love He gives that we're not earning,
Such a roaring, of His pouring,
He gives us when we believe.
By our acts we're not deserving,
But by race it's God we're serving.
On reflection, our direction,
Is God's tour that we receive.
He connects us, and directs us,
In a way we can't conceive,
With His Spirit we receive.

It is so difficult to comprehend the magnitude of God's love. He has poured His love into the hearts of each believer in such a way that is absolutely beyond our comprehension. But Paul tells us this is exactly what God has done. He has poured out His love into our hearts.

Most of us who are Christians try to live the Christian life. But it sometimes seems that the harder we try, the more difficult it is. Conversely, at other times it seems so easy to do what God wants us to do. There is a very simple explanation for the degree of difficulty we encounter as we attempt to live the Christian life. Someone has to be in control. If self is in control, the difficulty factor is astronomical. If God is in control, the decisions we make are spontaneous and in accordance with His will. Our nature is inherently evil, but by God's grace, He has poured out His love and His nature into the hearts of each of His children. If we will but step aside, remove self from the equation, "let go and let God," we will be absolutely amazed with the results.

Our prayer is that we will step aside and let God connect us and direct us in all areas of our lives through His indwelling Spirit and the outpouring of His love into our hearts, all for His glory through our Lord Jesus Christ.

August 19

IN THE BEGINNING

"In the beginning was the Word, and the Word was with God, and the Word was God." – John 1:1

HE IS TRULY DEITY

He was there in the beginning,
Loving us, despite our sinning,
On reflection, for election,
Our Lord died upon that tree.
God the Father did the sending,
Wracked with pain, His body bending,
There God gave us, Christ to save us,
His blood shed at Calvary,
Death defying, after dying,
He arose to set us free,
He is truly Deity.

There are many people in this world that believe Jesus Christ was a good man. There are also many people in this world who believe that what He taught was good, but this is the extent of their belief. The truth is Jesus Christ, the "Word" who was with God and was God from the very beginning, came to this earth as the second Person of the Trinity to die on a cross for our sins, that we might inherit eternal life with Him by simply putting our trust in Him. We also believe Jesus was a good man and that what He taught was good, but our belief extends far beyond that limited tenet. The primary difference in our belief and the world's belief is that we know that Jesus Christ was, and is, deity. John 1:14 tells us that the Word, the same Word who was with God, and who was God in the beginning, came to this earth as flesh. And that His glory was beheld as the only begotten of the Father, full of grace and truth. Therein lies the difference, and what a difference this is.

Our prayer is that as we walk down the pathway of this life, the Lord will give us the grace and determination to spread the gospel so that others might know Jesus Christ as their personal Savior. Our election to an eternity with Him depends upon our belief in Him. He shed His blood at Calvary, died and rose to set us free. He is truly deity.

August 20

BE STILL – PRESS ON

"Be still, and know that I am God." – Psalm 46:10
"I press toward the mark for the prize of the high calling of God in Jesus Christ." – Philippians 3:14

LET'S PRESS ON

There's a time for God's fulfillness,
As we wait in somber stillness,
There our yearning, turns to learning,
As God speaks to you and me.
Then, with vigor let obeyance,
Coincide with God's conveyance,
His connection, gives direction,
Let's press on to work, and be,
Always stressing, His great blessing,
Through blood shed upon that tree,
By our Lord at Calvary.

At first glance these two scriptures, one from the Old Testament and another from the New, seem to be a contradiction, but nothing could be farther from the truth. We have two distinct messages here. First, we should determine what God wants us to do, and this determination is almost impossible unless we pause long enough and still our soul long enough to hear what God has to say. Jesus gave instructions concerning privacy when we pray. In order to determine what God wants us to do, we must rid ourselves of distractions and be still enough to hear His message.

After we know what God wants us to do, then we need to implement His instructions with actions – vigorous actions. As Paul expressed it, we need to press on. We need to "Press toward the mark for the prize of the high calling of God in Jesus Christ." None of us knows how many days we have left on this earth. We can either dream about or be remorseful about yesterday. Tomorrow never comes, but we do have today. Our prayer is that by the grace of God, we are still enough to know what God wants us to do, then with vigor, we reason to do His will. Let's press on to work and be, always stressing, His great blessing, through blood shed upon that tree, by our Lord at Calvary.

LET US FIX OUR EYES

"Let us fix our eyes on Jesus, the Author and Perfecter of our faith." – Hebrews 12:2

OUR EYES ON JESUS

Let our eyes, with true fixation,
Focus through each situation,
So selection, and direction,
Is on Jesus day by day.
Not religious innuendo,
Nor the world's oblique crescendo,
But a growing, glowing knowing,
That our Lord's the only way.
No condition, just our mission,
As we travel earth's pathway,
To love Jesus, day by day.

Let us fix our eyes on Jesus. This is so simple to say, yet so difficult to actually do as we travel this earth's pathway. There are so many distractions. The ever-present growing crescendo of pressure that we face each day seems to tear our eyes away from the Lord. We become so wrapped up in our search for solutions to various everyday problems that our focus seems to be on everything except Jesus.

If we are fortunate enough to escape most of the worldly pressure each day and we actually take time to focus, there is another pitfall right in our pathway that we can so easily fall into. It is the pitfall of religion. In our heart, and in our mind, we want to do what Jesus wants us to do, but often we get so wrapped up by "do"-s and "don't"-s, by rules and regulations and by religion that we forget who the Author of our salvation and faith is. Jesus Christ is both the Author and the Perfecter of our faith. We must never permit anyone, however well intentioned, to deprive us of a personal relationship with our Lord by using religious innuendoes. Christianity is not a religion of rules and regulations, but a personal relationship with the Lord Jesus Christ.

Our prayer is that God will give us a sufficient amount of grace that the fixation of our eyes will be so powerfully focused on our Lord Jesus Christ, that neither the world's oblique crescendo, not religious innuendo can tear our eyes away from the Lord. May our eyes, with true fixation, focus through each situation, so selection and direction is on Jesus, day after day, after day.

August 22

THEY WILL TURN THEIR EARS AWAY

"They will turn their ears away from the truth and turn aside to myths." – 2 Timothy 4:4

LET'S RELY UPON HIS GRACE

Let's be careful how God sees us,
Let us follow only Jesus,
Let's not follow, any hollow,
Myths that contradict His Grace,
Let's be careful of deception,
Let us know at its inception,
Let's reject it, and correct it,
For our Lord, it does abase,
Let no notion, spawn emotion,
As we run this earthly race,
Let's rely upon His Grace.

Paul wrote Second Timothy as he languished in a cold dungeon in Rome. He knew that his work was finished and his life was almost at an end. This particular scripture was a part of Paul's charge to Timothy. He not only encouraged Timothy, but he cautioned him regarding what false teachers would teach, admonishing him to always refute this false doctrine and continually persevere as an evangelist with the teaching of the sound doctrine of truth. He predicted that a time would come when men, in order to suit their own desires, would gather around them a great number of teachers who would say what their itching ears wanted to hear. In Paul's ministry, he wore many hats in order to reach different segments of the people for Christ, but there was absolutely no compromise in Paul whatsoever regarding the truth of the pure gospel of grace.

Today, we observe Paul's prediction as reality. There are teachers who teach works instead of grace. Others teach universal salvation, and others teach "no virgin birth," or "no resurrection" or "no Hell for the lost." They tickle the itching ears of those who would succumb to myths instead of sound doctrine. They abhorrently compromise and relegate to insignificance the pure gospel of grace of our Lord Jesus Christ. Our prayer is that God gives us the grace and wisdom to recognize either compromise or distortion of the gospel, and that we steadfastly promote the teaching of the pure gospel, all for the glory of God, through our Lord Jesus Christ. Let no notion spawn emotion, as we run this earthly race. Let's rely upon His grace.

I AM WITH YOU ALWAYS

"And surely I am with you always, to the very end of the age." – Matthew 28:20b

WE WILL NEVER WALK ALONE

With us always is our Jesus,
Who has changed the way God sees us,
He's beside us, and inside us,
We will never walk alone.
Jesus Christ, who knows no rancor,
Is our deep and solid anchor,
There's no failing, our sailing,
Our homeport with Christ is known,
Let's not tarry, for we carry,
Seeds of love that He has sown,
We will never walk alone.

In this verse, Jesus gives His disciples, and us, a promise. That promise is that, in Spirit, He will never leave us. After he departed this earth to sit at the right hand of God the Father, He sent the Holy Spirit to indwell all believers. The Spirit is both a Guide and a Comforter. If we equate our journey on this earth to a voyage at sea, though we may encounter a multitude of turbulence on this stormy sea of life, He is our deep and solid anchor. With Him, we know our destination. Our homeport is in Heaven with Jesus forever and ever, throughout all eternity.

As we walk down this pathway of life, our personal relationship with Jesus through His indwelling Spirit will help us avoid the ditches, and when we insist on falling into one, He will gently pick us up and put us back on course. In Hebrews 13, we are promised that God will never leave us nor forsake us, and that Jesus Christ is the same yesterday, today and forever. However adverse our circumstances may be, the indwelling Spirit of Jesus Christ will see us through that adversity and give us comfort. What comfort it is to know our final destination, our homeport, but to also know that, in Christ, we will never again walk alone.

ABRAHAM BELIEVED GOD

"If, in fact, works justified Abraham, he had something to boast about, but not before God. Abraham believed God, and it was credited to him as righteousness." – Romans 4:2,4

BY BELIEVING, WE'RE RECEIVING

On this earthly path we travel,
With God's grace let us unravel,
God's selection, of election,
For our sure eternity.
Not by works are we receiving,
Saving grace, but by believing,
We're appointed, and anointed,
By our Lord, who's Deity,
For believing, we're receiving,
Life with Him, eternally,
Jesus Christ, who set us free.

During the ministry of Jesus, the Jews were teaching that Abraham, the great patriarch of the Jewish nation, was an example of a person being justified before God by works. But Paul, by reference to Genesis 15:6, was pointing out to them, and to us, that there was no mention of works in that scripture. In fact, it clearly states God justified Abraham because of his faith that God would keep His promises. Abraham had kept no law, nor had he rendered any service to God that would have earned him any credit. He simply believed what God had told him.

This passage of scripture sets forth the fundamental basis of the gospel. We are saved because we believe in Jesus Christ, not because of any works that we have done or will do. This is fundamental and basic. Christianity is set apart from religion in that our righteousness before God is credited to us by simple faith in Jesus Christ. Religion is a tenet with various beliefs, but always with works determining the destination, and/or end result. In Christianity, God's grace and our faith in Jesus combine to give us an eternity with our Lord. We're appointed, and anointed, by our Lord, who's deity, for believing, we're receiving, life with Him eternally, Jesus Christ, who set us free.

August 25

LET HIM WHO BOASTS

"Let him who boasts, boast in the Lord." – 1 Corinthians 1:30

THE SPIRIT OF GOD'S LOVE

Here's a sign, let us be posting,
Let us never be self boasting,
Let's be showing, that we're knowing,
All good things are from above.
With a change of disposition,
Let us curb our self-ambition,
Let's be growing, in the glowing,
Of the Spirit from above.
Christ connected, and directed,
For descending, like a dove,
Is the Spirit of God's love.

This directive by Paul reflects the difference in how the world thinks, and how we, as Christians, should think. The Greek philosophers in that era were held in great esteem. They projected wisdom far beyond the wisdom of the ordinary man or woman who lived in that time period, but as great as their wisdom was, it was only a worldly wisdom.

Paul points out to the Corinthians that the good things they had received, namely salvation – accompanied by righteousness, holiness and redemption – had been accomplished, not by anything they had done, nor by any wisdom they, or the world, had. It was a result of the power of God, working in the hearts and minds of every believer through the indwelling Spirit of Christ. He was telling them, and us, that if we boast, our boasting must be in what the Lord has done, not in what we have accomplished, because without Him, we really accomplish nothing.

Our prayer is that we might always remember that the wisdom of this world shrinks to absolute insignificance when compared to the power of God, through the indwelling Spirit of our Lord Jesus Christ. Let us always be Christ-connected and Christ-directed, for descending from above, is the awesome power and wisdom of God's love, our Lord Jesus Christ. If we boast, let's boast in Him.

I WILL GIVE YOU REST

"Come to Me, all you who are weary and burdened. And I will give you rest." – Matthew 11:28

LET US TURN TO HIM FOR REST

Our Lord changed the way God sees us,
Let's be resting in our Jesus,
Our souls dreary, bodies weary,
Let us turn to Him for rest.
Here on earth, our weakness growing,
Burdened down, fatigue is showing,
Dark clouds boding, strength eroding,
By ourselves, we fail the test,
But prevailing, in our failing,
Is our Lord, who gives His best,
When we turn to Him for rest.

In Matthew 6, Jesus tells us that in this world we will have troubles. In fact, He admonishes us not to worry about tomorrow, because today has enough troubles of it's own. In our scripture today, Jesus gives us a directive which will solve our problem of being burdened down and weary. He says to come to Him, and He will give us rest.

As we walk this pathway of life, from time to time we carry various burdens. These burdens may be mental, spiritual or physical, but in whatever form they appear, as we try to shoulder this load by ourselves the weight becomes staggering. Emotional frustration turns into a weakness and a weariness that seems to penetrate the very core of our soul, and our very being seems to cry out for rest. But the harder we try, the heavier the burdens become, and the weaker we become. But there is a solution, and that solution is Jesus

Whatever our burdens may be when we unload them on the Lord, we are, in effect saying, "Lord, I can't handle it, but You can, and I know You will." When this happens in our life, we then experience, through the love and grace of our Lord, the peace of our Lord, and we, at last rest in that peace. Our soul is no longer weary and burdened, but is resting in a peace that transcends all worldly understanding. We thank God for our Lord Jesus Christ, who gives us this rest and this peace.

August 27

HIS POWER WITHIN US

"Now to Him who is able to do immeasurably more than all we ask or imagine, according to His power that is at work within us." – Ephesians 3:20

THE POWER OF OUR GUIDE

When our days on earth go sour,
Let's depend upon His power,
Though we're reeling, with the feeling,
That despair resides inside.
Let's let Christ direct our thinking,
For He knows our soul is sinking,
Midst our musing, so confusing,
Let us trust in Him to guide,
Then the raining, of the paining,
Will dissolve as we abide,
In the power of our Guide.

The power of the living Christ residing within the hearts of believers is immeasurable. In this scripture, we are told that His power is more than we can ever imagine. When we think about His Spirit who resides within us, most of us usually think about how that Spirit gives guidance, and gives us comfort in our times of need. This, of course, is true. His Spirit is both our Guide and our Comforter. But what so many of us either don't comprehend, or don't believe, is the magnitude of the power of His Spirit which can do more than we can ask, or even imagine. This power is so great that it can not even be measured.

With our finite minds, we might equate this dynamo of power to a powerful 400 horsepower racing car. We are behind the wheel and the powerful engine is idling, waiting for us to step on the accelerator. This tremendous surge of power is at our disposal, but instead of stepping on the accelerator, we put our foot on the brake. Our prayer is that by the grace of God, we realize the power we have in Christ, and that in all areas of our life, we might minimize self, and maximizes Christ. Let's take our foot off the brake, place it on the accelerator and feel that tremendous surge of Christ-power that is at our disposal. Let's let Christ be our guide, and in Him, let us abide, and experience the power of our Guide, all for the glory of God through our Lord Jesus Christ.

OUR SUFFICIENCY

"Not that we are sufficient of ourselves to think any thing as of ourselves; but our sufficiency is of God." – 1 Corinthians 3:5

ALL SUFFICIENT DEITY

Let God's Grace within us flourish,
As His Word, we truly nourish,
All efficient, and sufficient,
Is His Grace for you and me.
Of ourselves, we're sadly lacking,
But by grace, and with His backing,
We're connected, and directed,
As His Spirit sets us free.
Let's be growing, in His glowing,
All-Sufficient Deity,
With His Grace for you and me.

As Christians, our task on this earth is to spread the gospel of Jesus Christ. In the second chapter of this letter, Paul tells us that as we spread the gospel, we are to God, the "aroma of Christ." To those who are being saved, we are the fragrance of life, but to those perishing, we are the smell of death. This is an awesome responsibility when we consider the fact that God has placed in our hands the means by which others will gain eternal life, or if we fail, will face eternal damnation. In and of ourselves, we are simply not up to the task. We would fail miserably. We are not sufficient. But the good news is that our sufficiency is not in ourselves, but in God, through our Lord Jesus Christ.

August 29

THAT THEY MAY BE ONE

"I have given them the glory that You gave Me, that they may be one as We are one." – John 17:22

WE ARE ONE WITH DEITY

Christ relates to us the story,
That He gives to us God's glory,
And the story, of God's glory,
Shows His love for you and me.
God the Father's one with Jesus,
And through Him is how God sees us,
Not rejected, but elected,
To spend all eternity,
Not with sorrow, nor with horror,
But with Joy and Ecstasy,
We are "one" with Deity.

Chapter 17 of the gospel of John relates to us the prayer that Jesus prayed just prior to His crucifixion. He prays first for Himself, then for His disciples and finally for all future believers. In verse 22, we are told that Jesus has literally given us God's glory that we might be one with the Father, just as the Son is one with His Father. In the following verse Jesus prays that we may be brought to complete unity to let the world know that He was sent by His Father, who loves us as He loves His Son.

In these passages, Jesus is stressing unity among the believers. "That they may be one, as We are one." He proclaims the unity of the Father and Son, then prays that those who have Jesus in their heart will be unified in spirit, letting the glory of God's indwelling Spirit prevail unto complete unity.

Various parts of the Bible are interpreted differently, but the gospel has a clear-cut message for believers. The blood of Jesus cleanses us, and by faith, we accept eternal life with Him. From that moment forward, we have a personal relationship with the Lord. Our prayer is that as Christians we realize who we are. We are one with Christ. Now, let us be one in His Spirit with our brothers and sisters, for the glory of God through our Lord Jesus Christ.

August 30

TO KNOW NOTHING EXCEPT...

"For I resolved to know nothing while I was with you except Jesus Christ and Him crucified." – 1 Corinthians 2:2

IT'S NOT WHAT, IT'S WHO

Not a wisdom, thus evolving,
Only Christ, is our resolving,
One direction, one connection,
With the One we hold so dear.
Not by chance, and WHAT we're knowing,
But by faith, and WHO we're knowing,
Our direction, a reflection,
Of our Lord, who's always near,
Thus resolving, our involving,
Makes our walk with Him so clear,
He will guide us while we're here.

It's not WHAT we know; it's WHO we know. This is the point Paul is trying to get across to the Corinthians in this scripture. The city of Corinth could be characterized as a city deeply involved with Greek culture. Its people were interested in Greek philosophy and placed a high premium on wisdom.

We know enough about Paul's background and his writings to know that he was exceptionally well educated and, in all probability, well versed in oratorical eloquence. Yet, his simple statement to the Corinthians was that eloquence or superior wisdom meant nothing without the resolve to know the Person of Jesus Christ.

Christianity is not religion. It is a personal relationship with our Lord Jesus Christ. All of the wisdom and eloquence in this world fade in comparison with our personal walk with the Lord. This is accomplished through His indwelling Spirit who gives us guidance and comfort. Our prayer is that we will always remember WHO we know, and never be sidetracked by WHAT we know, all for the glory of God, through our Lord Jesus Christ.

August 31

HE HIMSELF IS OUR PEACE

"For He Himself is our peace." – Ephesians 2:14

ABIDING IN HIS PEACE

Though this world is cold and maiming,
Peace from Christ is what we're claiming,
Love abounding, grace resounding,
He Himself becomes our Peace.
And, what ere our situation,
Jesus Christ is our foundation,
He's the blessing, we're confessing,
For His love will never cease,
And we're knowing, His Grace flowing,
Gives our troubled souls release,
We're abiding in His Peace.

Jesus Christ, Himself is our peace. What a beautiful truth this is; a promise from God to give us peace through our Lord Jesus Christ. Paul continues his dissertation by explaining that Christ, at the cross, destroyed the barrier, the dividing wall of hostility between sinful man and God. As believers, we don the mantle of His purity, reconciling us to God through Him. We are promised an eternity with Christ, guaranteed by His very Spirit which indwells all believers.

Romans 8:31 tells us that "If God is for us, who can be against us?" With these promises of God's love and grace for each believer, and knowing what our eternal destination is, regardless of our current situation, through Christ we can find peace. In fact, He IS our peace. The world out there may be cold and maiming, but peace from Christ is what we're claiming. We know that His love will never cease, and our knowing that His grace is flowing into our very being day, by day, by day, gives our troubled souls release, enabling each one of us to have the peace of God, through our Lord Jesus Christ. WE'RE ABIDING IN HIS PEACE.

September 1

HE WILL GUIDE YOU

"But when He, the Spirit of truth, comes, He will guide you into all truth." – John 16:13

HIS TRUTH HE WILL NOT HIDE

Now, the Truth is from our Jesus,
He's the One through whom God sees us,
Like bells knelling, in us dwelling,
In His Spirit, there to guide.
Now, all truth He will be showing,
And through Him we will be growing,
First induction, then instruction,
In God's realm, as we abide.
Spirit reaching, in us teaching,
For His truth, He will not hide,
As through Him, we're sanctified.

Our primary source of information and instruction regarding both our existence on this earth and our eternity is the Bible, which is God's word, almost literally breathed into existence by divine assignment to God's appointed designees. As we study these scriptures, we are made aware of yet another source, a divine source of guidance regarding the truth of God's word. This divine source is the Spirit of truth, the third Person of the Trinity, the Spirit of Christ, who indwells every believer. Today's scripture tells us that He will guide us into "all truth."

Does this mean that we should have complete knowledge, including specific details regarding such things as the date of the return of Christ or the Rapture? The answer, of course, is a definite NO, because our Lord has told us that no one will know that day or hour. But the scripture does promise that His indwelling Spirit will guide us into all truth. And in the process of our sanctification, He will guide us with God's wisdom if we will but respond with the Spirit instead of our mind. As we are being sanctified, each time that we respond with the Spirit we take a step forward toward our ultimate goal of complete unity with God's purpose for our lives. And any unanswered questions we might have will dissolve into obscurity as we become more and more in tune with the will of God. The very wisdom of God is at our disposal through our Lord Jesus Christ if we will only focus and follow with the Spirit instead of our mind, for as we are being sanctified, HIS TRUTH HE WILL NOT HIDE.

UNDER SUPERVISION OF THE LAW

"Now that faith has come, we are no longer under the supervision of the law." – Galatians 3:25

PEACE INSTEAD OF FEAR

Is our mind set on our Savior,
Or is it focused on behavior?
Our selection, of direction,
Is a choice we made down here.
With our faith we are connected,
With our Lord, who has directed,
That abiding, by His guiding,
Knowing He is always near,
Is our mission, and position,
While we work for Him down here,
Filled with peace, instead of fear?

First, let us consider what the scripture does not say. Neither in this scripture, nor in any other scripture in the Bible, are we told to break God's law. But in this scripture, we are clearly told that since faith has come, we are no longer under the supervision of the Law. Since faith has come, each believer is equipped with the indwelling Spirit of Christ. We are actually equipped to lead a perfect life with His Spirit, though each of us still possesses the old sin nature. This nature and the Holy Spirit are in constant conflict. As we grow in Christ our sin nature becomes more and more subordinate to the Spirit, and our spirit begins to have a oneness with His Spirit.

We make many decisions in this life, some good, some bad. By far, the best decision we have ever made was when we exercised faith in Jesus, thereby assuring us of an eternity with Him. But as we attempt to live the Christian life, we are also faced with many decisions. One of the most important choices we make as Christians is the focus of our mindset. We can focus on rules and regulations, or we can focus on Jesus. One focus produces fear, the other peace and joy. When we focus on Jesus, His Spirit and our spirit begin to have a oneness of purpose. This personal relationship with our Lord brings to fruition the massive diminution of our sin nature through His love and grace, enabling each one of us to enjoy the Christian life, filled with love, joy and peace. Our prayer is that by God's grace, we keep our mindset on Jesus.

September 3

THE RICHES OF GOD'S GRACE

"In Him we have redemption through His blood, the forgiveness of sins, in accordance with the riches of God's grace." – Ephesians 1:7

HE EXTENDS HIS GRACE

All God's Grace, we are receiving,
Through our Lord, when we're believing,
We're connected, not rejected,
As we run this earthly race.
On our own, we find the ditches,
But therein, we find God's riches,
All prevailing, never failing,
When our Lord, we do embrace.
His connection gives direction,
And in each and every case,
God, through Christ, extends His grace.

Because of God's love for each one of us, He extended His grace to us; first, with propitiation for our sin debt, accomplished by Christ at the cross, reconciling us to God while we were yet enemies (Romans 5:10). Then, as we exercised faith in Christ, we not only received forgiveness for our sins, but we were also redeemed through His blood.

With our endeavor to live the Christian life, we should never forget the magnitude of the extension of God's grace. Just as He cleansed us and saved us in accordance with the riches of His grace, through His Spirit, we are accorded an unlimited supply of His love and His grace, if we will only keep our eyes on Him. As we run this earthly race, on our own we seem to find more ditches than we do God's riches. However, as we grow in Christ, we begin to understand that God's true riches are found in the ditches. In the ditches, we find humility, and with a humble spirit, we experience the abundance of the riches of God's grace. When our Lord, we do embrace, His connection gives direction, and in each and every case, GOD, THROUGH CHRIST, EXTENDS HIS GRACE.

September 4

BE STILL

"Be still, and know that I am God." – Psalm 46:10

BE STILL AND KNOW

Whether evening, night or morning,
Let's be heedful of God's warning,
Let's be peering, and be hearing,
What God says to you and me.
Our souls "still," by His direction,
Gives our hearts, a Christ-Connection,
Then we're knowing, that we're growing,
For God's Love will ever be,
A connecting, and directing,
Flow of Grace from Deity,
Throughout all eternity.

I believe God gave us two eyes, with which to see, and two ears, with which to hear, but only one tongue, with which to speak, for a reason. This scripture is God's admonition to the nation of Israel to "be still, and know" that He is God, a declaration of His mighty sustaining presence. Now, as then, we need to be aware of His mighty sustaining presence in our lives. God has accomplished this with the third Person of the Trinity, the indwelling Holy Spirit, the very Spirit of Christ who guides and comforts each believer.

Also now, as then, we need to "be still and know," know that by God's grace, we will spend an eternity with our Lord. Whatever our situation might be, His grace is sufficient through our Lord Jesus Christ (2 Corinthians 12:9).

Our prayer is that before we use our tongue to speak, we will, by His grace, have a reverent stillness in our soul. So that our eyes might see, our ears might hear and our heart will know, not only God's saving grace through our Lord Jesus Christ, but the sufficiency of His presence in our daily lives. For we know that His love will ever be, a connecting and directing, flow of grace from deity, throughout all eternity.

September 5

I IN THEM, YOU IN ME

"I in them, You in Me. May they be brought to complete unity to let the world know that You sent Me, and have loved them even as You have loved Me." – John 17:23

WE DARE TO BE

While on earth, in Christ abiding,
He's within us, there residing,
Therein living, for God's giving,
All His love to you and me.
Now, this truth indeed is "heady,"
But the Lord's with us already,
His connection, gives direction,
And His Spirit sets us free,
But we're knowing, His Grace growing,
Is a dare, to you and me,
To be all that we can be.

This is an astonishing truth, a heady truth. The love of the Father is extended to each Christian through the indwelling Spirit of Christ. Though we yearn to be with the Lord when we leave this earth, the truth is that He's with us already. As time progresses, and our imperfect bodies are replaced by perfect glorified bodies, that event is not a goal to be realized, but a truth to be finalized. We already reside with the Lord, and His Spirit, who indwell search believer, not only gives us comfort and assistance, but guides us into all truth, giving us direction for our lives.

None of us knows the exact moment when we will see Jesus face-to-face. That will be a glorious time in our eternity. But as we walk this earthly path, we need to fully realize the magnitude of the splendor of our very personal intimate relationship with our Lord. We are blessed far beyond human comprehension. We can walk and talk with the Lord every day of our existence, throughout all eternity. With this ultimate gift of God's love and grace through our Lord Jesus Christ, I personally view it as a challenge, a dare to each one of us to be all that we can be for the Lord. Our prayer is that by God's grace, while we're on our earthly tour, and because of the preponderance of His grace, we dare to do just that. We dare to "be all that we can be" for the Lord, all for the glory of God, through our Lord Jesus Christ.

September 6

TODAY OR TOMORROW

"Now listen, you who say, today or tomorrow we will go…Why, you do not even know what will happen tomorrow." James 4:13a, 14a

LET US LOVE SOMEONE TODAY

Our Life filled with joy or sorrow,
Should we wait until tomorrow,
In all fairness, for awareness,
Or should we reach out today?
If our soul is Christ-connected,
Let our heart be Christ-directed,
Let's be knowing, that we're sowing,
Seeds of Love along the way.
In addition, let our mission,
Be for Jesus, day by day,
Let us love someone today.

As we go forward down life's pathway, attempting to lead the Christian life, we are faced with many decisions, some of which create a real factual and sincere dilemma in our thinking. We don't know which way to turn. We have the desire to do what the Lord wants us to do, but we simply cannot seem to get a handle on exactly what that is. Some of us very prayerfully "put out the fleece," just as Gideon did (Judges 6:37), but we seem to have a problem determining whether it is wet or dry. In the midst of our dilemma, sometimes we procrastinate instead of continuing to seek and search out God's guidance.

The fact that we need direction from our Lord is an absolute truth, but sometimes we need to do something in order to determine whether it is God's will. Regardless of the direction in which God is leading us, or the dilemma we face as we attempt to make that determination, there are certain things we can always do in obedience to our Lord's commands. And one of the most important directions we receive from Him is to love someone. As we begin each day, and with regard to passing the love of Christ on to others, the word, "procrastination," should not even be in our vocabulary.

As James teaches us in today's scripture, we have no knowledge whatsoever regarding what will happen tomorrow. All we have is today. Today our prayer is that by God's grace we reach out, Christ-connected, and Christ-directed, and sow seeds of His love along the way. Let us love someone today.

HE WILL DELIVER US

"He has delivered us from such a deadly peril, and He will deliver us. On Him we have set our hope (trust)." – 2 Corinthians 1:10

LET'S MAKE IT SIMPLE

Our Lord Jesus is the giver,
He's the One who will deliver,
There's no doubting, for He's routing,
Us to Heaven's Golden Gate.
He is now our Holy Temple,
While on earth, let's make it simple,
We receive Him, let's believe Him,
For His Grace will not abate,
Let life's crossing, be engrossing,
Since we know we have a date,
With our Jesus, at that gate.

The word rendered "hope" or "trust" in this scripture is the Greek word "elpis," the noun, or "elpizo," the verb. This word connotes a confident expectation. In Romans 15:13, God is referred to as the "God of hope," and we must remember that he is the Author of hope, not the subject of it. In Hebrews 6:19, hope is described as an anchor for our soul firm and secure.

In today's scripture, we are reminded that, as Christians, we have been delivered from such a deadly peril (the fate of the unbeliever). And we are assured that our deliverance will be completely brought to fruition. Consequently, we are instructed to "set our hope" on, or "trust completely" in the Lord.

As we attempt to live this Christian life, we make it so complex. Our very nature seems to seek out complexity. We completely trust the Lord for our eternity, but we seem to have a problem trusting Him for today. Let's make it simple. He, who spoke into existence the universe, loved us so much He sent His only Son to die on a cross for our sins, then gave us eternal life, is certainly capable of taking care of our today. Our prayer is, Lord, we trust you for our eternity. By Your grace, let us live each day simply trusting you. Let our thoughts be like that of a small child, looking up to his father, knowing that his father will take care of him. Lord, help us make it simple, trusting You completely, all for Your glory through our Lord Jesus Christ.

I HAVE POWER

"No man taketh it from Me, but I lay it down of Myself. I have power to lay it down, and I have power to take it again. This commandment have I received of My Father." – John 10:18

LET US ABIDE

Though His life He would be losing,
He embraced His father's choosing,
With selection, of direction,
He took up His cross and died.
On that cross men would abuse Him,
But He chooses to let God use Him.
With no ration, of compassion,
He expired, then death defied,
Godhead merging, Power surging,
He arose, let us abide,
For He's always at our side.

In this scripture, Jesus is proclaiming His deity, in that He states that no one can take His life from Him, except, and unless, He permits it. Then He states that He has the power both to lay His life down, and to take it up again, thus proclaiming His power of resurrection. His last statement proclaims that He, indeed, is the Son of God, indicating that the power of resurrection was given Him directly by the Father. But we also note one other truth in His statement, and that is that He knew His Father's will, and God's will was for Him to go to that cross and die.

Jesus walked this earth both as a man and as deity. His mission on this earth was to die for the sins of all mankind, cleansing our sins in order that we might be acceptable to God the Father. But Jesus had a choice. There was no way the agony of the cross was something to look forward to, and Jesus knew the pain and humiliation that awaited Him, but He also knew what God wanted Him to do, and He did it.

As we attempt to live the Christian life, and we know what God wants us to do, do we do it, or do we think about the personal hardship that might result in our obedience? Do we put self first, or do we put God first? Our prayer is that by God's grace we always put Him first, and in loving obedience, do what He wants us to do, and be who He wants us to be, all for the glory of God.

DRAW NEAR TO GOD

"Come near to God, and He will come near to you." – James 4:8

GOD WILL DRAW NEAR TO US

As we look at our behavior,
Are our eyes upon our Savior?
Is attitude, mere platitude,
Is He near to us out there?
Do we focus on His Lordship,
Or complain about our hardship?
Our direction, needs connection,
Though our souls to Him we bare.
Let's draw nearer, ever nearer,
He, in turn, with Grace so rare,
Will draw near with loving care.

As Christians, the only intermediary we have between us and God is our Lord Jesus Christ. We also have the indwelling Holy Spirit guiding us and giving us comfort. Even so, there are times when God seems SO far away. We seem to be in a vacuum with no gravitational pull in any direction. We just float from one point of conflict to another, with no anchor to stabilize our soul, drifting farther and farther from the nearness of God. We are acutely aware of our problems, but seemingly oblivious to the love and grace of God. What is our problem and, of utmost priority, what is the solution?

Our problem is the direction and object of our focus. We either encounter a problem, or, more likely, we anticipate a problem. Either way, we become focused on the troubled area, and on self, instead of on the promises of God. We seem not to be able to see the forest for the trees. Fearful anticipation does not breed reality. Our reality is in the Lord, so the solution to our problem is to completely realize who we are in the Lord, then to focus on Him and His grace, instead of on self and our problems. When we do this, it is absolutely astonishing how near God is to us. Our vacuum dissolves as we feel the secure anchor of God's love and grace through our Lord Jesus Christ. Though our souls to Him we bare, let's draw nearer, ever nearer. Then He, in turn, with grace so rare, will draw near to us, with loving care.

September 10

LET HIM WHO BOASTS

"Let him who boasts boast in the Lord." – 1 Corinthians 1:31

OUR STRENGTH IS IN THE LORD

If our works lead us to boasting,
It's the Lord we must be toasting,
For when weakness leads to meekness,
Then we're pleasing to the Lord.
And what ere our situation,
We're the Lord's; we're His creation,
For the tower, of his power,
Sinful man can not retard.
He aligns us, and assigns us,
Then He gives us our reward,
And our strength is in the Lord.

In this scripture, we are issued a warning. Verse 29 summarizes the fact that God chose the foolish and the weak things of this world to shame the wise and the strong, so that no one may boast before Him. And today's scripture tells us that if we must boast, we must boast in the Lord, not in ourselves. Note that, in this scripture, we are not told to boast, but we are warned that if we do our boasting has to be about what God has done, not about what we have done.

When we think of the word "boast," we think of some haughty statement made by someone regarding his accomplishments. The word "boast" is also rendered "glory" in the King James Version. In 2 Corinthians 12:10b, Paul writes, "When I am weak, then I am strong." In a prior verse, he tells us that he will boast about his weakness, in order that the power of Christ may rest on him.

The Lord cannot use us in our own strength, because in and of ourselves, we have none. But when we completely realize this and go to the Lord in meekness, our weakness turned to meekness suddenly transforms us from a vessel of ineptness to a recipient of the power and strength of Christ in order to do His will. Only when we are truly humble, and open our heart to Him are we pleasing in His sight. Then His power will flow through us, permitting us to do good works for Him. If we ever do any boasting, it must be about our weakness, or about His strength, because what ere the situation, we're His creation, and through the tower of His power, he aligns us, and assigns us, then He gives us our reward, and OUR STRENGTH IS IN THE LORD."

September 11

PUT ON THE ARMOR OF God

"Finally, be strong in the Lord, and in His mighty power. Put on the full armor of God." – Ephesians 6:10

LET'S PUT IT ON

God's full armor is for using,
May we never be refusing,
An attitude of gratitude,
Will demand we put it on.
We encounter evil forces,
But we fight with God's resources,
Christ-connected, we're directed,
As we fight the dark unknown,
Cold or warmer, it's God's armor,
It's His armor, all alone –
That protects, LET'S PUT IT ON.

After this admonition, Paul explains that the struggle is not against flesh and blood, but against the evil forces of the spiritual world. His exhortation coincided with the armor of the Roman soldier, and the sequence in which the armor was put on – all being for defensive purposes except for the final "taking-in-hand" of the sword, an offensive weapon, thus described as the "sword of the Spirit," the word of God. The "putting-on" of the full armor of God obviously refers to how Christians can overcome the many temptations so prevalent in this evil world during the life-long process of sanctification. Paul says that with this armor to stand firm. This armor includes the belt of truth, the breastplate of righteousness, feet fitted with the readiness of the gospel, the shield of faith, the helmet of salvation and the sword of the Spirit.

The great truth in Paul's exhortation and admonition is that Christians have at their disposal the full armor of God. They know the truth, possess the righteousness of Christ and have responded to the gospel. God's grace has given them faith – they know they have eternal salvation and the indwelling Spirit of Christ to guide them. Now they must understand that they can't do it, but HE CAN. By simple exertion of their will they must focus on "Christ" instead of "self." Then they will be protected by the "full armor of God," for it's His armor, and His armor alone that protects them. By His grace, LET'S PUT IT ON.

September 12

#1 – BELT OF TRUTH

"Stand firm then, with the belt of truth buckled around your waist." – Ephesians 6:14

FREE TO WIN THIS RACE

We prepare ourselves for living,
With the belt of truth God's giving,
And we're finding, that this binding,
Sets us free to run this race.
Not the freedom to be sinning,
But the freedom to be winning,
And we're winning, from beginning,
As God's Spirit, we embrace,
Love for others, sisters, brothers,
And for God, who gives us grace,
Set us free to win this race.

Before the Roman soldier put on his armor, he first girded himself with a belt around his waist. In the days of Jesus, all garments were loose and flowing. In order to prepare for war, play or battle, these garments had to be girded around the waist in order to give freedom of movement to the individual. In fact, the word "girding" is often used in the Bible as a metaphor, denoting preparation prior to action.

Paul is telling us that before we "put on the full armor of God," we must first gird ourselves with truth – the truth of knowing who we are in Christ and the truth of our integrity in Christ, that is, the truth of our sincerity. When we gird ourselves with these things, we are prepared to go forward. This "belt of truth" enables us to have ease and freedom of movement with God, with others, and with ourselves. Thus, we are then fully prepared, and free to put on the full armor of God.

Our prayer is that by God's grace, we are girded with this belt of truth, which will give us the ease of freedom to, not only put on the full armor of God, but to stride forward for God in all areas of our lives. May our God, who gives us grace, through His Spirit we embrace, give us the grace, not only to run this race, but the grace to win this race, all for the glory of God through our Lord Jesus Christ.

September 13

#2 – BREASTPLATE OF RIGHTEOUSNESS

"With the breastplate of righteousness in place." – Ephesians 6:14b

LET'S OBEY WITH WORD AND DEED

We are righteous through his dying,
Then his act of death defying,
And He's living, in us giving,
Us the guidance that we need.
But, we must let Him direct us then
Our actions will protect us.
We'll be winning, over sinning,
With each kind and loving deed.
Righteous living, is His giving,
But, we have a choice, indeed,
Let's obey, with word and deed.

After the Roman soldier girded his waist with a belt in order to ensure freedom of movement, he began to put on his armor. The first piece of armor he put on was a breastplate. This protected his heart and other vital organs from the enemy's attack, whether it was a barrage of arrows, a sword or a lance.

Paul tells us that, as Christians, after we gird ourselves with the belt of truth, the truth of knowing who we are in Christ and the truth of our sincerity and integrity in Christ, we are then free to put on the full armor of God. And the first piece of armor is the "breastplate of righteousness." The righteousness Paul tells us about in this scripture is not the righteousness of Christ that we receive when we are justified, but rather the righteous acts that we do in God's sanctifying process. The point he is making is that, just as a soldier's breastplate protects him from the enemy, so does righteous living protect us from the attacks of the enemy. We know that we will continually have the opportunity to sin. However, Paul tells us that righteous living will protect us from the temptation to sin. Paul is making two points with this illustration. First, if we are busy enough doing good we don't have that much time to sin. Second, if we are focused on Christ and what He wants us to do, the "arrows of temptation" will be blunted, and not penetrate the breastplate of the righteousness of Christ.

Our prayer is that by God's grace, we put on this "breastplate of right-eousness," for only the righteousness of Christ keeps us winning over sinning, and though righteous living is His giving, we have choices, indeed.

September 14

#3 – THE READINESS OF PEACE

"And with your feet fitted with the readiness that comes from the gospel of peace." – Ephesians 6:15

KNOWLEDGE OF HIS PEACE

There must be no reservation,
We stand firm on our foundation,
We're connected, and directed,
Through His peace that we embrace.
For, the gospel is a blessing,
It's a blessing we're confessing,
Footing stable, makes us able,
Our temptations to erase,
Not by sinning, but beginning,
Each temptation that we face,
With the knowledge of His grace.

In this scripture, the Greek word "hetoimasia" is rendered "readiness" or "preparedness." It is also found in the Septuagint with the specific meaning of "a firm foundation," or "sure footing." This could be interpreted as a readiness to spread the gospel. But since Paul's admonition was to put on the full armor of God in order to "stand firm," we must interpret this word in light of a defensive, rather than an offensive, piece of armor.

Just as a house built on sand will fall (Matthew 7:26), and a soldier without a firm footing will fall when attacked by the enemy, we as Christians, without a firm foundation of the gospel, will fall when confronted with temptation. Just as a Roman soldier wore hobnailed sandals when going into battle in order to have sure footing and to stand firm when the enemy attacked, we as Christians must be equipped with the gospel of peace with an undergirding foundation giving us knowledge of, and dependence upon, the gospel. Thus, when faced with temptation, we are equipped to stand our ground, to stand firm with the peace of Jesus Christ in our heart.

Our prayer is that we put on the full armor of God, with full knowledge of, and dependence upon, the gospel of peace – a peace we have only through our Lord Jesus Christ. Then our temptations we will erase, not by sinning, but by beginning each temptation that we face with the knowledge of His grace.

#4 – THE SHIELD OF FAITH

"In addition to all this, take up the shield of faith with which you can extinguish all the flaming arrows of the evil one." – Ephesians 6:16

FAITH WILL SHIELD US

There are times, we're not denying,
When a flaming dart is flying,
Not at brothers, or at others,
But directly at our heart.
But regardless of direction,
Faith in Christ will give protection,
We're not yielding, with His shielding,
But we have to do our part.
Let's be showing, that we're knowing,
That His Grace He will impart,
Faith will shield us from that dart.

Just as the armor of the Roman soldier would not be complete without a shield in place, the "full armor of God" includes the "shield of faith." In New Testament times, darts were often dipped in pitch and set on fire when being used. The wooden shields were covered with leather and linen in order to extinguish them quickly. Paul equates the wiles of the devil with these fiery darts. There is no doubt in Paul's mind that these flaming arrows, or fiery darts, will be launched at us. These darts could represent temptations regarding morality, fear, doubt, injustice or disappointment, all directed toward us to burn and destroy.

Another fact regarding the soldier's shield is that it was used in such a manner that it could be moved to intercept these fiery darts. It protected not only the soldier himself, but also his armor. The breastplate protected the heart and other vital parts of the body, but the shield protected even his breastplate. We might say that the shield was the soldier's first line of defense. In like manner, faith is our first line of defense.

Our prayer is that for whatever circumstance or reason the fiery dart is flying directly at our heart, by God's grace we do our part. And we use the shield of faith, showing that we're knowing that to us, His grace He will impart, and faith will shield us from that dart.

#5 – THE HELMET OF SALVATION

"Take the helmet of salvation." – Ephesians 6:17a

CHRIST CONNECTED AND PROTECTED

With the helmet of salvation,
We are saved for the duration,
This foundation, our salvation,
Is God's gift to you and me.
Through our Lord, we are elected,
When, by Faith, we're Christ-connected,
Is a gift, by Grace, it's free,
Thus connected, we're protected,
Let's thank God for Calvary,
Where Christ died, for you and me.

Paul continues his instructions to us regarding his admonition to put on the full armor of God. The last piece of defensive armor put on by the Roman soldier was his helmet. There was a reason for it being last. It was uncomfortable, but as he prepared for battle, as he prepared to "stand firm," he immediately protected his head from harm with his helmet. The head is the most vulnerable part of the body. A head wound can immediately render its recipient either unconscious or dead, and in the heat of hand-to-hand combat, unconsciousness usually results in death.

In this verse, the word "take" is not a suggestion. The Greek work for "take" is an imperative. Paul's admonition to us to take up the helmet of salvation is an order, a command. This is imperative if we are to stand firm in victory, instead of falling in from the penalty of sin. However, in the imperative context, we are reminded that without the helmet of salvation, the Christian does not have the full armor of God with which to "stand firm." In order to be protected from the power of sin, we must know who we are in the power of God's saving grace through our Lord Jesus Christ. We are "God-elected" by being "Christ-connected," and with this connection, we have protection. Let's thank God for Calvary, where Christ died, for you and me.

September 17

#6 – TAKE THE SWORD OF THE SPIRIT

"Take the helmet of salvation and the sword of the Spirit, which is the word of God – and pray in the Spirit on all occasions." – Ephesians 6:17-18

WE MAKE OUR STAND

Now, the word of God is given,
And His sword is Spirit-driven,
We're commanded, to be candid,
And to take His Sword in hand.
By His Grace, He will befriend us,
And His Spirit will defend us,
He'll correct us, and protect us,
As the Spirit's fire is fanned,
As we're growing, let's be knowing,
Where that line, is drawn in sand,
With His Sword, we make our stand.

After the soldier has put on his full armor, he takes up his sword. The sword is principally an offensive weapon, however, in personal combat, it also becomes a defensive weapon. Although his shield is the soldier's first line of defense, if he is skilled in the use of his sword, with it he can parry, block and turn aside his opponent's sword thrusts even before they strike his shield.

In this scripture we have another imperative, "take," and the subject is "the sword of the Spirit," defined as "the word of God," and we are commanded to "pray in the Spirit" on all occasions. By definition, the Greek "logos," which is all encompassing, is not the word used here for "word of God." Rather, the Greek "rhema" is used, denoting that which is spoken, or, we might say, that which is specifically applicable to a given situation. An illustration would be when Jesus was tempted and tested by Satan (Matthew 4:1-10), and won the battle, using the sword of the Spirit, specific scripture from the word of God.

As Christians, especially with regard to either morality or the truth of the gospel, we need to fortify ourselves with both a knowledge and understanding of God's word. Then, with God's grace, draw a line in the sand, a point beyond which, WE WILL NOT GO. Our prayer is, that, as the Spirit's fire is fanned, we'll be growing, in the knowing, of exactly where that line is drawn in the sand. AT THAT POINT, WITH THE SWORD OF HIS SPIRIT, WE MAKE OUR STAND.

THE SEVEN CHURCHES

"The seven stars are the angels of the seven churches, and the seven lamp-stands are the seven churches." – Revelation 1:20b

LET'S BE ALL THAT WE CAN BE

Now, our Lord, who reigns in Heaven,
Sometimes uses number seven,
He's beseeching, as He's teaching,
And He's reaching you and me.
We're His Church, for the duration,
He now gives us information,
And, with living, loving, giving,
He gives Grace that we might see.
Let's be lurching, forward, searching,
For His truth, which set us free.
Let's be all, that we can be.

The book of Revelation is apocalyptic, a type of writing that is highly symbolic. It is a prophetic writing concerned with the end of the world, but also has instructions for us today, both as individuals, and especially, as a church body. The number seven is used 52 times in this book, and though at times, seven might be the exact count, symbolically, it denotes fullness, or completeness.

Almost all Bible scholars believe that the author of Revelation was the apostle John, son of Zebedee. In this particular scripture, John is repeating what Jesus is revealing to him regarding different church bodies. We believe these were actual churches in Asia Minor, and the evaluation of each was real. In addition, some Bible scholars see the seven letters as a preview of church history, as it spirals downward to the lukewarmness of the church at Laodicea. Others interpret them as characteristic of present time. Regardless of how much symbolism we attach to these seven churches, we have instructions directly from the Lord regarding how to live, both as an individual, and as a member of the body of Christ.

With a prayerful attitude and thanksgiving, let us proceed with the study of these seven letters to the seven churches. As He's teaching you and me, with His living, loving, giving, give us the grace that we might see. Let's be lurching forward, searching, for His truth, which set us free. LET'S BE ALL THAT WE CAN BE.

September 19

CHURCH #1 – EPHESUS

"I know your works, your labor, your patience, and that you cannot bear those who are evil. And you have tested those who say they are apostles and are not, and have found them liars; and you have persevered and have patience, and have labored for My name's sake and have not become weary. Nevertheless, I have this against you, that you have left your first love. Remember therefore from where you have fallen: repent and do the first works or else I will come to you quickly and remove your lampstand from its place – unless you repent. But this you have, that you hate the deeds of the Nicolaitans, which I also hate." – Revelation 2:2-6

PUT HIM FIRST

Works and deeds, we are assessing,
And for Jesus, they're a blessing,
Our abiding, with His building,
Let us work, with love and care.
But, in every situation,
Loving Him, for the duration,
Is His teaching, as we're reaching,
To embrace the saints out there.
Let's not ration, His compassion,
Loving Him, must not be rare,
Put Him first, with loving care.

This congregation was commended for their deeds, their hard work, their intolerance of evil, their perseverance, the hardships they had endured, and their hatred for the practices of the Nicolaitans, which included immorality and the practice of idolatry. Yet, there was condemnation in this letter because of one thing. The church, individually, and as a body, had forsaken their "first love," their love for Jesus, and their love for each other. They had become so busy with the entanglement of what they were, they had forgotten who they were.

Christianity is a love relationship with our Lord Jesus Christ, which in turn, becomes a love relationship with each other, for the Lord. We, both as individuals and as a church body, need to do good deeds, to persevere in the faith, to be intolerant of evil, to work hard, and to endure whatever hardships we encounter in our Christian walk, but never to the exclusion of our first love, our love for Jesus and each other. Loving Him must not be rare, LET'S PUT HIM FIRST, WITH LOVING CARE.

CHURCH #2 – SMYRNA

"I know your afflictions and your poverty, yet you are rich. Do not be afraid of what you are about to suffer. Be faithful, even to the point of death, and I will give you the crown of life." – Revelation 2:9-10

CROWNS OF LIFE

Midst our trial, and persecution,
Our Lord gives us the solution,
Have faith longer, have faith stronger,
There will be a day of rest.
And, though poor in earthly travel,
Through our Lord, this will unravel,
And our hardship, for His Lordship,
Will, at last, be for the best,
For the Living, Lord is giving,
All the Saints, who pass the test,
Crowns of Life, and all the rest.

The Christians in the church at Smyrna were extremely poor. They were also being persecuted by both pagan Gentiles and hostile Jews. In fact, the synagogue in Smyrna was referred to as the synagogue of Satan. Yet, these Christians remained faithful to the Lord. The message to these Christians was that, though they were poor and were experiencing extreme persecution, yet they were rich – rich in the Lord.

This letter was the first of only two, out of the seven letters to the churches in Asia Minor, in which there was absolutely no condemnation. There was only commendation for standing firm and faithful in the midst of such adverse circumstances. It is interesting to note that these Christians were not promised that circumstances would improve for them on this earth. In fact, they were promised that the persecutions would escalate, even to the point of death, but they were exhorted to continue to be faithful. Their riches were found in the Lord, not in circumstances.

Our earthly tour is but an iota of time, when referenced to eternity. Our prayer is that with God's grace, we fully realize that any hardship we might experience in this life, means nothing compared to His Lordship in our life, for the Living Lord, is giving, all the saints, who pass the test, CROWNS OF LIFE AND ALL THE REST.

CHURCH #3 – PERGAMUM

"I know where you live – where Satan has his throne, yet you remain true to My name, and remain faithful. But some hold to the teaching of Balaam, and some to the teaching of the Nicolaitans. Repent." – Revelation 2:13-16 (synopsis)

LET OUR DOCTRINE BE PURE

Let our church, with all it's preaching,
Reject evil, with it's teaching,
While we're reaching, let's be teaching,
That our morals should be pure.
Let not "Truth" be our revising,
Let us not be compromising,
But be preaching, and be teaching,
What is right, and what is sure.
For our Jesus, as He sees us,
While we're on this earthly tour,
Let our doctrine, be pure.

This letter to the church at Pergamum first acknowledges that the city itself is where Satan lives, a veritable sewer of immorality. And in the midst of this adversity, the church, as a whole, had kept the faith and had remained true to the Lord. However, some among them had not. The letter states that some among them held to the teaching of Balaam, and/or the Nicolaitans. These designations identified these groups as heretical sects within the church, who had worked out a compromise with the pagan society. One of these sects, the Nicolaitans, was apparently teaching that spiritual liberty gave them the right to practice idolatry and immorality. This departure from the gospel and compromise with immorality would corrupt the church, as was later evidenced in the third century. This letter was a warning to the church against any and all deviation from the doctrine of Christ, the pure gospel of grace.

Today, as in the day of the church in Pergamum, Christianity is faced with corruption within the church. Anytime and anywhere, groups within the church depart from the doctrine of the pure gospel of grace and decide that compromise with the world is the proper way to spread the gospel. Our prayer is that with God's grace, our reaching, and teaching, will be what is right, and what is sure. Let not truth be our revising, let us not be compromising.

CHURCH #4 – THYATIRA

"I know your deeds, your love and faith, your service and perseverance. You are now doing more than you did at first, but you tolerate that woman Jezebel. I will make those who live under her teaching suffer intensely, and strike her children down, unless they repent." – Revelation 2:18-29 (synopsis)

OUR LORD HATES SIN

Some grow stronger; they are winning,
This life's battle, against sinning,
Others falter, at the altar,
Living daily, sin within.
For the ones whose lust is sinning,
There must be a new beginning,
God has anger, for sin's languor,
In the hearts and minds of men,
And disaster, from the Master,
Could result from sin within,
Our Lord hates to see men sin.

Apparently, the church at Thyatira was a small congregation, and a self-proclaimed "prophetess" was influencing the church. The name "Jezebel" suggests the worship of the god, Baal. Throughout Israel's history, the Baal cults had challenged the worship of the one and only true God. Their rites consisted of, not only sexual immorality under the guise of the fertility god, but even such abominable acts of child sacrifice. They had utter disregard for God's Laws. They lived in a state of moral turpitude, their debauchery rampant, spawned by Satan through a false prophet, or prophetess.

In this letter, the woman called Jezebel could, or could not, have been a member of the church, but it is very evident that she was in a position to influence the members. This letter begins with a commendation to those members who remained faithful, who, in fact, were doing more for the Lord now, than at first. They had grown in their faith. However, they seemed to represent only a remnant of the church body. The tone of condemnation contained in this letter suggests harsh retribution by the Lord against this cultic group unless they repent.

In churches today, it would be rare to see a cultic group being so prominently and openly evil. However, it is not rare to find many who are willing to comprise basic beliefs in order to be accepted by the world.

CHURCH #5 – SARDIS

"You have a reputation of being alive, but you are dead. Wake up. Strengthen what remains, and is about to die, for I have not found your deeds complete in the sight of my God. You have a few people in Sardis who have not soiled their clothes. They will walk with Me, dressed in white." – Revelation 3:1-6 (synopsis)

ONLY CHRIST CAN MAKE IT WELL

A church dead, instead of living,
Lacks the Spirit, Christ is giving,
For He's knowing, they're not growing,
They are just a hollow shell.
They may look as if they render,
All the grace, of our Lord's splendor,
But this sighting, is a blighting,
And is like a cancer cell,
That has landed, then expanded,
And is headed, straight for Hell.
Only Christ can make it well.

In the vernacular, this church, indeed, seemed headed straight for Hell, certainly not the remnant who were Christians, but the church itself, which once alive, was not pronounced dead by the Lord. This church had a reputation for being alive, but that reputation was all that was left. The Spirit of the Lord was no longer in their midst. Without the predominance of the Holy Spirit, no church can fulfill its destiny. It becomes a hollow shell. The gospel is not preached, and members become satisfied and content with the status-quo, lax in their approach to discipleship, and alienated from the truth of the gospel. Currently, we might equate this condition within a church to be the country club attitude, all show and no go where members are more concerned with looks than with actions, and more concerned with social events than they are with spiritual truth.

That attitude within a congregation can, indeed, become like a cancer cell, which has entered the body, has landed, then expanded. And regarding the effectiveness of the church that cancer cell will multiply and expand to such a degree that, metaphorically speaking, we can envision that church going straight to Hell, and ONLY CHRIST CAN MAKE IT WELL.

CHURCH #6 – PHILADELPHIA

"I have placed before you an open door that no one can shut. I know you have little strength, yet you have kept My word. Since you have kept My command to endure patiently, I will also keep you from the hour of trial that is going to come upon the whole world." – Revelation 3:7-13 (synopsis)

THEY WERE HIS FOR EVERMORE

Weak, but "Strong" with Christ in Glory,
Was to be their final story,
To be captured, and be raptured,
With the Lord for evermore.
They had won their earthly testing,
With the Lord, they would be resting,
He was saying, since obeying,
They would be with Him before,
Tribulation, for duration,
He gave them, an open door,
THEY WERE HIS, FOR EVERMORE.

In this letter, Jesus had nothing but praise for the church at Philadelphia. He made note of the fact that they had little strength. However, they had endured, kept His word, and had not denied His name. They had kept the faith. In this scripture, Jesus uses the analogy of an open door to describe entry into the heavenly realm, a door that only Jesus can either open or close. He declares it open for members of this church, and then reminds them that what He has opened no one can close.

Jesus also makes a promise to members of this church, and to each one of us who are in Christ. He tells them, and us, that we will be kept from that hour of trial that will come upon the whole world. In other words, we will be raptured to be with the Lord forever before that terrible seven years of tribulation is thrust upon this earth. This is one of the verses in the Bible that solidifies the belief in the pre-tribulation Rapture of the church; that is, a belief that the Rapture of the church will occur prior to the Great Tribulation.

Our prayer is that though we are weak, by God's grace, we may be strong in the Lord now. For we know that, as Christians, our final story will be fulfilled with Christ in glory. We'll be raptured and we'll be captured by our Lord. He will lead us through that open door, and WE'LL BE HIS FOR EVERMORE.

CHURCH #7 – LAODICEA

"You are neither cold nor hot. I wish you were either one or the other. So because you are lukewarm, neither hot nor cold, I am about to spew you out of My mouth." – Revelation 3:15-16

LET THE SPIRIT'S FIRE BE FANNED

Now, lukewarmness, was in season,
With no zeal for Christ the reason,
No ambition, for a mission,
Just an apathetic stand.
Neither hot, nor cold with caring,
Nor with evidence of sharing,
No attitude, of gratitude,
And no line, drawn in the sand.
Our position, and our mission,
Is in Christ; let's make our stand.
Let the Spirit's fire be fanned.

Our Lord first makes a statement of fact concerning the church at Laodicea. The church as a congregation, and its members individually, were neither cold nor hot. They were lukewarm. He then makes an astonishing statement. He says that He wished they would either be one or the other, for He is about to spit them out of His mouth. How could the Lord prefer that we be cold, instead of just lukewarm? The answer lies in the Lord's wisdom and knowledge of our thought processes.

The person who is either hot or cold at least takes a stand. He has convictions, whether they are right or wrong. And one who has convictions, even if they are wrong, can be led to repentance. A great example of this is the apostle Paul, who after his repentance, was used mightily by the Lord. But, the one who is lukewarm is apathetic. He simply does not care one way or the other. This state of mind can be applied to both salvation and sanctification. The Lord leads; He does not force.

As Christians may we never be lukewarm in our love for the Lord. Our prayer is that, by God's grace, we exhibit an attitude of gratitude, and draw a line in the sand, with our position, being a reflection of our mission, which is in Christ. And upon Him, let us make our stand. LET THE SPIRIT'S FIRE BE FANNED.

September 26

AGES OF THE SEVEN CHURCHES

"Write, therefore, what you have seen, what is now and what will take place later." – Revelation 1:19

'ORE THE AGES, SATAN RAGES

Work for Christ in church did follow,
Some were true, and some were hollow,
'Ore the ages, Satan rages,
As each church, is put to test.
Some receive a commendation,
Others only condemnation,
Let's be wary, reasons vary,
But His truth will pass the test.
Let His living, loving giving,
Inspire us, to do our best,
In His loving arms, we rest.

The book of Revelation is apocalyptic, that is, written in a way that is highly symbolic and prophetic concerning the end times. Many Bible scholars have attempted to parallel the conditions existing in the seven churches with circumstances surrounding the church in various stages and ages, from its inception until the current day. This scripture, in which John received his instructions, tells him to write about not only what is now, but also what will take place later. And this admonition gives credibility to prophetic interpretation. Much of the information, dates and data contained in today's devotional, and the following seven, is assimilated from Arnold G. Fruchtenbaum's ***Footsteps of the Messiah***. His frame of reference is pre-tribulation, dispensational pre-millennialism. The dates in church history corresponding with the seven letters are as follows: 1) Ephesus 30-100, 2) Smyrna 100-313, 3) Pergamum 313-600, 4) Thyatira 600-1517, 5) Sardis 1517-1648, 6) Philadelphia 1648-1900 and 7) Laodicea 1900 to present day.

We know that the rages of Satan have been directed toward the church throughout the ages, and only the truth of Jesus Christ will allow us to pass the test. Let's be wary, reasons vary, but His truth will pass the test. Let His living, loving, giving, inspire each one of us to do out best, then and only then, in the loving arms of our Lord Jesus Christ, WE REST.

September 27

#1 – EPHESUS – 30-100

"Yet I hold this against you. You have forsaken your first love." – Revelation 2:4 (synopsis)

THE SITUATION

In the church, the situation,
In the second generation,
Was to swerver, from the fervor,
They at first exemplified.
Our Lord first, had been their teaching,
And with vigor, they were reaching,
But now slackness, and a lackness,
Of their love, for Christ who died,
Caused a turning, from the burning,
Love they first exemplified.
In His love, let us abide.

The word "Ephesus" means, "desired." The apostolic church began in about 30 AD, and the author of this letter, John, died in about 100 AD. During this period of time, the "desired" apostolic church began with its members fervently loving and working for the Lord. As they years passed, they continued rejecting evil, doing good works, enduring hardships, and identifying false teachers. They, in fact, had kept the doctrine pure and for all of these things, they were being commended. However they were rebuked for having forsaken their "first love," the Lord Jesus Christ.

When the church first began, the members had a burning love for the Lord. As the church progressed, the second generation of Christians continued to work hard, refute evil, endure hardships and keep the doctrine of the gospel pure, but they had lost something. They had lost that burning love for the Lord, and for this, they were rebuked.

There is a lesson for every Christian contained in this letter to Ephesus. Our Lord wants our hands, our feet and our head, that we might proceed with His work as we walk down the pathway of life, but most of all, HE WANTS OUR HEARTS. He wants our earthly tour to be a love relationship with Him. Our prayer is that in whatever capacity we serve the Lord, we first give Him our heart. Then He can use our hands, our feet and our mind. May there never be a turning, from a burning love for our Lord Jesus Christ. In His love, let us abide.

#2 SMYRNA 100-313 AD.

"Do not be afraid of what you are about to suffer. You will suffer persecution for ten days but I will give you the crown of life. He who overcomes will not be hurt at all by the second death." – Revelation 2:8-11 (synopsis)

AN ETERNITY OF REST

This church, under persecution,
Knew the Lord, was their solution,
And His Lordship, through their hardship,
Gave them strength, to pass the test.
Yes, they knew they would be dying,
But just once, then death-defying,
Faith-connected, resurrected,
By the Lord, Who gives His best.
Christ connected, and directed,
Through the Lord, they passed the test.
AN ETERNITY OF REST.

The word "Smyrna" means "myrrh," a sweet perfume used for embalming dead bodies. The church, beginning in approximately 100 AD, and extending to about 313 AD, was a church continually faced with persecution by the Romans. In fact, during that period of time, 10 Roman emperors officially attempted to obliterate Christianity. An emperor of Rome was considered to be a god, thus demanding that his subjects, including Christians, bow down before him. Their refusal resulted in martyrdom, even unto cruel death, for many Christians. Some Bible scholars have equated the "ten days of persecution" in this letter to these "ten emperors." Whether or not this is an accurate assessment, the fact remains that the church, during this time period, endured and remained faithful under extremely adverse circumstances. The name "Smyrna," indicating a sweet smelling perfume, would certainly be appropriate in this instance. The faithful testimony of the church was like a sweet smelling perfume to the Lord. The use of this perfume in the embalming of bodies could be equated with the preservation of the body of believers until eternal life with the Lord. There would be no second death.

Our prayer is that we as Christians keep the faith in our daily walk. While on this earth, let His connection give us direction, then at last, with no second death, with our Lord WE WILL ENJOY AN ETERNITY OF REST.

#3 – PERGAMUM 313-600 AD

"Nevertheless I have a few things against you. You have people there who hold to the teaching of Balaam. Likewise you also have those who hold to the teaching of the Nicolaitans." – Revelation 2:12-17 (synopsis)

LET US KEEP THE GOSPEL PURE

It's the cross of Christ we carry,
Church and state should never marry,
Let's being caring, and be sharing,
Let us keep the Gospel pure.
Let no group within be changing,
Moral laws, at their arranging,
By insistence, and resistance,
As we make this earthly tour,
Let our teaching, and our preaching,
Be that Truth in Christ is sure.
Let us keep the Gospel pure.

The word "Pergamum" means, "thoroughly married." In 313 AD, the Emperor Constantine made Christianity the official state religion of the Roman Empire, thus the church was married to the state. This condition existed until approximately 600 AD. People all over the empire were baptized into the church without any real regard to personal faith. They simply added Jesus to their list of gods, bringing their pagan practices with them, which included abject immorality. Thus, they qualified as holding to the teachings of Balaam. Also, during this period of church history, a distinction began to emerge between clergy and the laity, with different sets of laws and regulations for each group. A priestly order was set up in the church which further corrupted and laid the foundation for what was to follow in the next phase of the church age. Thus, they qualified as those who were holding on to the teachings of the Nicolaitans.

There are two distinct messages in these verses for every Christian. First, never compromise the truth of the gospel, including morality, for any expediency. Second, always remember that Christ is Head of the church, not a state, not an organization and not a pastor. Ours is a personal relationship with God, through our Lord Jesus Christ. As we make this earthly tour, let our teaching, and our preaching, be that only truth in Christ is sure. LET US KEEP THE GOSPEL PURE.

#4 – THYATIRA 600-1517 AD

"I know your deeds, your love and faith, your service and perseverance, and that you are now doing more than you did at first. Nevertheless, I have this against you: You tolerate that woman Jezebel." – Revelation 2:18-29 (synopsis)

A SAD, SAD DAY

In the church, now that it's later,
Works and faith, for some were greater,
But a hateful, and a fateful,
Jezebel led them astray.
Works, not faith, was instituted,
Saved by grace, was executed,
And her teaching, therein reaching,
Was enforced, in that sad day.
Church requirement, Grace retirement,
Was infused, along the way,
For the church, a sad, sad day.

The word "Thyatira" means "continual or perpetual sacrifice," a fitting description of the church in the dark ages between 600 AD and 1517 AD. Among other new, manmade rules and regulations, a doctrine of continual sacrifice in Mass was instituted, the theology being that when the priest blessed the bread and the wine, they became the real body and real blood of Jesus. This doctrine is called transubstantiation. In the celebration of Mass, Christ is sacrificed again, even though Hebrews 10:18 clearly tells us that "there is no longer any sacrifice for sin." Different rules for clergy and laity were also observed. The laity could partake of the bread only, while the clergy would partake of bread and wine, the theology being that since the wine had become the real blood of Jesus, the laity might accidentally spill it. In these dark ages, the church became a religious system, bearing little resemblance to the New Testament church. Ten major new doctrines were introduced into the church, one of them being justification by works, not by faith in Christ with the gift of God's grace.

These were the dark ages in the history of the church. Works, not faith, was instituted, and saved by grace was executed. This was, for the church, indeed, A SAD, SAD DAY. By the grace of God, may our theology remain pure, all for His glory, through our Lord Jesus Christ.

#5 – SARDIS – 1517-1648 AD

"I know your deeds; you have a reputation of being alive, but you are dead. Wake up." – Revelation 3:1-6 (synopsis)

A BURNING, CHURNING YEARNING

Now pure doctrine has potential,
But God's Spirit is essential,
For on-going, Christian growing,
Or a church will surely die.
When a church is state-connected,
Then that church is state-directed,
And there's lurking, only shirking,
For God's Spirit, they defy,
There's no burning, churning, yearning,
To obey our Lord on high,
And that church will surely die.

The word "Sardis" means "those escaping," and could be representative of the church of the Reformation, which began in 1517 with Martin Luther's posting of his 95 thesis, and continued until about 1648. The period began with a purification of doctrine, and a breakaway from the Roman church, thus their reputation for being alive. However, they failed to cure one very basic problem, that of unity of church and state, and they eventually became dead churches because they also became state churches. Children of members were baptized into the church without any requirement for personal faith in Christ. Thus the church eventually had many members who were unbelievers. To use a metaphor, we might say that the church was well equipped for heating, but there was no fire in the furnace. They were equipped with pure doctrine, but as more and more unbelievers formally joined the church, the church as a body, became spiritually dead.

These scriptures contain a very basic truth for each and every Christian. Spiritual life is impossible without good doctrine, but GOOD DOCTRINE WITHOUT SPIRITUAL LIFE IS DEAD. BOTH ARE NECESSARY. May our church never be state-connected or state-directed, but spiritually alive, with a BURNING, CHURNING, YEARNING in each one of us to be all that God wants us to be, all for His glory, through our Lord Jesus Christ.

#6 – PHILADELPHIA – 1648-1900 AD

"What He opens no one can shut. I will also keep you from the hour of trial that is going to come upon the whole world." – Revelation 3:7-13 (synopsis)

LET JESUS BE OUR GUIDE

This church, in our Lord abiding,
Was the product of His guiding,
They were teaching, and were reaching,
And that door was opened wide.
There would be no tribulation,
There would only be elation,
Christ-connected, and directed,
They would be at our Lord's side.
May our teaching, and our reaching,
Before Jesus, who once died,
He now lies, and is our guide.

The word "Philadelphia" means "brotherly love," a very fitting symbol for the church during the great missionary movement, which occurred between the years 1648-1900. In the eighteenth and nineteenth century, there was an "open door" policy in almost every country for missionary work. During that period of time, the church took advantage of this opportunity and, in turn, helped others find that open door that leads to an eternity with our Lord. In addition to bringing Gentiles into a saving relationship with the Lord, by 1900 approximately 250,000 Jews came to Christ.

With a pre-tribulation frame of reference, in this letter, the promise that the Lord is going to keep the church from the hour of trial that is going to come upon the whole earth, could be His promise that the church will be raptured prior to the Great Tribulation period. Regardless of one's frame of reference, when we are at last "with the Lord," there will be only elation, with no trace of tribulation. Let each one of us be, not only Christ-connected, but also Christ-directed, that we might continually be teaching, and reaching for unbelievers, to help direct them through that open door. Let Jesus, who once died, then arose to defy death, always be our guide all for the glory of God through our Lord Jesus Christ.

#7 – LAODICEA – 1900 – PRESENT DAY

"So, because you are lukewarm, neither hot nor cold, I will spit you out of my mouth. You say: 'I am rich, I don't need a thing,' but you do not realize that you are wretched, pitiful, poor, blind and naked." – Revelation 3:14-22 (synopsis)

THROUGHOUT ALL ETERNITY

Now, a church is apathetic,
When its members are heretic,
No fire burning, just a turning,
From the truth that sets us free.
For lukewarmness, Christ is hating,
That's the truth, there's no debating,
He's commanding, that we're standing,
In His truth, that we might be,
Ever living, through His giving,
Love and grace, to you and me,
Throughout all eternity.

The word "Laodicea" means "people ruling," and in contrast to Christ ruling, this is an apt description of such a large segment of the church, beginning in the early 1900s. This might be identified as the age of apostasy in the church. The word "apostasy" is defined as "the departure from the truth that one PROFESSED to have," not necessarily that one had. Seldom do apostates actually possess the truth. During this time period, there came into existence many cults, in addition to many so-called "churches," all of whom deviated from the gospel by either denying the deity of Christ or embodying a "different Christ" within their organization. Theirs was, and is, lukewarmness toward Christ, an apathetic attitude in regard to spiritual things, rather a sense of well being in material possessions, and a comfortable follow-the-leader approach within the church with regard to manmade rules and regulations. In so many churches, this has indeed been a period of "people ruling," instead of Christ ruling. The Spirit of Christ is nowhere to be found and in this scripture, because of that apathy, Jesus says that he is about to "spit them out of His mouth."

Lord, by Your grace, let us know Your truth, and reject error, never being in the least apathetic, but continually being filled with Your Spirit.

October 4

A MUSTARD SEED

"If you have faith as small as a mustard seed, you can say to this mountain, 'move from here to there,' and it will move. Nothing will be impossible for you." – Matthew 1:20,21

LET US DARE

If the will of God's directing,
With our Lord, are we connecting,
He will seize us, our dear Jesus,
And will answer fervent prayer.
Though we know we're insufficient,
Our dear Lord is all sufficient.
He's the tower, of all power,
And by faith, if we but dare,
Though we're sighing, He's replying,
With a "yes;" He answers prayer,
Let us ask Him; let us dare.

In order to interpret this scripture, let us first be knowledgeable concerning a mustard seed, and then analyze the phrase, "to move a mountain." A mustard seed at that time was the very smallest seed known, yet when planted under favorable conditions, it would grow to a height of ten feet or more the first year. To "move a mountain," or "remove a mountain," meant in Jewish idiom, "to remove difficulties," thus Jesus was apparently speaking metaphorically. He was rebuking the disciples for lack of faith, and giving them instructions for future ministries. His message to them, and to us, was and is, that we must have faith in Him, and in what He can accomplish through us. True faith will expand and increase rapidly, just as the mustard seed rapidly becomes a tree. If we are truly in God's will, any hindrance to our ministry for Christ will be removed. We merely have to pray in faith, and in His will.

Our prayer is that God will give us the grace to always pray in faith, and in accordance with His will, removing selfish desires from our prayers, always keeping our eyes focused on Jesus, and what he wants us to do. Then that mustard seed of faith can grow and grow into maturity. Though we are insufficient, we know that our Lord is all sufficient. He's the tower of all power. With faith, let us to go to Him in prayer, for though we may be signing, we know he will be replying, with a "yes." He answers prayer. Let us ask Him, LET US DARE.

BOUGHT AT A PRICE

"You are not your own. You were bought at a price." – 1 Corinthians 6:19-20

HE SOUGHT US, THEN BOUGHT US

Bought by blood, our Lord is saying,
Not our own, so start obeying,
For He sought us, then He bought us,
With His blood, upon that tree.
Though He freed us, He's beseeching,
Telling us, to go out reaching,
For our brothers, sisters, other,
That their blinded eyes might see,
By believing, we're receiving,
Our Lord's gift, to you and me,
Life with Him, eternally.

In this scripture, we are reminded that we're really not our own, because we were bought and paid for by the blood of Jesus. He died on that cross for our sins. In Philippians 2:7 we are told that "our attitude should be the same as that of Christ Jesus," Who though He was deity, made himself nothing, taking the very nature of a servant. Paul, in Romans 1:1, identifies himself as a "servant of Jesus Christ." Galatians 5:1 tells us that Christ set us free, to be free, and Romans 6:4 tells us that we now "walk in the newness of life." These various verses may seem to be incongruent, but nothing is farther from the truth.

The truth is that Jesus did buy us at a price, and that price was His precious blood shed on that cross for the sins of all mankind. By believing in Him, our sin-debt is paid and we will spend eternity with Him. However, both before and after our conversion, we are set free to have choices. First, we choose to either accept or reject Him as our Savior, then we have choices during the sanctification process. We should never serve Him out of fear, but always in love. This scripture is a reminder of how very much He has done for us. And we should, out of love and gratitude, become a willing servant for Him. Though He freed us, He's beseeching, telling us to go out reaching for our brothers, sisters, others, that their blinded eyes might see, by believing, we're receiving, our Lord's gift to you and me, life with Him eternally.

October 6

FREE INDEED

"So, if the Son sets you free, you will be free indeed." – Romans 8:36

HIS GRACE HAS SET US FREE

Jesus Christ, who did the freeing,
Will direct our very being,
He's inside us, there to guide us,
Guiding grace, for you and me.
By that grace, let us be ridding,
Thoughts that some should do our bidding,
For He's gifted, each saint lifted,
With a conscience, that is free,
Free of rancor, He's our anchor,
And the only guide we see,
For His grace has set us free.

Even for Christians, or perhaps I should say, especially for Christians, one of the most difficult character traits to overcome is the impulse, even craving, to urge others to conform to our views. As Christians, we are Spirit led. As we continue to seek the truth, we form opinions regarding interpretation of various scriptures, and for us, this message is from the Lord. Conversely, other Christians, who are also Spirit led, seem to have a different message from the Lord because their interpretation does not exactly coincide with ours. How can this be? They must be wrong. We need to change their thinking. We need to straighten them out. These are thoughts that race through our mind as we let our human nature block out our spiritual nature. This is not what God intended. We sometimes have a tendency to fence God in. He must be amused by our efforts, but the truth is that God cannot be fenced in.

It seems to take God forever to straighten out the thinking of some of us. Our tendency is to think that those who don't see things exactly like we do are wrong. We try to fence God in. We tend to forget that God also set them free through our Lord Jesus Christ. Let us never forget that it's Christ who does the freeing, as He guides our very being, and by His grace, let us be "ridding," thoughts that others should do our bidding. Rather let us realize that He has gifted each saint "lifted" with a conscience that is FREE, a guiding grace for you and ME. Let Jesus be the only guide we SEE, for HIS GRACE HAS SET US FREE.

I WILL GIVE YOU REST

"Come unto Me, all you that labor and are heavy laden, and I will give you rest." – Matthew 11:28

OUR ENHANCER IS THE ANSWER

Now, what ere the path we're taking,
Is our body tired and aching?
Are we laden, heavy-laden?
Has the fire, within us died?
Do we moan so loud we hear it?
In our body, soul and spirit?
Can our testing, turn to resting?
What on earth, can turn this tide?
Our Enhancer, is the Answer.
Christ is always at our side.
He gives rest, when we abide.

We can be "heavy laden," that is "burdened down," in our labor, not only in our body, but in our very soul and spirit also. As we become more mature, perhaps we are more keenly aware of a physical burden. As our body experiences a certain amount of aches and pains, at any age, we can experience a burdening down in our soul and in our spirit. We have disappointments. We have failures. A big dark cloud seems to envelop our very being, blotting out all light. Our very soul and spirit feel the weight of this darkness, a burden too heavy to carry. We look for solutions, perhaps a resting from this testing. In any event, we are tired in both our soul and our spirit. We are exhausted. We need some rest. In this scripture, Jesus gives us the solution. He says "Come unto Me, and I will give you rest."

When we walk with the Lord, not every day is filled with sunshine. There are days, and times, when a dark cloud seems to envelop us, and we are heavy laden and burdened. Our very soul and spirit become exhausted. We need some rest. What a wonderful promise this is from our Lord. For whatever reason we are burdened, we can turn to Him, and that burden is lifted. We thank God for this solution. We know that Christ is, not only our Enhancer, but He's also the answer to the burdens we have in this life. He is always at our side and IN HIM, WE HAVE REST, WHEN WE ABIDE.

CONSIDER HIM WHO ENDURED

"Consider Him who endured such opposition from sinful men, so that you will not grow weary." – Hebrews 12:3

LET'S CONTINUE WORKING HARD

As we work in His connection,
We so often find rejection,
We grow weary, tired and weary,
As we struggle for the Lord.
But, a look in His direction,
And the scope of His rejection,
Should not tire us, but inspire us,
To be faithful to our Lord.
Our behavior, for our Savior,
Should reflect that we're His wards.
Let's continue working hard.

It seems that the more we try to do for the Lord, the more opposition we encounter. Many of those we called "friends" seem to have just faded away. Rejection seems to rear its ugly head at every turn. We are misunderstood, maligned and mistreated. We grow weary with the apparent futility of our efforts. How can we regain that spiritual momentum we once had?

The solution to this condition of spiritual stagnation is, of course, to "set our hearts and our minds on things above" (Colossians 3:1-2). We need to focus on Christ, not on ourselves. But today's scripture gives us instructions that are even more specific. We need not only to set our hearts and minds on Christ, but we need to remember what He endured. He was not only rejected, misunderstood, maligned and mistreated; He was betrayed, even denied and abandoned for a time by His friends. He also was spat upon, scorned and crucified and enduring an agonizing death on the cross. Any opposition and/or rejection we might face on our journey for the Lord will fade into insignificance when compared with what Jesus endured.

As we encounter difficulties in our ministry for the Lord, let us look in His direction, at the scope of His rejection, being ever mindful to be faithful to our Lord, that our behavior, for our Savior, will reflect that we're His wards. LET'S CONTINUE WORKING HARD.

October 9

THE WILL OF GOD

"And He made known to us the mystery of His will according to His good pleasure, which He purposed in Christ." – Ephesians 1:9

GOD'S WILL FOR YOU AND ME

Now, the will of God, we treasure,
And His grace, we cannot measure,
So tremendous, it's stupendous,
With His love for you and me.
All "The Saints" are his adoptions,
But, by Grace, He gives us options,
Our selection, of direction,
Can be one, or two, or three,
If connected, then directed,
By our Lord, who set us free.
That's God's Will, for you and me.

As Christians, what is God's will for our lives? If we are truly in Christ, and Christ is in us, we have an overwhelming desire to live our lives within the will of God. There are some Christians who, because of their devotion, spend much of their life "putting out the fleece," in order to be sure that each decision, and each action, is exactly what God wants them to do. This is an admirable trait, showing sincere devotion to the Lord, but many Christians become so engrossed with specific detailed instructions from the Lord, that they spend their lives putting out the fleece, instead off stepping out in faith.

With regard to living our life in accordance with God's will, in most scriptures the meaning is to live our life under God's gracious design, rather than under His determined resolve. And, very graciously, He designed a means by which we can enjoy an eternity with Him, and in the present enjoy a very personal spiritual relationship with His Son, our Lord Jesus Christ. In the midst of this relationship with Jesus, God gives us options within His will, a will that we treasure, filled with so much grace, that we can't even measure. And though our selection, of direction, may be either one, or two, or three, if we're connected, and directed, by our Lord, who set us free, THAT'S GOD'S WILL FOR YOU AND ME.

THE PRIDE OF LIFE

"And the pride of life is not of the Father, but is of the world." – 1 John 2:16b

BUT FOR HIM, OUR PRIDE IS NAUGHT

Pride of life, will make us hollow,
It's the Lord, that we must follow,
As we're learning, let's be turning,
From the world, to what He taught.
We thank God for His connection,
Let us work, at His direction,
He's the Tower, of all Power,
Saving Grace, through Him was wrought.
Let our weakness, turn to meekness,
Through His blood, our souls He bought,
But for Him, our pride is naught.

In this world, even Christians, or perhaps we should say, especially Christians, seem to have a tendency to take pride in accomplishments. In the worldly sphere, worldly accomplishments are duly noted, and accolades are heaped upon the ones whose expertise in a particular field enabled them to produce an outstanding result. They are recognized, and most of them thoroughly enjoy the recognition, in fact, human nature being what it is, most people take great pride in their accomplishments and want others to know about them. As we move from the worldly sphere to the spiritual realm, too often we encounter the same situation. A person, truly godly, will seem to excel in some phase of spiritual endeavor. Next, comes recognition, then pride of accomplishment seems to rear its ugly head, thus the Christian succumbs to the same entrapment of pride in the spiritual realm, that is an every day occurrence in the worldly sphere.

Today's scripture clearly teaches us that pride of accomplishment is not of the Lord, unless, of course that pride is in the Lord. As Christians, all of us need to realize that the only power we have is the power and strength provided by the Lord. Pride of life will make us hollow; it's the Lord, that we must follow. He's the tower, of all power, and saving grace, through Him was wrought. Through His blood, our souls He bought. BUT FOR HIM, OUR PRIDE IS NAUGHT.

YOU ARE NO LONGER A SLAVE

"So you are no longer a slave, but a son, and since you are a son, God has also made you an heir." – Galatians 4:7

HE WILLS US ETERNITY

Now a slave, may work for merit,
But a slave, will not inherit,
Our Lord's teaching, that He's reaching,
To adopt a family.
Then, each member has His Spirit,
We can feel it; we can hear it,
He's inside us, there to guide us,
He gives Grace, to you and me.
And we're glowing, with the knowing,
We're an "heir" to Deity,
He "wills us" Eternity.

What an exhilarating truth this is. When we accept Christ as our personal Savior, our status immediately changes. We become members of the family of God. We are adopted into God's family through our Lord Jesus Christ, and as sons and daughters, we automatically become heirs to the family fortune. And what a fortune, indeed, a wealth of riches, beginning with His love, mercy and grace, culminating at our death with a spiritual bodily resurrection that we might be with the Lord, for all eternity.

As we complete our time on this earth, equipped with His love, mercy and grace, we realize that we are no longer slaves, slaves to fear and anxiety. Thought we may be objects of misunderstanding, mistreatment and maliciousness, we have His indwelling Spirit to guide and comfort us. And most of all, we have a sure hope of an eternity with Him. We know, beyond any doubt, that He's inside us, here to guide us. He gives His love, His mercy and His grace to you and me, and we're just "glowing" with the "knowing," WE'RE AN HEIR TO DEITY. HE WILLS US ETERNITY.

October 12

SERVE ONE ANOTHER

"Serve one another in love." – Galatians 5:13b

"I tell you the truth, whatever you did for one of the least of these brothers of Mine, you did for Me." – Matthew 25:40

"My Father will honor the one who serves Me." – John 12:26b

LET'S SERVE HIM TODAY

Do we serve our Lord and Master,
Do we wait, 'til morning after,
Does our talking, turn to balking,
Or, do we serve Him today?
Let us, with our Christ connection,
Serve our Lord, at His direction,
Loving others, sisters, brothers,
That we meet along life's way.
Let our mission, be submission,
To His will, as we obey,
Let us serve our Lord TODAY.

We are admonished to "serve one another in love," that is, His love. We serve others, not because they are so lovable, but because of our love for the Lord. Jesus tells us that whatever we do for the very "least of these," we do for Him. We know, what to do, and how to do it, so what do we do? WE PROCRASTINATE. Today, we just simply don't have enough time. We have other things scheduled. Today, it is just too inconvenient. We will do it tomorrow, then when tomorrow arrives, it becomes today and again we procrastinate.

At this point, there is something that we might consider. What if our Lord had decided that dying on the cross just did not fit His schedule? He would do it tomorrow, but today and of course tomorrow never becomes a reality as tomorrow, because, when it arrives it becomes today.

We might ask ourselves, do we really serve our Master, or do we always wait till morning after? Are we proficient at talking about it, then remiss, as our talking turns to balking? Our prayer is that God will give us the grace to serve our Lord and Master today, not the morning after, and that we let our mission in life be submission to His will, as we obey. LET US SERVE OUR LORD TODAY.

October 13

OUR MEASURE

"When they measure themselves by themselves, and compare themselves with themselves, they are not wise." – 2 Corinthians 10:12b

"And become mature, attaining to the whole measure of the fullness of Christ." – Ephesians 4:13b

MEASURE ONLY BY GOD'S SON

Let's not look around and measure,
Let us look up to the Treasure,
Let us measure, by the Treasure,
Jesus Christ, God's only Son.
For, in others, truth will vary,
By God's Grace, let us be wary,
Our Enhancer is the answer,
As this earthly race is run,
Let's be growing, in His glowing,
And, when all is said and done,
Measure only by God's Son.

In these scriptures, we are first admonished to never measure, or compare ourselves with others. There are two basic reasons for this counsel. First, if we think we are in some way superior, pride rears its ugly head. Second, if we think we are in some way inferior, envy becomes a reality. Neither pride nor envy has an acceptable place in the Kingdom of God. Our second admonition from these scriptures is to become mature by attaining to the whole measure of the fullness of Christ.

In this world, in various fields of endeavor, whether it's the business world, the athletic world, the political world, and yes, even the religious world, we seem to have a tendency to place certain people on a pedestal. In our Christian walk, we see a particular leader who really seems to "have it all together," with knowledge of the Bible, eloquence of speech and apparent commitment to spreading the gospel of Jesus Christ. Our immediate tendency, even if we are reluctant to admit it, is to place that particular person on a pedestal. The problem is that in this world, too many pedestals are "built on sand." Something happens and that particular person, pedestal and all come tumbling down, then the truth of God's word suddenly becomes a very vivid reality. Our only measure is Christ. Our prayer is that we attain to the measure of Christ.

October 14

THE SCRIPTURE

"All scripture is God-breathed and is useful for teaching, rebuking, correcting and training in righteousness, so that the man of God may be thoroughly equipped for every good work." – 2 Timothy 3:16-17

LET'S TEACH JESUS EVERY DAY

God, through scripture, is revealing,
To the Saints, He's not concealing,
He's beseeching, reaching, teaching,
Us to use His Word today.
For, through scripture, we are gaining,
Words of wisdom, as we're training,
Let all teaching, reaching, preaching,
Be what scripture has to say.
Let correction and direction,
Please our Lord, as we obey,
Let's teach "Jesus" everyday.

When Paul admonished Timothy to rely on and use all of the scripture as he worked for the Lord, we might note, at that time, the only scripture we know for sure that was available was the Old Testament. Perhaps some of the epistles were already accepted as scripture, but this is pure conjecture. Today, with our complete Bible, how much more we are in a position to be trained by the word of God.

As we study God's Word, we discover a complete blueprint, not only for salvation, but also for the living of each day. Jesus, not only saves us for all eternity, He walks with us day, after day, after day. He leads us through the valley of the shadow of death, and we fear no evil, for He is with us. As He gives us that sure hope of salvation, He also comforts us and gives us peace. What a wonderful Savior and companion He is. Our prayer is that, with God's grace, we will spend more and more time with Jesus, both in prayer and in the reading of the scripture, for through the scripture, we are gaining, words of wisdom, as we're training. As we're reaching, let's be teaching, what the scriptures have to say. Let's please our Lord, as we obey. LET'S TEACH JESUS EVERYDAY.

HIS LOVE IN OUR HEARTS

"God has poured out His love into our hearts by the Holy Spirit, whom He has given us." – Romans 5:5b

LET'S HAVE A BALL

As we travel down earth's highway,
Looking up to Heaven's skyway,
Let us never, never, ever,
Be so smug, we know it all.
Now, there is no need to panic,
For our Lord, is a romantic,
He's insisting, He's existing,
In our spirit, heart and all.
With His giving, loving living,
We are beckoned by His call.
With our Lord, let's have a ball.

We know that we are admonished to "study the scripture" (2 Timothy 3:16, 17), that the scripture is God-breathed and a blueprint for both salvation and the living of the Christian life. However, a certain danger exists as we delve deeply into the scripture. This danger coexists with our sin nature. As we probe the depths of God's word, we must always guard against overkill, that is, a tendency to substitute the Bible for Jesus. We must remember that it is only a blueprint, pointing us to our Savior and our Lord. The Bible is not a thing to be worshipped. It is a source of both information and instruction, together with the indwelling Spirit, that gives us direction in our life, and by study of the scripture, we are pointed directly toward Jesus. Let us never be so saturated with knowledge of the Bible that our focus is on scripture, instead of Jesus.

God has truly poured His love into our heart with the indwelling Holy Spirit.

As we travel down this earth's highway, leading up to Heaven's skyway, let us never, never, ever be so smug with knowledge of the Bible, that we think that we know it all. There is no need to panic, for Jesus is a romantic and with His living, loving, giving, we are beckoned by His call. WITH OUR LORD, LET'S HAVE A BALL.

PRAY TO YOUR FATHER

"But when you pray, go into your room, close the door and pray to your Father, who is unseen. Then your Father, who sees what is done in secret, will reward you." – Matthew 6:6

HE WILL GIVE US OUR REWARD

Let us pray where no one sees us,
To the Father of our Jesus,
He will hear us, for He's near us,
And through Christ, we are His wards.
Let no pride in self be showing,
For our dear Lord is all knowing,
Our Enhancer, then will answer,
He's our Savior, and our Lord.
Our prayer given, Spirit-driven,
Will be answered by the Lord,
He will give us our reward.

This scripture is a prelude to what we refer to as the Lord's Prayer, through in fact, it was a model prayer for His disciples. This prayer was and most prayers are, addressed to the Father and in some instances in the New Testament, prayer was addressed to Jesus, but in no instance addressed to the Holy Spirit. Prayer was prayed through the Spirit, but not to the Spirit. God the Father and God the Son both reside in Heaven, while the Spirit resides within each believer.

The primary thrust of truth in this scripture is that when we pray, our motivation should be pure. The Pharisees delighted in public appearances for prayer. Their prayers became a display for men to see, rather than a petition for God to hear, consequently, they received their full reward from men and no reward from God. In this scripture, we are promised a reward from God if our prayer is truly in the Spirit. That reward is answered prayer. The answer may be "yes," or "no," or "wait," but our prayer will be answered, and if our prayer is within God's will, the answer will be a resounding, "yes." So, when we pray, let us pray where no one sees us, to the Father of Jesus, for through Christ, we are His wards, and our payer given, Spirit-driven; will be answered by the Lord. HE WILL GIVE US OUR REWARD.

October 17

CONTROLLING ANGER

"In your anger do not sin, do not let the sun go down while you are still angry." – Ephesians 4:26

LET US NOT WAIT

Like a storm upon the ocean,
Anger is a strong emotion,
Storm clouds brewing, rage ensuring,
'Til, at last, the winds abate.
But, our Lord, from the beginning,
Tells each one to keep from sinning,
He's extolling, our controlling,
Any rage, or wrath, or hate.
Let us fashion, with a passion,
God's great Love, instead of hate,
By His Grace, let us not wait.

Anger is perhaps the very strongest of all human emotions or passions. Just as storm clouds evolve from a darkened sky, into turbulence and finally into a full-blown roaring typhoon. Anger, if not resolved quickly, can evolve into rage, hate or even a mindset of wrathful revenge. To be angry is not necessarily a sin. In fact, there are many instances of righteous anger in the scriptures, This particular scripture instructs and admonishes us in the manner and expediency of our response to anger. This admonishment is two-fold: First, "in your anger, do not sin." And second, "Do not let the sun go down on your anger."

When we are angry, this passionate emotion seems to take us out of the Spirit directly into our sin nature. Our thoughts, instead of being directed by the Spirit, seem to be controlled by emotion. And the embodiment of God's love, and grace and peace are for a time overpowered by the passion of anger. And in this state of mind, we might say we are sin just waiting to happen. This scripture tells us to expel this emotion before the sun goes down. In other words, now, not later. If we focus on the Lord, His love and grace will literally obliterate this emotion of anger. Then we can resume our fellowship with Him, enjoying His peace that surpasses all understanding. So, with storm clouds of anger brewing and possible rage ensuring, let us turn to the Lord, and focus on His great love, not on hate, and by His grace, let us do it now. LET US NOT WAIT.

PRAISE

"For they loved praise from men more than praise from God." – John 12:43

"Well done, good and faithful servant." – Matthew 25:23

LOOK TO CHRIST FOR HIS AMEN

Do we covet praise from others?
From our sisters, and our brothers,
As we're working, is there lurking,
As desire for praise from men?
As we live and curb behavior,
Let our works be for our Savior.
Let's be growing, with the sowing,
Of his seeds of Love, and then,
Look directly, quite correctly,
Not for accolades from men,
Look to Christ, for His "Amen."

Ephesians 2:10 tells us that we are God's workmanship, created in Christ Jesus to do good works. As we attempt to do good works for our Lord, perhaps we should ask ourselves two questions. First, should the work we do for the Lord be out of fear or should we work for our Lord because we love Him and want to obey Him. That question is answered so brilliantly in 1 John 4:18, which tells us that "there is no fear in love, but perfect love drives out fear, because fear has to do with punishment, and the one who fears is not made perfect in love." Second, is our primary desire to be recognized by men for any good works we might accomplish, or do we correctly, look directly to the Lord for His approval? In other words, exactly what is our agenda? Are we longing to please God, or do we crave accolades from men? On that day when we meet our Lord face-to-face, will we hear, "Well done, good and faithful servant?"

Our prayer is that by God's grace, any accomplishments we might have or any good works we might do will be with the Lord, to the Lord, and for the Lord. Let us never covet praise from others, but be growing, with the sowing of His seeds of love, never for accolades from men but always for our Lord, and for HIS AMEN.

October 19

MAKE EVERY EFFORT

"And I will make every effort to see that after my departure you will always be able to remember these things." – 2 Peter 1:15

ABIDING IN HIS WILL

With our Lord, let our position,
Extend farther than contrition,
Let's be reaching, with His teaching,
That His Will, we might fulfill.
True, we're sorry for our sinning,
For our sinning, from beginning,
Once it bound-us, but he found-us,
Now, we're free to do His Will.
Let our mission, be ambition,
To proclaim His truth until,
We're abiding in His Will.

Peter knew that he had very little time left on this earth. He would soon meet Jesus, face-to-face. But, he was using what time he had left working for the Lord. We can almost feel the immense urgency that consumed Peter as he both proclaimed the gospel of Jesus Christ and by instruction and admonition provided a road map for Christian living. The potential that only Jesus had seen in Peter had now come to fruition. He wanted to be sure his message would be remembered long after his death, and he worked diligently toward that goal. He wanted to do something for the Lord. He was reaching, with his teaching, proclaiming the truth of the gospel, abiding in the will of God.

In our Christian walk, perhaps we should take a page out of Peter's book. Unlike Peter, most of us don't know how much longer we have to spend on this earth, but like Peter, let each one of us press forward with whatever labor of love we are now involved with the Lord. Our prayer is that the Lord will imbue us with, not only the ability and power to do His will, but also the urgency of accomplishment for Him. Whatever our work for the Lord may be, by His grace, let us be reaching, with His teaching that His will, we might fulfill. Let our mission be reaching, with His teaching that His will, we might fulfill. Let our mission be to proclaim His truth until, we know for sure WE'RE ABIDING IN HIS WILL.

ASK AND IT WILL BE GIVEN YOU

"Jesus did this, the first of His miracles. He showed His glory." – John 2:11

"Ask and it will be given you." – Matthew 7:7

WE NEED ANOTHER MIRACLE

Lord, we're not being satirical,
But Lord, we simply need another miracle.
We're so tired; our very soul seems mired,
But there's no rejection.
That's not meant, Lord, we're simply spent,
We're looking to You for direction.
You said "ask," Lord so we're asking,
In Your Grace only, are we basking,
Please lift us up, Lord
Once again, let our heartstrings be lyrical,
What we're saying is:
Lord, we need another miracle.

Our walk with the Lord is an exhilarating experience. When we first believed, it seemed that the sun was shining twenty-four hours each day. His Spirit seemed to lift our very soul to undreamed-of heights. We were literally basking in the radiance of His grace. As our walk continued and we became more mature in Christ, our pathway led us, not only to the mountaintops but also into the valleys. And most of our maturity in Christ was realized on the low road, not on the high road, because as our very soul became mired in foreboding circumstances, each time as we turned to the Lord, we experienced miracle after miracle after miracle. With His love, mercy and grace, He lifted us up sometimes it seemed, to soar with eagles.

We have found another valley, Lord and again our soul seems mired, but there's no rejection. That's not meant Lord, we're simply spent and we're looking to You for direction. You said, "ask," Lord and we're asking. In Your grace only, are we basking. Please lift us up, Lord. Once again, let our heartstrings be lyrical. What we're saying is, LORD, WE NEED ANOTHER MIRACLE.

LOVE ONE ANOTHER

"A new command I give you: love one another." – John 13:34

WE JUST DON'T UNDERSTAND IT

Our supply is growing, Lord,
We just don't understand it.
But You said to hand it
Out to others; sisters, brothers,
And this tiny ember of love,
After You fanned it,
With the gentle breeze of Your Spirit,
We passed it on, and Lord,
It seems to have burst into a
Roaring, soaring, blaze of Grace.
Your love given us, has driven us
To new heights, for now we're full of it.
Our supply is growing, Lord,
We just don't understand it.

One very basic truth in the law of supply and demand is that, as demand increases, supply decreases. Whatever our inventory may be, as we assign those possessions into the market place, the more we dispose of, the less we have left. If we sell or give away enough of our possessions, we will have none left. This is true in the secular world and in the business world, but not in the spiritual world. In the spiritual world, the law of supply and demand, as we know it does not exist – especially as it pertains to love.

God, through our Lord Jesus Christ, has put love into our hearts and has commanded us to "love one another." This is not a request. It is a command – His command. But when we obey Him, a strange thing happens. As we pass His love on to others, the more we give away the more we have left. Our supply of love seems to increase, beginning like a small ember, then fanned by the gentle breeze of His Spirit, this tiny ember of love suddenly erupts into a roaring, soaring, blaze of His grace. And His love given us has driven us, to new heights and now we're full of it. Our supply of love is growing, Lord to such an extent that we simply don't understand it, but Lord we thank you for it.

October 22

YOU ARE AWESOME, LORD

"Through Him, all things were made." – John 1:3

"In Him was life and that life was the light of men." – John 1:4

YOU TAKE TIME TO BE MY FRIEND

You are "Awesome," Lord,
You created the whole universe and now,
You must be busy, running it
So much to do, all up to You,
Yet, you befriend me; You gave me life,
You bend men, then mend me, then send me,
Out on life's highway, to do Your will.
I know you're busy, Lord, but You take time to
Walk with me, talk with me, and pour Your love
Into my heart, we're not apart, You are with me
Every minute, of every hour, of every day
You are "Awesome," Lord, so busy yet
You take time to be my friend.

Our Lord is indeed awesome. When we think of the magnitude of His creation, the immensity, the vastness of the universe, the cosmos, much of which is an immeasurably eons of light years away, we can only marvel at His miraculous creation. Yet He loved us so much, He took time to come to this earth and die on a cross for our sins. And now that our faith is placed in Him, He has given us, not only life in His name for eternity, but also His love, which He pours into our hearts, and His grace and mercy, which He extends to us along this pathway of life. As busy as He has to be, taking care of all creation, He still takes time to bend us to His will, mend us when we need mending, both physically and spiritually, then send us out to do His will, but not alone. His Spirit indwells us and He walks by our side every minute, of every hour, of every day there to both comfort and direct us. We're indeed have an awesome Lord, so busy yet HE TAKES TIME TO BE OUR FRIEND.

October 23

YOUR GRACE

"My grace is sufficient for you." – 2 Corinthians 12:9

WE KNOW ALL ABOUT YOUR GRACE

We know all about your grace, Lord.
Just a little bit sprinkled here and there would be sufficient.
But, Lord, You're so efficient, not just a drop or two,
But a whole, rushing, gushing, outpouring
Seems to come our way, just, when we least expect it.
You lift us from the doldrums of darkness and despair,
And our soul soars upward, upward, as if on the wings of eagles.
We see the sun, bursting through the clouds,
An unbelievable brightness, magnified a thousand-fold,
With a generous helping, layer upon layer, of grace,
Upon grace, upon grace, 'til at last we're back in Your embrace.
Yes, Lord, we've been there,
We know all about Your grace.

Being a Christian is exciting. We are not only assured of our final destination, but as we face each day, we are also assured of the sufficiency of God's grace through our Lord Jesus Christ. On this earth, we will face days that are dark and dreary and our very soul will agonize in despair and despondency. But the good news is that our Lord has promised that His grace is sufficient for our every need, and indeed how sufficient His grace truly is. When we turn to Him from the doldrums of despair and darkness, our very soul seems to be "lifted up," soaring as if on wings of eagles reaching higher and higher, basking in the brilliance of His grace, a radiance indescribable as it permeates our very being.

Lord, we thank You for this. You just keep piling on such a generous portion of Your grace, just layer after layer, of grace, upon grace, upon grace, until we are at peace, again resting in Your embrace. Yes, Lord we've been there. WE KNOW ALL ABOUT YOUR GRACE.

POWER FROM GOD

"But we have this treasure in jars of clay to show that this all-surpassing power is from God, and not from us." – 2 Corinthians 4:7

STRONGER – JUST A LITTLE LONGER

Please, Lord, for You let me be stronger,
Just a little longer.
I know my body is merely a jar of clay,
Subject to being battered, and shattered,
And finally cast aside with decay.
But Lord, that's okay because
Inside that jar is something special.
You gave it to me, and it's there to stay.
I know time and age will take their toll,
But Lord, right now we're on a roll.
You're the Tower of strength and power,
And my weakness is completely submerged,
In Your strength, making me stronger,
So, I'm asking You,
Lord, please let me be stronger,
Just a little longer.

In this scripture, Paul analogizes using "jars of clay" to represent mankind. In those days, it was customary to conceal treasure in clay jars. The jars themselves had very little value and no beauty, however the contents could be most precious both in value and in beauty. The clay jars represent human frailty and unworthiness, however; the treasure contained within represents the all-surpassing power of God, through our Lord Jesus Christ. This sharp contrast exhibits the truth of man's absolute insufficiency and God's total sufficiency.

Our strength is in the Lord. As we walk down the pathway of life, our body becomes battered, then finally shattered with decay. But that's okay, because our body is merely a temporary shelter for our eternal spirit. We receive His power, and His strength, and as our body becomes weaker and weaker, through the power of His Spirit we become stronger and stronger. Lord, we know that when we submerge our weakness in your power and strength, You make us stronger, so we're asking, Lord, PLEASE LET US BE STRONGER – JUST A LITTLE LONGER.

October 25

FREE INDEED

"So if the Son sets you free, you will be free indeed." – John 8:36

I'M SO GLAD I SPROUTED WINGS

My soul seems to have sprouted wings, Lord.
And each day they seem to grow, longer and stronger.
You said I was free to soar,
And pour Your Love out to others,
To my sisters and brothers.
But Lord, at first, when I tried to fly,
Some weight kept pulling me back to earth,
Perhaps guilt, or sin.
But Lord, You lifted that,
And now it seems almost weightless.
These wings are growing, Lord,
Not yet at full strength, but each day growing,
Longer and stronger, lifting me higher and higher,
In the freedom of Your Grace.
One day, Lord, these wings You gave me,
When You set me free,
Will carry me all the way up through those pearly gates,
And we'll meet, face-to-face.
You've given me so much, Lord,
Love and mercy, and other things By Your Grace.
I am "so" glad I sprouted wings.

The legalist wants to ignore this scripture, just as he would like to ignore many others, including Galatians 5:1, but this is a very basic truth of the gospel. We are not only set free from the burden of our sins through our Lord, but by His grace, we are also set free from the burden of the Law. We no longer look with fear at the Law. We now look with love to our Lord. We have the freedom to focus on who we are in Christ, instead of what we are in the religious realm.

Some of us were indoctrinated in a legalistic church in our youth, and the focus was on fear of the Lord instead of love for the Lord. As we begin to understand the truth of the freedom we have under the umbrella of God's love we are lifted above and beyond the burden of both our sins and the Law. And as we pass His love on to others, we seem to soar higher and higher.

October 26

NEVER WILL I LEAVE YOU

"Never will I leave you; never will I forsake you." – Hebrews 13:5b

YOU JUST KEEP HANGING AROUND

You just keep "hanging around," Lord, You promised
Never to leave us, You told us You would hold us and
Mold us, to Your Image, but Lord,
There are times when we're forgetful, or careless,
Or perhaps, just rebellious, we strike out "on our own."
We set our sights on things, other things, many things,
We get mired in circumstances, at times
Painful circumstances, and it hurts, Lord,
The eyes of our soul seem to focus inward, instead of
Outward, and downward, instead of upward, instead of
Outward, and downward, instead of upward but, Lord,
As we languish in self-anguish, We suddenly feel a
Presence. A gentle voice says, You're "near me," now
"hear me;" "My Grace is Sufficient" so, From our
Lord, with body broken, come these words, so gently
Spoken, and His Grace fills our soul, to a veritable apex
Of ecstasy. Lord we're so thankful that You just keep
"Hanging around."

As Christians, we have this promise from our Lord, that He will never leave us, nor forsake us. There are so many times that we seem to forget this promise. We strikeout on our own. Sometimes we're on the high road, and sometimes we're on the low road. On the high road, often we are so full of ourselves that we don't focus on the Lord. But as we plunge down to the low road and become mired in painful circumstances, we begin to look to the Lord for help. And He's there, near us. He hasn't left us. We may have ignored Him, but He was always there, and He gives us His assurance that His grace is sufficient for our every need. As we hear His gentle, loving voice, our very soul seems to fill with His grace and His peace, for we know that He walks with us, even through the valley of the shadow of death to lead us to still water. What a gracious blessing this is. Though we at times are not very lovable, He continues to love us, day after day, after day. Lord, we're so thankful that You just keep hanging around.

ASK IN MY NAME

"And I will do whatever you ask in My name, so that the Son may bring glory to the Father." – John 14:13

WE'RE BETTER ACQUAINTED NOW

Lord, we're so glad we're better acquainted now.
When we first met, we knew You, but not very well. You
Came here to save us. We asked in Your name and You
Gave us life, Your life, then we began our journey, and
Lord, we found valleys so many valleys, but a miracle
Occurred we asked for help in Your Name, and then, we
Discovered, You're always the same, beside-us, there to
Guide us. When we faltered, You strengthened us, when
We stumbled and fell, You picked us up; we plunged into
Deep, deep ditches of despair, and Lord, in those
"Ditches," we found Your true "riches," Your love, Your
Mercy, Your grace, and Your peace, and now, You are,
Not only our Savior, but our most trusted "Friend."
Lord, we're so glad we're better acquainted now.

A great truth is embodied in this scripture. When we make a request within God's will, our answer will always be a resounding "yes." As new Christians, we trust the Lord for our eternity, and for most of us, this is an exhilarating experience. We look forward to some day being with the Lord, and sharing an eternity with Him, but the truth is that our eternity with the Lord begins the very moment we put our trust in Him. He is not only our Savior, but also a constant companion; our most trusted Friend. And when we turn to Him for help, He is always there. When we ask in His name, we discover He's always the same; kind, gentle and loving, and He does answer prayer. When we falter, He gives us strength. When we fall down, he picks us up.

As we progress toward spiritual maturity, we become nearer, and nearer to the Lord. By personal experience, we know more about Him, and we depend on Him more and more. He is truly our Friend, and He wants the very best for each one of us. As we review our walk with the Lord, we can remember miracle after miracle, and blessing upon blessing. We now, not only know Him, but we know Him well, and in all candor, we can say, LORD, WE'RE SO GLAD WE'RE BETTER ACQUAINTED NOW.

I AM THE LIGHT OF THE WORLD

"I am the Light of the world. Whoever follows Me will never walk in darkness, but will have the light of life." – John 8:12

THE LIGHT OF THIS WORLD

It's so dark, Lord; thick, inky blackness engulfs us.
Our load is heavy, and we're stumbling, Lord, our feet
Entangled in the undergrowth of circumstances,
Our very soul mired in the quicksand of despair.
We can't see, and we can't move, We need light
So, at last we ask, Lord, and miracle of all miracles,
As we turn to You, we see a spark, a flicker, then a
Flame, and Lord, as our eyes continue to look for You,
That flame suddenly erupts into a bursting brilliance of
Brightness. We can see, and we can move. Our burden
Becomes as a feather, wafting in the summer breeze.
As your light guides us away from the undergrowth of
Circumstance and the quick-sand of despair, we have a
Spring in our step and a lilt in our heart. Our very
Soul soars with ecstasy. Yes, Lord, You are truly the
Light of this world.

The primary truth in this scripture deals with salvation, in that those who follow Jesus and believe on Him will have eternal life. In other scripture, God's holiness is expressed in terms of light. But in this scripture, light refers, not so much to God's holiness, but to the revelation of his love in Christ Jesus. The permeating of that light, that love into lives darkened by sin. The secondary truth revealed in this scripture is that God's love, the embodiment of His grace, His mercy and His peace is ours through our Lord Jesus Christ, who is the Light of the world.

As we walk down the pathway of this life, we become entangled with circumstance not to our liking; perhaps of our making, but not to our liking. Our load seems so heavy, and we become mired in the darkness of despair. It seems that we can't move because we can't see. But the good news is that when we turn to the Lord, His light will burst into a brilliant brightness of love, mercy, grace and, yes, even peace for our soul. And as long as we keep our eyes on Him, He will ease our burdens, light our way, and our very soul seems to soar with ecstasy. Yes, Lord, You are truly THE LIGHT OF THIS WORLD.

October 29

THE WEDDING FEAST

"Let us rejoice and be glad and give Him glory. For the wedding of the Lamb has come and His bride has made herself ready. Fine linen, bright and clean, was given her to wear." – Revelation 19:7

COULD WE WAIT JUST A LITTLE WHILE?

We look forward, Lord,
To that wedding feast, a festive occasion
First, our hearts You capture
Then our souls You Rapture.
At last, we're with You, Lord,
At Your side, as Your bride.
We dream, Lord, of Your majesty,
Your loving smile, all the while
No ups and downs there, Lord,
All ups, no downs
Our Joy will have no bounds.
We're ready, Lord, to finish this race
To meet You face-to-face, see Your Grace,
But Lord, we ask in order to complete
Our earthly file, Lord, could we wait,
Just a little while?

In the days that Jesus walked this earth, the wedding ceremonies were somewhat different than they are today. Normally, the bridegroom, with his entourage, would go to the home of his betrothed and bring her to his home for the wedding ceremony, followed by the wedding feast and this wedding feast was a very festive occasion. The bridegroom and his friends would engage in jubilant celebration of the occasion.

In this scripture, Christ is depicted as the Lamb, and we who are Christians are depicted as the bride of Christ. When our days on this earth are over, the Lord takes us home to be with Him. And when this occurs there will be much celebrating, like unto a wedding feast, because just as the bridegroom and his friends celebrate his union with the bride, Jesus and His saints will celebrate our eternal union with Him.

Lord, we look forward to that wedding feast with You. We're ready to finish this race and see You face-to-face, see Your grace.

TODAY, NOT TOMORROW

"Why, you do not even know what will happen tomorrow." – James 4:14

PLEASE HELP US DO OUR PART

Lord, You are so special, so good to us.
First, You save us, then You gave us
Life, Your Life, Eternal Life.
You walk with us, and talk with us
When we stumble, You hold us up
When we're sad, You gladden our heart.
Lord, You have done so much for us
We don't know how many tomorrows we have,
But we do have today, and until we see You
Face-to-face forever to be in Your embrace,
Lord, until that time, by Your Grace,
Let us do something special for You.
We don't need to worry, Lord,
We just need to hurry.
This request is from the heart,
Today, Lord, please help us do our part.

This scripture gives us a great truth and teaches a good lesson. So many of us have good intentions. We are going to do all of these great things for the Lord, but not today. Today, we are too busy. We will have more time tomorrow. The problem is—we may never see tomorrow on this earth. We may draw our last breath before tomorrow ever arrives. All we have is today – in fact, all we truly have is right now.

When we think about how very much the Lord has done, and is doing, for each one of us, most of us earnestly desire to do something special for the Lord. We have good intentions, in fact, we may even talk about what we are going to do, but actions speak much louder than words. Our prayer is that we not worry, just hurry to do that something special for the Lord. Our request is for the heart. Today, Lord, please help us do our part.

October 31

I AM THE WAY

"I am the way and the truth and the life. No one comes to the Father except through Me." – John 14:6

A FAULTY COMPASS

We seem to have a faulty compass, Lord,
We pointed it toward You in Heaven's skyway,
And received Life, but now, on earth's highway,
As we run this race, the hand of our compass seems
To be fluttering all over the place, We seek Your way
On earth's highway. We point our compass toward You,
Our Lodestar, but then the lodestones of circumstances
Seem to exert such a pull, our heart is full, Lord of
Wanting to do Your will, As we climb each hill, our very
Soul, You fill, with Your love, Your mercy and Your
Grace, but still, the hand of our compass seems to be
Fluttering all over the place. We need a new one, Lord.
We ask that this faulty compass of ours, You replace
Please give us one, Lord, completely saturated with
Your grace.

In this scripture, Jesus tells us that He is the truth, that He gives us life, and that He is the only way to the Father. We believed this truth and received His life because, He not only showed us the way, He was and is the Way. Now, that we have eternal life in His name, all we have to do is finish our tour here on earth. It sounds simple, but is it? As we walk down this highway of life, looking forward to Heaven's skyway, Jesus is still the only way we can have an abundant life.

As Christians, we want to be in God's will. We set the compass of our hearts, minds and eyes on Jesus. And our pathway seems to widen with His abundance of love, mercy, grace and even His peace in our soul. But as we progress, the lodestones of circumstances at times seem to exert such a magnetic pull that the hand of our compass seems to flutter all over the place. We take our eyes off Jesus and focus on self. We have a faulty compass and we need a new one. We need one that will continually focus on Jesus, instead of on circumstances. Our prayer is, Lord, we ask that this faulty compass of ours, You replace. Please give us one, completely saturated with YOUR GRACE.

TO EACH ONE GRACE

"But to each one of us grace has been given." – Ephesians 4:7

YOU'RE NEVER STINGY WITH GRACE

We've learned a lesson, Lord; we've known You for years,
Many years, through highs and lows, ups and downs,
Whatever the circumstances, Your Grace abounds.
At times we're on the mountaintop, the air so pure,
Then into the valley where nothing seems to be for sure.
But there's one constant, Lord, You never leave us
You're always near, allaying our fears, drying our tears,
And Lord, the lesson we've learned throughout the years
Is high or low, up or down, there is one thing for sure
In each and every case
You're never stingy with Your Grace.

This scripture is a statement of fact, that each one of us has been given God's grace through our Lord Jesus Christ. Prior to His ascension, Jesus promised to send His Holy Spirit to all believers. A portion of the grace of God is that we possess His indwelling Spirit, Who guides us and comforts us. We receive God's grace on the mountaintop, but an even greater portion of His grace is evident as we topple from our mountaintop into the valleys. With our very soul crying out for relief, God's grace multiples and magnifies, with such an outpouring that it becomes a crescendo of love and mercy, lifting our spirit upward, ever upward, to reunite with His Spirit, there to again rest in His peaceful, loving embrace.

Yes, Lord we have learned a lesson. Through highs and lows and ups and downs, we know Your grace abounds, for throughout the years, as you allayed each fear, dried each tear, we learned that there is one thing, for sure. In each and every case, You're never stingy with Your grace.

November 2

OUR ENEMY, THE DEVIL

"Be self-controlled and alert. Your enemy the devil prowls around like a roaring lion looking for someone to devour." – Peter 5:8

"Because He Himself suffered when He was tempted, He is able to help those who are being tempted." – Hebrews 2:18

PLEASE LORD, JUST STOMP ON HIM

He's out there again, Lord, just prowling around
Looking for someone to chew on.
When he's near, we feel fear; he's so much stronger than
We are, but we call on You, and You bash him, Lord.
He wants us to sin, Lord, to worry, to take our eyes off
You and focus on circumstances, to doubt, all about,
Your love and mercy and grace, but Lord, by Your
Grace, we won't do that, so again, we call on You.
He's near now, we can sense it. he's getting closer and closer, Lord,
please grab him again, and bash him, and
This time, when You bash him please don't stop, just
Keep on, bash him mash him, lash him smash him.
This time, Lord please don't let him get up again,
Just stomp on him.

The devil is alive and well, and the way he operates, he seems to not realize that he was defeated on that cross at Calvary. These scriptures teach us that first, the devil is prowling around like a roaring lion, just looking for someone to devour. Second, Jesus, Who resisted temptation and suffered for it, is able to help us when we are tempted.

Temptation to sin covers a multiplicity of situation. When we think of being tempted, our first thoughts perhaps are thoughts concerning immorality, and that is certainly sin, but the truth is that we are tempted by much more than immorality. When we take our eyes off the Lord and focus on circumstances and self, the temptation of anxiety becomes a reality. Being anxious leads to fear and doubt. We worry about tomorrow, instead of being thankful for today. As each bothersome circumstance presents itself, we can almost literally feel the devil sneaking up on us. He is much stronger than we are but we have the solution and that solution is the Lord. We call on Him and His strength and His power will subdue the devil.

November 3

HE WASHED THEIR FEET

"He poured water into a basin and began to wash His disciples' feet." –
John 13:8b

"Unless I wash you, you have no part of Me." – John 13:8b

LET US WASH SOMEBODY'S FEET

You not only washed my feet, Lord,
You washed me all over, all of me,
From head to toe, high and low.
You chose to go to that cross for me, Lord,
There to endure pain, suffering, humiliation.
On that cross, with the blood You shed,
You cleansed me; You made me pure,
Eternally secure. Lord, You set an example for us,
To follow. It's too late to wash Your feet, but on this
Dusty pathway of life, we pray today, let us obey,
For You, Lord, today among those we meet,
Let us wash somebody's feet.

These scriptures reveal at least one great truth, and Jesus also gives us a
great example to follow. The great truth revealed is that, unless He cleanses us,
we are not a part of Him. (13:8b) In other words, we are cleansed of our sins
only by the cleansing blood of Jesus which was shed on that cross, leading us to
eternal life with Him. The great example He gave us to follow was His washing
the disciples' feet. The washing of feet was a lowly, menial task, normally performed only by a servant. As Jesus performed this task, his teaching was two-
fold. First, He was teaching humility, and second, He was teaching service to
others. His greatest service to us was when He humbled Himself, and suffered
the cruel indignity of the cross, all for our sake. He then arose, that we might
have life in His name.

Just as Jesus symbolically exhibited an attitude of humble service to others by washing His disciples' feet, we pray, Lord, today, let us obey. Give us the
grace that we might serve You by serving others. On this dusty pathway of life
for You, Lord, today among those we meet, let us wash someone's feet.

I AM WITH YOU ALWAYS

"And surely I am with you always, to the very end of the age." – Matthew 28:20b

YOU WERE WITH US ALL THE WAY

Looking backward, Lord, We're young again.
We know You, but not very well. We're full of vim and
Vigor and vitality. We have dreams, it seems, to conquer
The world, Let's go forward.
We had found a ditch or two, but no gulches yet.
We charge forward, then suddenly there's a gulch, a real
Deep gulch. We plunge down, down, down into the depths.
There's no way out, it's too deep, we can't get a handhold,
Then miraculously You appear. You lift us up, up, up,
Out of the gulch, back on life's highway again.
After that, there was a time, we though, You were only in the
Gulches. But, not true, it was just that in the gulches
We got better acquainted. Now we know, You never left
Us, You were with us, all the way.

As we reflect on the highway of life we have traveled thus far, our thoughts sometimes go back to our youth. There was a point in time when we accepted Christ, and our eternity was secured, but with the energy and aspirations of youth, we launched out with our assault on this world we would conquer. We had minor setbacks on our journey, just little ditches that we stumbled into, then got out of, but suddenly there loomed something much more serious – a real deep gulch darkened with disappointment, defeatism and despair. We plunged down, down, down into its very depths. We tried to climb out, but we couldn't. It was in the very depths of our despair that we really got acquainted with the Lord, for it was there that we learned first hand all about His love, mercy and grace.

Now, as we reflect on our highway of life, we stumbled into many ditches, and a few deep dark gulches, but in each and every case, we weren't alone. The Lord was with us. He picked us up and put us back on life's highway. He eased our pain, and gave us peace and hope. We're better acquainted now, and we know that He never left us. He was with us – all the way.

November 5

A FLAME IN OUR HEART

"You are the light of the world. A city that is set on a hill cannot be hid. Neither do men light a candle and put it under a bushel, but on a candlestick." – Matthew 5:14a, 15a

LET THAT FLAME NEVER FLICKER

When we trusted You, Lord, with our life,
You lit a candle in our heart, a flame,
A beacon for others to see so that they, too,
Might know You. Lord, we know You gave us life,
But sometimes we don't do our part.
At times, with eyes on You that flame will
Flare into brilliant brightness for others to see.
But, at other times, with eyes on self, that candle
Will flicker and the flame will almost go out.
We pray, Lord, by your grace, let us do our part,
With that candle You lit in our heart.
May we always love, and never bicker,
And do it now, or even quicker,
Rich or poor, well or sicker
Let that flame never flicker.

When Jesus walked this earth, He was the Light of the world, and though the darkness rejected Him, His light was a bright beacon for others to see. Now that He is seated at the right hand of God the Father, He uses each one of us who are Christians to spread the gospel of salvation. In fact, His Great Commission to each one of us is to go into the world and tell others about the saving grace of God through our Lord Jesus Christ. We have received His light, love, mercy and grace. Now, we are to pass this opportunity of eternal salvation on to others by letting His light shine through us, that others might see Jesus in us.

Try as we might, at times when we focus on self instead of Jesus, that flame will flicker, but when we keep focused on Jesus the flame of His light seems to burst forth and flare where others can see and be brought into a loving relationship with the Lord. Our prayer is that by His grace, we keep our eyes on Him. May we always love, and never bicker. Let that flame never flicker.

November 6

NO OTHER NAME

"Salvation is found in no one else, for there is no other name under Heaven given to men by which we must be saved." – Acts 4:12

OUR ARMS WERE TOO SHORT

Father, we looked for You.
We reached and beseeched looking for You.
This came from the heart,
But our arms were too short, then
Miracle of all miracles,
We looked around and there we found
You had already reached down
And given us Jesus. We touched Him
And He touched us. He gave us life,
His life, eternal life,
Now He walks with us, and talks with us.
He gives us His Love, His Mercy and His Grace.
And one day soon, He'll take us home.
We reached, Lord, but our arms were too short.
We're so glad
Your arms are longer than ours are.

This scripture is one of many scriptures in the Bible that give us the one and only essential ingredient for salvation. Salvation is through Jesus and Jesus alone. We find the Father through the Son. Many people reach for God, some with good works, some with good intentions, others with worldly wisdom, and many in desperation. But the truth of the gospel is that access to God the Father is only through His Son, our Lord Jesus Christ. As this scripture tells us, "There is no other name under Heaven given to men by which we must be saved."

As we reach up for God, we find that our arms are too short. But the good news is that He has already reached down to us through Jesus. By faith in Him, we receive His life, eternal life, and while we're on this earth, He walks with us and talks with us, giving us an abundance of love, mercy and grace. And one day soon, He will take us home. With eternal gratitude we can say, Lord, we're so glad Your arms are longer than ours are.

November 7

THE EYE IS THE LAMP OF THE BODY

"The eye is the lamp of the body. If your eyes are good, your whole body will be full of light." – Matthew 6:22

"Set your hearts on things above. Set your minds on things above." – Colossians 3:1a, 2a

PLEASE HELP US FIND OUR GLASSES

We were near-sighted, Lord. Our eyes were failing,
But You gave us glasses, glasses to look through to see You.
And Your light illuminated our path with love, mercy, grace and peace.
With those glasses, Lord, our vision was better than 20/20,
It was perfect, perfected by You.
But, Lord, somewhere along that pathway we took
Our eyes off you and dropped our glasses. We intended to
Take just a peek at our circumstances, just one short
Sideline glance, but our eyes became focused on self and
We stumbled and fell into the under growth of circumstances,
And Lord we dropped our glasses.
We know in our heart that Your Love, Your Mercy, and
Your Grace continue to be ours, day after day after day,
But our sight is a little fuzzy now, so Lord, in order to also
Have Your Peace; we want to ask You for one small favor.
Lord, will you please help us find our glasses?

This scripture from Matthew tells us that the eyes are the lamps of the body. If our eyes are good, our whole body will be full of light and the scripture from Colossians instructs us to set our hearts and our minds on things above. Jesus used many parables and much analogy in His teaching. He did this in order that the people might better understand His gospel of truth.

The analogy used in today's devotional may seem to be quite ridiculous, especially to those who have never had trouble with their vision. But to those who have, perhaps it will help define a very simple truth regarding our walk with the Lord. That truth is that when our focus is on self and circumstances instead of on Jesus, even though we know we have His love, mercy and grace, we no longer have His peace. So our prayer is that by God's grace, we return our focus to the Lord, or by analogy, we might say, "Lord, will You please help us find our glasses?"

THE TONGUE IS A FIRE

"Consider what a great forest is set on fire by a small spark. The tongue also is a fire." – James 3:5b, 6a

LET'S PUT IT TO SHAME

Now, the tongue is so proficient,
Let us pray it's more efficient,
Let us maim it, or let's tame it,
For its sparks will cause a flame.
And the flame that we're assuming,
Is a flame that's all consuming.
First it's flaring, then it's blaring,
Spewing out both guilt and blame.
Let's not claim it, let's just tame it,
So before ours does the same,
Let us put our tongue to shame.

We are all guilty of speaking before we think, in fact, in retrospect, we might sometimes wonder if our tongue is even connected to our brain. In this scripture, James gives an indication of how powerful this very small part of our body really is. He equates it to a small rudder steering a large ship, and a small fire consuming an entire forest.

As Christians, we know that the reason we are placed on this earth is to honor the Lord, with what we think, what we do and what we say. Our prayer is that with His help, we make sure that our tongue is connected, not only to our brain, but also to His loving Spirit. Before it sparks into a roaring flame, spewing out guilt and blame, let's not claim-it, let's just tame-it, so before ours does the same, Let us put our tongue to shame.

November 9

DO NOT WORRY

"So, don't worry about tomorrow. Tomorrow will take care of itself. Each day has enough troubles of its own." – Matthew 6:34

HELP US WAIT UNTIL WE GET THERE

We have a small problem, Lord.
There's a big bridge out there, and we just know
We'll have to cross it tomorrow. So guess what, Lord
We worry, and we hurry, and
We've already crossed it fourteen times today
That's the big one, Lord, in addition to all the little
Bridges that we "had" to cross today.
What's our problem, Lord? We don't even know for sure
We will "ever" have to cross that "Big One."
Our prayer is that by Your Grace, we have enough
"Faith" that we don't worry, and hurry to cross that
"Big One" today, the one that "may" not even be there tomorrow.
Lord, help us wait until we get there.

For most of us, I believe this admonition by our Lord not to worry about tomorrow is one of the most difficult of His commandments to keep. It seems that in our humanity, we just thrive on projecting what tomorrow may bring, and when our finite minds tune into secular things, rather than spiritual things, we become anxious. We worry. Our projection focuses on self and circumstances, instead of on the Lord and His promises. To worry is perhaps a polite way of saying to fear. In most instances, when we worry, we fear either getting something we don't want, or not getting something we do want. We visualize a big bridge that we think must be crossed tomorrow. So in our anxiety, we cross that big one, time after time, today.

Our prayer is that by God's grace we have a sufficient amount of faith not to worry about tomorrow, enough faith that we don't worry, and hurry to cross that big bridge time after time today, for tomorrow that "big one" may not even be there. Lord, help us wait until we get there.

PUT ON THE FULL ARMOR OF GOD

"Put on the full armor of God." – Ephesians 6:11a

"And with your feet fitted with the readiness that comes from the gospel of peace." – Ephesians 6:15

"My peace I give you. I do not give as the world gives. Do not let your hearts be troubled, and do not be afraid." – John 14:27

PLEASE HELP US FIND OUR SHOES

Lord, You have been so good to us.
You not only gave us eternal life,
You armed us for this life with Your armor, Lord;
The belt of truth, breastplate of Righteousness,
Shoes of peace, shield of faith, helmet of Salvation
And sword of the Spirit.
And Lord, everything seems to be in place most of the time,
Except for one item, those "Shoes of peace."
We keep losing our shoes.
We're talking to You, and suddenly we're distracted.
We glance over at circumstances, and the next thing we know
Our shoes are gone.
Lord, will You please help us find our shoes?

The Lord has indeed been good to us. We look forward to an eternity with Him, and with our loved ones. What a glorious gift this is. He also arms us for the living of this life with His indwelling Holy Spirit, who guides us and gives us comfort. We know His truth. We possess His righteousness. Through His blood, by faith, we have salvation, and with this knowledge of His love, mercy and grace, we receive His peace. Jesus tells us that the peace he gives is not as the world gives. He also tells us to not let our hearts be troubled, and to not be afraid.

Paul, in Ephesians, tells us to put on the full armor of God, and in sequence, his third directive is to have our feet fitted with the gospel of peace. Our problem is, we put on these "shoes of peace," and our joy seems to have no bounds as we stand in His peace. Then we are distracted by circumstances, and take our eyes off Jesus and suddenly we lose the peace that we had.

November 11

JUDGING OTHERS

"Why do you look at the speck of sawdust in your brother's eye and pay no attention to the plank in your own eye?" – Matthew 7:3

THAT PLANK OUT THERE

Lord, there is this Christian brother of mine,
He must have eye trouble.
the rest of him seems to be okay, just his eyes.
each time I look at him his eyes are red and bleary.
there must be something in his eyes,
something small, perhaps just a speck,
But it's there. He needs to get it out.
Lord, I'm glad my eyes are not like his eyes.
My vision seems to be great.
at least, it's great when I can see.
But there is something I don't understand.
I keep rubbing my eyes, trying to get the right focus.
There are times when I can't see anything
anything, that is except that big "plank" out there.
I don't know exactly where it is,
but it's there somewhere.
Perhaps in some other brother's eyes.
Lord, that plank couldn't be in my eye, could it?

Jesus often taught with metaphors or parables. In this scripture, he is teaching us to not be habitually critical of others, continually trying to change them, especially without first evaluating our own life. Metaphorically, He illustrates with the "speck" in our brother's eyes, and for effect, He uses a strong hyperbole "plank" in our own eye.

Even though we are Christians, and have the very Spirit of Christ living in us, in our humanity it is so much easier to recognize the faults of others than it is to realize what our own shortcomings are. Our eyesight seems to be 20/20 as we see the speck in our brother's eye, but we seem to be blind to the plank in our own eye.

Our prayer is that with the Lord's help, we spend our time taking inventory of, and correcting our faults, instead of looking for faults in others. Let's get that plank out of our eye today.

November 12

THAT YOUR JOY MAY BE COMPLETE

"I have told you this so that My joy may be in you. And that your joy may be complete." – John 15:11

PLEASE LORD, CUT IT LOOSE

Our spirit is lagging just a bit today, Lord,
Not real sad, and not too bad, just sagging a bit.
We feel as if we're dragging something behind us,
Something we found, and it's dragging us down.
In fact, Lord, whatever it is it seems to be getting
Heavier and heavier and heavier
And our spirit seems to be getting lower and lower and lower.
Our spirit wants to be free, like a little boy leaping
And "jumping with joy" on the playground.
But Lord, our spirit's not "jumping" too high today.
Whatever it was we found, just keeps dragging us down.
So we're asking a small favor today.
Lord would you please cut it loose?

The great truth Jesus relates to us in this scripture is that He has literally given us His joy, that our joy might be complete in Him. His love for us is so great that He wants the very best for each one of us. And He gave us His Spirit that we might be comforted and guided along the way, experiencing His love, peace, grace and joy. But as we travel down life's highway, we seem to have a habit of picking something up that drags us down. In our humanity, perhaps, it's a little resentment toward one of our Christian brothers or sisters. Or perhaps we feel slighted by someone, or perhaps a sin of omission regarding something we should do, and don't. Whatever it is, it begins to drag us down, and our spirit begins sagging and we begin to lose that joy we were experiencing. But the good news is that there is a solution and that solution is found in Jesus.

Lord, we know we took our eyes off You for a little while, and without Your guidance, we picked up something along the way that we shouldn't have picked up, and whatever it was is getting heavier and heavier. Our spirit is no longer jumping with joy. So Lord, whatever it was that we found, that something that's dragging us down, would You please cut it loose?

November 13

NO ONE CAN SNATCH THEM

"I give them eternal life, and they shall never perish; no one can snatch them out of My hand." – John 10:28

PLEASE GRIP US JUST A LITTLE TIGHTER

Lord, we know you have a good grip on us,
And wherever we go, you won't let go,
And someday You will take us home.
But Lord, this pathway of life is so uncertain.
At times the path is broad, and paved with sure footing,
At other times it's narrow, and slippery with no footing.
And Lord, we're on that narrow path right now.
It's narrow, and it's right on the brink of a huge cliff
Overlooking a deep, dark abyss.
And it's slippery, Lord.
Our feet are slipping and sliding all over the place,
And we seem to be sliding toward the edge.
We know You have a good grip on us.
You told us that and we can feel it.
Sometimes it feels firm and sometimes lighter.
But Lord right now, would You please
Grip us just a little tighter.

In this scripture, our Lord promises us eternal life, and He tells us that no one can snatch us out of His hands. Metaphorically speaking, we are in the hands of Jesus. That grip He has on us will not only take us home, but will also provide strength and guidance for us as we travel down this pathway of life.

As we attempt to live the Christian life, sometimes we seem to have no obstacles in our way, and at that point in time, His grip on us perhaps feels a little lighter. At other times, we seem to face so many barriers in our path that we instinctively turn to Him and feel His grip tighten and become firm. We know He's with us, giving us an abundance of His love, mercy and grace. There are also times when it seems we have an exceptionally huge obstacle to overcome. Although we know He has a good grip on us, at this point we seem to say, "Lord, right now, would you please grip us just a little tighter?" And the good news is that He can and he does.

ETERNAL LIFE

"Whoever believes in the Son has eternal life." – John 3:36

ALIVE NOW, AND WE KNOW IT

We're alive now, and we know it, Lord.
There was a time when we were dead and
We didn't know it.
We just plodded along, no song in our heart,
No hope in our soul.
But then, Lord, we met You
And You made us whole.
You saved our soul.
Now we have a spring in our step,
A song in our heart and, Lord,
Now it seems that our very soul
Is soaring to new heights,
Day, after day, after day,
We're up here with the eagles now, Lord.
We remember when You came to us
And offered to sow the seed of Your life in our soul.
And we said, "Yes, Lord, please sow it."
And You did.
And Lord, we're alive now and we know it.

The greatest gift that has ever been given, or will ever be received, is the gift that was given us by our Lord Jesus Christ, and that gift is eternal life. Eternal means "forever, never ending," so we know we will be with Jesus forever and ever. But the exciting thing is that we don't have to wait to be alive. We received his life the very moment we accepted Him as our Savior and His indwelling Spirit gives us guidance and comfort day after day.

There was a time before we met Jesus that we were dead, and probably most of us didn't even know it. We just assumed that life was supposed to be dull and dreary, and then we met Jesus. How things changed! We became alive, with a song in our heart, a spring in our step and a purpose in our life. We were once dead, and perhaps we didn't know it, but by the grace of God, through our Lord Jesus Christ, we're alive now, and we know it.

I AM THE LIGHT OF THE WORLD

"I am the Light of the world." – John 8:12

THE SON WILL SHINE IN THE MORNING

Lord, at the moment we seem to be engulfed in total darkness
We're fraught with despair, and weary with wear.
Our very soul seems to be caught up and gripped
With a warning of doom and gloom.
We're in its clutches, Lord, and there's no light here.
We're tired and we're cold, and we're no longer bold.
We're turning to You, Lord; we need Your help,
Please help us.
Is that a light I see, Lord, Your light?
It seems to be getting nearer and nearer,
Brighter and brighter.
And now, Lord, it's bursting into a brilliant brightness,
The spawning of Your dawning,
You have turned night into day.
Yes, Lord, we get the message.
Midst the darkness of night, the gloom with no light.
Though our soul is gripped with a warning You give release,
And You give us Your Peace,
For the Son will shine in the morning.

Even Christians get tired, cold and no longer bold. When we take our eyes off Jesus and look at circumstances, we sometimes seem to be engulfed in darkness and we become fraught with despair and weary with wear. In this scripture, we see a great truth unfold. Jesus is the Light of the world. Not only is He the Light that saves, He is also the Light that we can turn to in our darkest hour, and when we ask for help, His response is so gracious. He will turn our darkest night into day with the brilliant brightness of His grace, for we know that whatever our circumstances may be, "the Son will shine in the morning."

November 16

THE NARROW ROAD

"But small is the gate and narrow the road that leads to life, and only a few find it." – Matthew 6:14

JUST DRAG US BACK

We found it, Lord, that narrow road
You told us about.
And now we have life, Your life.
But Lord, as we travel down this road of life,
Sometimes it seems so narrow and so hard,
And sometimes we see a fork in the road, Lord,
A super highway that looks so wide and easy.
We see others enjoy the ride, drive with pride,
And with never a sigh, pass others by.
We've been told it's a shortcut,
But not by You, Lord.
You said to stay on the narrow one,
And to stop along the way
To help others stay on the right road.
And Lord we want to obey, so we're asking You,
If we should turn off onto that other road for any reason,
Please get us back on the right road.
Just turn us around and reroute us.
And Lord, if there is any resistance on our part,
If we balk, or try to make excuses, or just persist to resist,
Please Lord; don't pay any attention to the willpower we lack.
JUST DRAG US BACK.

This scripture has to do with salvation. And the message is that the road that leads to salvation is narrow. That is, only a few will believe in Jesus and be saved. But in the sanctification process, as we travel down this road of life, our road sometimes seems so narrow and so hard. And we see a fork in our road that looks so wide and so easy. It looks like a superhighway, a shortcut. We see others on that road that seem to be enjoying the ride, paying no attention to others and just intent on pleasing themselves.

Our prayer is that if we come to that fork in the road, by Your grace, we recognize which is the right road, and which is the wrong road.

November 17

HE MADE HIS HOME WITH US

"If anyone loves Me, he will obey My teaching. My Father will love him and We will come to him and make Our home with him." – John 14:23

JUST A LITTLE TIGHTER, LORD

You are so good to us, Lord.
First You save us, then You gave us
Your life, eternal life.
Then You made Your home with us.
You walk with us, talk with us,
And whatever burden we bear, You care.
And You make it lighter, Lord.
Just today, the load we were carrying
Seemed so heavy.
And You put Your loving arms around us,
And squeezed us, and made it lighter.
But Lord, it's still a little too heavy for us to carry.
And even though You made it lighter,
Lord would You please squeeze us
Just a little tighter?

As Christians, we obeyed the teaching of Jesus and by faith accepted Him as our Lord and our Savior. This scripture promises us that He will then make His home with us, and He has done just that with His indwelling Holy Spirit. Now He walks with us, and talks with us and whatever burden we might have, He puts His loving arms around us and makes it lighter.

As we walk down this pathway of life, there are many burdens that we must bear. But the good news is that we don't have to bear them alone. Jesus is with us day after day, every step of the way. When the load seems to get too heavy, He puts His loving arms around us, and makes it lighter. But there are times when that load we carry still seems to be too heavy, even though He has made it lighter. So we ask, "Please, Lord, would You squeeze us just a little tighter?" And He does, and miracle of all miracles, our burden is lifted and we have His peace. How can we ever thank Him enough for this?

HE WILL NOT SPEAK ON HIS OWN

"But when He, the Spirit of Truth comes, He will guide you into all truth. He will not speak on His own; He will speak only what He hears." – John 16:13

GIVE US THE GRACE TO CHANGE PLACES

We're out on life's highway, Lord,
And the traffic is heavy.
We see wrecks all over the place,
No one seems to know what the speed limit is,
Or which lane to drive in.
We just avoided a head-on collision, just barely.
You're with us Lord, but we have you in the passenger seat,
And You should be behind the wheel,
Where You could do the driving.
Lord, please give us the grace to change places.

In this scripture, Jesus gives us information regarding the work of the Holy Spirit. We are promised His Spirit the moment we accept Him as our Savior and our Lord. He will remain with us to comfort us and to guide us along the way, but Jesus makes it very clear that He will not force us to do anything. We have choices. We must ask.

When we, as Christians, drive down this highway of life, we have Jesus with us in the form of His indwelling Spirit. But all too frequently, He is not behind the wheel. He is in the passenger seat because we insist on doing the driving ourselves. And the truth is, we are not very good drivers. And if we stay behind the wheel long enough, we will probably have a head on collision. We need to let Him do the driving, and we need to get in the passenger seat. Our prayer is that we realize this, and that He gives us the grace to change places.

November 19

ADOPTED INTO GOD'S FAMILY

"In love, He predestined us to be adopted as His sons through Jesus Christ, in accordance with His pleasure and will." – Ephesians 1:5a

"So you are no longer a slave, but a son; and since you are a son, God has made you also an heir." – Galatians 4:7

LET THEM KNOW WE'RE RELATED

Father, through Jesus, You have adopted us.
We're no longer slaves, but members of Your family.
We're Your sons and Your daughters, and Lord,
Besides that, we are heirs to the "family fortune."
And what a "fortune" that is.
We will inherit, completely without merit,
a mansion next door to You, to live in
Forever and ever—with no monthly payments all bills
Paid for and plenty of spending money.
Lord, while we're still on this earth, let us act like a
Child of Yours. Let us pass Your love on to others, as
We tell them about Jesus. Help us be good Sons and
Daughters, and reach-out to others. Lord, we pray, since
We are in Your family, as we reach out to others, and
They see us, don't let our efforts be ill-fated
Please, Lord, when they see us, let them KNOW we're related.

What an exhilarating truth this is that is revealed in these scriptures. When we accept Jesus, we are adopted into the family of God, and our status immediately changes. We are no longer slaves. Now we are sons and daughters of God the Father, having full privileges as children, and we are heirs to the family fortune, an eternity with our Lord in a place that He has already prepared for us.

In gratitude for this position we have in Christ, may we look and act like God's children as we walk down this pathway of life. Let us reach out to others, and sow the seeds of His love in their hearts. Our prayer is, Lord let others see Jesus in us, and as we reach out, don't let our efforts be ill fated – when they see us, Lord let them KNOW WE'RE RELATED.

BUT GOD MADE IT GROW

"I planted the seed, Apollos watered it, but God made it grow. So, neither he who plants nor he who waters is anything, but only God, Who makes things grow." – 1 Corinthians 3:6-7.

COULD WE HAVE A BUMPER CROP?

Have we failed You, Lord? We've been telling
Others about You, about Your Saving Grace,
Your love and mercy too, and so far—
Nothing has happened—
We've tried to be true, Lord but now,
What do we do? —Yes, Lord we hear you—
Loud and clear—Our job is to do the sowing, and
Watering too, but leave the growing to You.
Yes, Lord we'll do that-We will drop the Seed of
Your Gospel into the fertile ground of unbelievers--,
Then continue to water it—but Lord,
One small favor we ask---perhaps we're a bit selfish, but-
In this fertile ground of unbelievers, for Your Glory,
When the seed of Your Gospel we drop, please Lord,
COULD WE HAVE A BUMPER CROP?

As Christians, we walk down this pathway of life with a desire to please God, to be all that we can be for the Lord. In this capacity, we tell others about Jesus, about His saving grace, love and mercy. This is not only a privilege, but also an obligation (Mark 16:15). We obey the Lord, and present His gospel to others. We tell them about Jesus, about how He has changed our life and how He can do the same for them. But so often, we see no results. We feel like a failure. What did we do wrong? The answer is found in today's scripture.

We did nothing wrong, except perhaps anticipate the results with too much expectation, for this scripture teaches us that we are to tell others about Jesus, and continue to tell them. In other words, we are to plant the seed and then continue to water. Our job is to do the sowing, because only the Lord can do the growing, and He does and He will. Even so, in our humanity, and perhaps a bit selfishly, but all for His glory, we make a request, which is "Lord, in this fertile ground of unbelievers, when the seed of Your gospel we drop, Lord, – COULD WE PLEASE HAVE A BUMPER CROP?"

November 21

GOD'S GRACE IS GIVEN TO US

"I always thank God for you, because of His grace given you in Christ Jesus." – 1 Corinthians 1:4

JUST SMEAR IT ALL OVER US

We have walked together a long way, Lord,
And we know all about Your love, Your mercy
And Your grace, especially Your grace.
You have led us, and guided us
And sometimes even carried us.
You have never left us, You have been with us,
All the way, day after day.
But Lord, speaking of Your grace today,
We seem to need a little "extra helping."
We are seeking some solutions,
And our thinking seems to be a little "fuzzy."
So again we seek Your grace.
And Lord, this time we need to "lot of it."
So as You give it, will You please give more
Than just an "extra helping."
Give us a "bunch of it," just pile it on thick
Layer after layer in fact today, Lord, please
JUST SMEAR IT ALL OVER US.

In this scripture, Paul is thanking God for extending His grace through Christ Jesus to members of the Corinthian church, both for salvation and for the living of the Christian life. This truth regarding the grace of God is as real today for each one of us, as it was for the Christians in Corinth.

Some of us have had a long journey with the Lord and during that journey we have experienced God's love, mercy and grace through our Lord Jesus Christ – especially His grace. But there are days when we seem to need a little extra helping of grace. In fact, at the moment we want more than just an extra helping. We want a bunch of it, so we ask and it seems a miracle occurs. We receive so much of it that we have grace leftover, and that leftover grace gives us peace that surpasses all understanding and although we don't understand it, we can thank Him for it, and we do.

NO ONE CAN SNATCH THEM

"My sheep listen to My voice; I know them and they follow Me. I give them eternal life and they shall never perish; no one can snatch them out of My hand." – John 10:27-28

LORD, PLEASE US BOTH HANDS

You have given us eternal life, Lord,
And You've told us that no one can snatch us
Out of Your hand.
So we know for sure that we're secure in Your hand,
And that at the end of our road, You'll take us home
To be with You forever and ever.
But Lord, it's been raining lately,
And on this road we're traveling,
We just ran out of pavement.
It's narrow, and it's going downhill,
And it's slick, Lord.
We're slipping and sliding,
And there are some deep ditches on both sides.
And Lord, even though we know You hold us,
And that Your hand will never let go, one small favor we ask.
Right now, Lord, would You please use both hands?

This scripture is one of many scriptures in the Bible that guarantees the believer eternal security, so we know our salvation is secure, however, the sanctification process is a different matter. Although we know for sure what our ultimate destination will be, we still have an earthly road to travel. Sometimes that road seems like a super highway with wide shoulders and no ditches. But at other times, it seems so narrow and slick, with ditches on both sides. We become embroiled with circumstances beyond our control, perhaps of our own making, or perhaps the Lord is teaching us a lesson, but for whatever reason, we realize that we need help – His help.

Metaphorically speaking, although we know He has us in His hand, at that point we feel like asking Him to use both hands. So, we ask, and He responds with His guidance, and once again, we marvel at the magnitude of His generosity, love, mercy and grace. In response to our request, He has truly used both hands.

November 23

JESUS GIVES FORGIVENESS

"For He has rescued us from the dominion of darkness and brought us into the kingdom of the Son He loves, in whom we have redemption, the forgiveness of sins." – Colossians 1:13-14

FORGIVENESS IS FOREVER

A simple truth, Lord, so difficult for us to understand,
You forgive our sins, all of them, while others don't.
And the most difficult task, it seems, is for us to forgive ourselves.
By your blood, through Your grace, and with the faith You give us,
We are cleansed.
You wash us "white as snow."
And Lord, You must use a powerful detergent because,
Even as we go out and find a little dirt here and there,
It continues to keep us clean.
No, we don't understand it, Lord.
We step forward with our best endeavor, and we fail miserably.
But Lord, You're with us all the way.
When we fail and fall, You pick us up,
Dust us off and put us back on the right road,
The road that leads home.
Yes, Lord, You have taught us a simple truth,
And please help us understand it.
Though we may fail and fall in our endeavor,
Your forgiveness is forever, and we thank You for this Lord.

When we accept Jesus as our Savior and our Lord, some miraculous things happen. We immediately receive His Spirit as a deposit, guaranteeing us eternal life (Ephesians 1:14), but at the same time, we are forgiven and cleansed of all sin – past, present and future. This is so difficult for us to understand. Perhaps we can understand how we can be forgiven for past sins, perhaps even present sins, but how are we now forgiven and cleansed for future sins?

The simple fact is that when we truly accept Christ, His Spirit within us, while guiding and directing us, is continually keeping us clean. We are actually equipped with the Spirit to not sin at all. But in our humanity, we take our eyes off Jesus and, through our own endeavor, we fail miserably.

WE'LL MEET THE LORD, FACE TO FACE

"And the dead in Christ will rise first, after that, we who are still alive and are left will be caught up together with them in the clouds to meet the Lord in the air, and so we will be with the Lord forever." – 1 Thessalonians 4:16b-17a

A FACE FULL OF GRACE

Lord, we are now running an earthly race,
But You have promised us that, whether alive or dead,
When You appear in the clouds, we'll see You face to face.
We long to see Your face, Lord,
We visualize; we paint a picture of Your face.
A sad face, sad because of all the sin in the world;
A compassionate face, full of loving kindness;
A pained face, a reflection of the agony of the cross;
A wise face, full of all knowledge and wisdom;
A smiling face, becoming with all radiance.
But Lord, as we run this earthly race,
Whatever our circumstances may be,
When we seek Your face, in each and every case,
WE SEE A FACE FULL OF GRACE.

In this scripture, we have our Lord's promise that at the Rapture, whether we are alive or dead, if we are His, we will at last meet Him face to face, then we will spend an eternity with our Lord. What a glorious promise. As we run this earthly race, we often reflect on the various faces of our Lord. We see many: His expression of sadness for the sin in the world; the pain with the agony He suffered on the cross for each of us; to a wise face, full of compassion and loving kindness; to a smiling face, beaming with all radiance as He welcomes us home. But the great truth is that however we visualize His face, in each and every case, WE SEE A FACE FULL OF GRACE.

A BEGINNING AND AN END

"But the day of the Lord will come like a thief. The heavens will disappear with a roar; the elements will be destroyed by fire, and the earth and everything in it will be laid bare." – 2 Peter 3:10

"I give them eternal life, and they shall never perish; no one can snatch them out of My hand." – John 10:28

A BEGINNING, BUT NO END

We were just thinking, Lord, about Your promise.
You give us eternal life, a life that will never end.
All other things on this earth had a beginning
But they have an end; the birds in the air,
The fish in the sea, all life on this earth will cease to be.
We could be prone to tears and sorrow,
For a roaring fire, with all its horror,
Will consume this earth and destroy it.
The riches of today will be gone tomorrow.
Yes, Lord, these things had a beginning,
And they have an end, but we don't.
We had a beginning with You, and now, there is no end.
We will be with You, together with all the Saints,
Not by our endeavor, but by Your grace,
We'll be together for all eternity.
And "Eternity is Forever," there is no end.
And we thank You for this, Lord.

These scriptures present two basic truths. First, ultimately this earth will be laid bare and everything in it will be destroyed. The things we see today will be gone tomorrow. They will be destroyed and consumed by a roaring fire. This destruction is referred to as the "Day of the Lord." No one except the Lord knows when this will happen, but the good news is that when it does, we won't be here; because the second truth we find in these scriptures is that, in Christ, we have eternal life. Although all things on this earth had a beginning, we also know they have an end. But for those of us who had our beginning in Jesus, there is no end. He has promised us an eternity with Him, safe and secure in His loving arms, with no sorrow, and no tears, just joy in our heart forever.

November 26

TURN THE OTHER CHEEK

"But I tell you, do not resist an evil person. If someone strikes you on the right cheek, turn to him the other also." – Matthew 5:39

ONCE MORE

They did us wrong, Lord, and You know it.
We came to You and You said, "Turn the other cheek,"
And we did.
And guess what Lord, they hit us again.
And we came back to You and You said, "Turn the other
Cheek, once more," and we did.
And Lord, and they hit us once more,
And this time, harder.
And this has happened several times Lord,
And You kept saying "once more."
And just like before, they hit us once more.
And Lord, now both cheeks are sore.
What do we do now, Lord? We're asking.
Can we retaliate? Can we make their cheeks sore?
Yes, Lord, we hear Your answer loud and clear.
Just like before, "Turn the other cheek once more."
Yes, Lord we hear.
And although both of our cheeks are already sore,
For You, we won't keep score,
We'll turn the other cheek once more.

In this scripture, Jesus is exhorting us to respond to someone who does us a personal wrong, not with retaliation contained within our humanity, but with the humility embodied in His indwelling Spirit. When someone does us a personal wrong, in our humanity our first and foremost impulse is to get even. And in our mind, we can devise all kinds of ways to even the score. But Jesus tells us not to retaliate, rather, to turn the other cheek. 1 Peter 2:23 tells us that when they hurled their insults at Him, He did not retaliate. When He suffered, He made no threats. Instead, He entrusted Himself to Him Who judges justly.

November 27

HE CALLS THEM BY NAME

"He calls His own sheep by name and leads them out." – John 10:3b

YOU ALWAYS REMEMBER OUR NAME

What a memory You have, Lord.
We met years ago, and You still remember our name.
There was nothing special about us.
We came to You with neither fortune nor fame,
Full of guilt and blame, our spirit laggard and lame.
Then we met You, and Lord, all we had was faith,
And You gave us that.
But Lord, You took that little bit of faith we had,
And You made it grow and grow,
And now we love You so.
And Lord, we're special now,
Not for anything we've done,
But because we know You.
And Lord, we still don't have fortune or fame,
But also, we no longer feel guilt and blame,
And our spirit is no longer laggard and lame.
In fact, Lord, right now we're excited.
We not only know You, but You know us,
And we know You know us,
Because since You came,
You always remember our name.

During the days that Jesus walked this earth, shepherds would abide in the fields, taking care of their sheep. There was something special about the relationship between the shepherd and his sheep. In the morning, he would lead them out to water and good pasture, and in the evening, he would bring them into a safe place. The shepherd would often gave each of his sheep a name, and he would call each one by name and they would follow him anywhere he led them.

In this scripture, Jesus is using allegory to emphasize a truth, and the truth is that if we belong to Jesus, He knows us very personally and intimately. In fact, regardless of the size of His flock, He can call each one of us by name. He takes us out to pasture each day and keeps us safe each evening.

November 28

LOVE YOUR NEIGHBOR

"And if by grace, then it is no longer by works; if it were, grace would not be grace." – Romans 11:6

"Love your neighbor as yourself." – Matthew 22:39b

"For we are God's workmanship, created in Christ Jesus to do good works." – Ephesians 2:10

PLEASE LORD, JUST SHOVE US

We love You so much Lord,
You've done so very much for us,
We can never repay You.
But in gratitude, we would like to try
To do our best for You before we die.
There is something on our heart, Lord,
That we need to do for You today,
An extension of Your love to a Brother,
And we have good intentions,
But we've been so busy
Time seems to pass so quickly.
We need some help, Your help, Lord.
We have procrastinated, we need
A gentle nudge from You to get started.
No, more than a nudge, Lord,
Something more forceful, perhaps a shove.
Yes, Lord, that's it, a shove.
We know You're with us, in us, and above us.
And we know You love us, but Lord,
In order to get us started today,
Will You please JUST SHOVE US?

First, we are saved by grace, not by works. Second, we are admonished to love one another. And third, we are created in Christ Jesus to do good works. And if we're in the Lord, and the Lord is in us, out of gratitude for what He has done, not fear of what He might do, we strive to please Him. But sometimes we become so entangled with circumstances, so busy doing other things that we have a tendency to put off until tomorrow what we should be doing for the Lord today.

November 29

THAT YOU MAY BE WITH ME

"In my Father's house are many mansions; if it were not so, I would have told you. I am going there to prepare a place for you. And if I go and prepare a place for you, I will come back and take you to be with Me, that where I am, you may be also." – John 14:2-3

HEAVEN IS WHERE YOU ARE

Lord, there are so many skeptics in this world,
Who make no decision, but have only derision for You.
They ask weighty questions, Lord.
For instance, "Exactly where is this Heaven of yours located?"
And Lord, we don't know, the universe is so vast,
And You own all of it, and we don't know the exact location,
You haven't told us.
But Lord, one thing we do know for sure, because You have told us,
We know Who will be there.
So Lord, our response to the question is, and has to be,
"We don't know for sure exactly where Heaven is,
But we do know for sure Who will be there."
Because, large or small, near or far, Heaven is where You are.
And You're waiting with open arms to welcome us home.
Lord, please help all of us understand that the importance of Heaven
Is not "where it is" but "Who will be there."

Our Lord, through the Bible, has answered many, many questions. But there are some questions that will not be answered until later. To some extent, we are all curious. And there is nothing wrong with having a curiosity. But as we search the scriptures for answers, spiritual discernment guided by the Holy Spirit must be used. And we find that there are some questions that will be answered only when we meet our Lord, face to face. We believe one of the unanswered questions is, "Exactly where is Heaven?"

There are times when the unbeliever, especially one who derides the Lord, will tauntingly ask the believer questions that cannot be specifically answered, an example, "Exactly where is Heaven?" Of course, the Bible does not give us a specific location, but the Bible does give us information that is much more important. The exact location of Heaven pales into insignificance when compared to Who will be there, because Heaven is where Jesus is.

FOR THE LORD TO SEE

"Everything they do is done for men to see." – Matthew 23:5

"It is the Lord who judges me." – 1 Corinthians 4:4b

"When they measure themselves by themselves and compare themselves with themselves they are not wise." – 2 Corinthians 10:12b

HELP US MIND OUR OWN BUSINESS

We look around Lord and see others who seem to be doing
Something special for You and we know You told us not to,
But, in our humanity we judge and we compare—and the
Result is we either feel a great sense of inadequacy, or we
Question their motives. Help us obey You Lord.

By Your grace, and through Your power, let us do
Something for You, something special, not for men to see,
But for You to see – not for men to judge, but for you to
Judge. In our heart, let us be sure, our motive is pure – with
No hidden agenda – never desiring accolades from men, but
Always seeking only "Your Amen." Let whatever we do Glorify You, Lord. You are
the "Tower of all Power." By Your grace, and through Your power, as our work for
You
Is unfurled, in this world, let our selection of direction
Always be with Your connection, all for Your glory,
Through our Lord Jesus Christ, and Lord, also please
HELP US MIND OUR OWN BUSINESS.

The scriptures give us, not only the gospel, but also situational guidelines for living the Christian life. As we walk down this pathway of life, there are two sign posts that say don't judge others, and don't compare ourselves with others. The Lord has been so special to us, we would like to do something special for Him. Even in our fervor for the Lord, at that moment we are in danger of disregarding both of these signposts. We have all we can handle, just being sure our motives are pure, so as we attempt to do something special for the Lord. Let us never forget that there are times in our Christian walk when we can best serve the Lord by simply minding our own business.

December 1

DO YOU LOVE ME?

"For I seek not to please Myself but Him who sent Me." – John 5:30b

"Do you love Me? Feed My sheep." – John 21:17

LET US FOLLOW WHERE HE LEADS

God the Father, through Christ sees us,
Let us follow only Jesus,
Through Him working, never shirking,
Then our soul, His Spirit feeds.
Without Christ, the One we follow,
All good causes would be hollow,
So let's never, never, never,
Make Him second, to our deeds.
His connection and direction,
Give a purpose to our deeds
Let us follow where He leads.

Two very basic truths are revealed in these scriptures. First, Jesus has a very personal relationship with the Father, and at all times, He strives to please Him. Second, His admonition to Peter, and to those of us who love Him, is to feed His sheep, in other words to tell others about Jesus.

As Christians, we certainly have an obligation to tell others about Jesus, but even more than an obligation, we have the privilege of telling others about Him. Just as Jesus had a personal relationship with the Father, we have a personal relationship with Jesus. Our efforts should always be to help others know more about Jesus, rather than promoting a particular doctrinal belief. Doctrinal beliefs are too frequently substituted for personal beliefs. When this happens, the focus is on a cause, and not on Jesus. Keeping our eyes on Jesus, and our very intimate relationship with Him, will result in being directed by Him, then by God's grace through our Lord Jesus Christ, have purpose for our deeds. Let us always follow where He leads.

December 2

HE STRENGTHENS ME

"I can do all things through Him who strengthens me." – Philippians 4:13

IN HIS STRENGTH

Let us understand our weakness,
Then approach the Lord in meekness,
He's the tower of all power,
He's our Lord, God's only Son.
With regard to our earth's mission,
Let's be sure He's our ignition,
With Him merging, power surging,
In His strength, our race is run.
As our weakness turns to meekness,
He gives strength to get things done,
In his strength our race is won.

It is a well-documented fact that most athletes are in their prime between the ages of 25 and 30. After they pass 30 years of age, their strength begins to decline and their skills diminish. In whatever sport in which they are participating, they gradually become less and less effective. They are experiencing "power failure."

As Christians, our physical bodies are no different from those of the athletes. But regardless of age, spiritually, we experience a strange phenomenon. Even as we become weaker physically, when we go to the Lord in meekness, we receive a tremendous surge of power, Christ-power. And this power gives us the strength and the skill to successfully complete whatever the Lord has for us to do. Instead of experiencing power failure, we are spiritually in our prime. Our prayer is that we continue to go to the Lord in meekness, then let this surge of Christ-power be used daily by each one of us, all for the glory of God through our Lord Jesus Christ.

December 3

ASSEMBLING TOGETHER

"...not forsaking our own assembling together." – Hebrews 10:25b

"For when two or three come together in My name, there am I with them." – Matthew 18:20

CHRISTIAN FELLOWSHIP

With regard to our direction,
Let's be wise in our selection,
This December, let's remember,
Christian fellowship is best.
For, when Christians we are greeting,
Someone else is at that meeting,
It's a blessing, we're confessing,
For our Jesus is the guest,
And together, we can weather,
Any storm, and all the rest,
With our Lord, we pass the test.

Jesus tells His disciples that when two or more of them are gathered in His name, He will also be with them. At the time, Jesus gave them this promise; they had not yet received the Holy Spirit. They had Jesus instead. But, as Christians, we now have His Spirit indwelling us, so we might ask the question, "How can Christ be with us any more than He already is, simply by having fellowship with other Christians?" This is a difficult question to answer because Jesus may have been promising His presence in a certain situation prior to His sending His Spirit to indwell us. However, regardless of the interpretation of this verse, our personal experience proves to us that having fellowship with other Christians enhances our love for, and devotion to the Lord. Just as passing His love on to others increases our supply instead of depleting it when we have fellowship with other Christians, His Spirit within us seems to magnify with His love and His presence. In fact, we can truly say that we're confessing this fellowship is a blessing, because fellowship is always best, when Jesus is the guest.

December 4

WE TRUST IN THE LIVING GOD

"For therefore we both labor and suffer reproach. Because we trust in the living God." – 1 Timothy 4:10b

"Praise be to the God and Father of our Lord Jesus Christ, who has blessed us in the heavenly realms with every spiritual blessing in Christ." – Ephesians 1:3

THE ULTIMATE BLESSING

We have so many blessings, Lord,
And each one comes from You,
Not because we're due
And not because of what we do,
Just loving "grace gifts" from You.
At times Lord, we don't even know it's a blessing
We think it's a reproach, and perhaps it is,
But You know it's a blessing and that's what counts.
But Lord, we have a simple request to make.
By Your grace, let our "trust" never be misdirected.
Let our trust always be in You, not in Your blessings.
Let us be so well acquainted with You
That our trust is not in "what" You will do,
But in "Who" You are.
Then we will never have to take our eyes off You.
We can just marvel at Your presence in our lives,
And praise You day, after day, after day.
We can go about our work for You
Always with love, never with fear.
And Lord, while we're down here,
That will be the ULTIMATE BLESSING.

There are great truths revealed in these scriptures. First, we have already received every spiritual blessing in Christ, and second, even though we continue to receive His blessings day after day, our trust should always be in Him, not in His blessings.

If our trust becomes misdirected and is centered on what the Lord will do, instead of Who the Lord is, with our finite minds, we will have our focus on circumstances instead of on Jesus.

GOD'S WILL FOR YOU AND ME

"Be joyful always. Pray continually. Give thanks in all circumstances, for this is God's will for you in Christ Jesus." – 1 Thessalonians 5:16-18

GOD'S GIFT TO YOU AND ME

Since we know our own hereafter,
Let our hearts be filled with laughter.
As we're walking, let's be talking,
With our Lord, who set us free.
Let's continually be praying,
Giving thanks, as we're obeying,
Joy increasing, never ceasing,
In His will for you and me.
God now sees us, through our Jesus,
And His gift to you and me,
Is a SURE ETERNITY.

In these verses, Paul, in summary, is telling us how God wills us to live the Christian life. He admonishes us to be joyful and pray continually, always giving thanks regardless of our circumstances. For most of us, this is much easier said than done.

As we walk this pathway of life, an adverse circumstance will rear its ugly head. If we take our eyes off Jesus, and look at the circumstance, our joy seems to depart; we forget to pray and when we do pray, we are not thankful for that particular circumstance. God understands this. He didn't tell us to be thankful for that particular circumstance. He told us to be thankful regardless of circumstances. There is a difference, but what we must do in order to regain our joy, is to re-focus on the Lord. When we are having difficulty living within the will of God, we need to remember the gift of God, our Lord, Jesus Christ, through whom we are guaranteed a sure eternity. As we sincerely express gratitude, we are again living within the will of God, walking and talking with the Lord, counting our blessings and giving thanks for each and every one of them. May we never, even for a moment, forget the gift of God, then with eyes focuses on Jesus, by His grace, let us live within the will of God, all for His glory, through our Lord Jesus Christ.

December 6

EVERYONE DESERTED ME

"Everyone deserted me. But the Lord stood at my side and gave me strength." – 2 Timothy 4:16b-17a

HE'S STANDING AT OUR SIDE

There are times when friends will hurt us,
There are times when they desert us,
For believing, and receiving,
Jesus Christ, the crucified.
They not only don't believe us,
They reject us, and they leave us,
But God sees us, there with Jesus,
For, in Him do we abide,
And the tower of His power,
Gives us strength, so deep and wide,
For He's standing at our side.

In Hebrews 13, we are reminded that the Lord will never leave us nor forsake us. In today's verse, Paul reaffirms that truth. He is chained in a cold, damp dungeon like a common criminal, soon to die and deserted by many of his coworkers. His simple statement of truth was that though he was deserted by others, the Lord stood at his side, and gave him strength.

This statement of truth is as applicable today as it was in the days of Paul. We may not be in a cold, damp dungeon, but when we proclaim our faith in Jesus, we invite the ridicule of others, and frequently, the ones who hurt us and desert us, are those whom we though were friends. Friends can disappoint us, and they can desert us, but the one constant we have in this life is Jesus. Regardless of circumstances, if in Him we do abide, the tower of His power gives us strength, so very deep and wide, for He never leaves us. He is always standing at our side. What a blessing this is.

December 7

THE LORD IS MY HELPER

"God has said, 'Never will I leave you, never will I forsake you,' so we say with confidence: 'The Lord is my helper: I will not be afraid. What can man do to me?'" – Hebrews 13:5b-6

FAITH INSTEAD OF FEAR

When a storm brews on our ocean,
Let's not yield to our emotion,
Let projection, of direction,
Be with faith, instead of fear.
Though the sky is dark and dreary,
And our spirit, worn and weary,
Our Enhancer, is the answer,
And He's always standing near,
Right beside us, there to guide us,
And our prayer, He'll always hear,
Yield to faith, instead of fear.

As we walk down this pathway of life, we will face many situations that are unpleasant. Circumstances, at times, will cause apprehension and anxiety. At that point, we are looking right into the face of fear, but we have options. We can either yield to that fear or yield to faith – faith in the promises of God.

Today's scripture gives us several assurances. The Lord will never leave us. He will never forsake us. He will be our Helper. So with His strength and power available, who or what is there to fear? The answer, of course, is that there is nothing to fear except fear itself. Our prayer is that as we confront each unpleasant circumstance, we remember these promises. And by the grace of God, through our Lord Jesus Christ, may we always YIELD TO FAITH INSTEAD OF FEAR.

REDEMPTION THROUGH HIS BLOOD

"In Him we have redemption through His blood, the forgiveness of sins, in accordance with the riches of God's grace." – Ephesians 1:7

HE BOUGHT US OUR ETERNITY

Grace and mercy are in Jesus,
For through Him our Father sees us,
And God's vision made provision,
For His death upon that tree.
There, to pay for mankind's sinning,
To give each a new beginning.
We trust Jesus, then God sees us,
He's as just, as just can be.
Though He loves us, truly loves us,
Our Lord's blood upon that tree,
Bought us our eternity.

Much is said and written about the love, grace and mercy of God. And this is as it should be. However, let us never forget that He is also a just God. And in order to satisfy His righteousness, He sent Jesus to shed His blood for our sins, that by faith in Jesus, we might receive His righteousness and receive the gift of salvation. We are forgiven, not simply because God loves us, but because Jesus has paid the price for our redemption.

December 9

WE HAVE BEEN MADE HOLY

"And by that will, we have been made holy through the sacrifice of the body of Jesus Christ once for all. Because by one sacrifice He has made perfect forever those who are being made holy." – Hebrews 10:10, 14

WE ARE BEING MADE HOLY

Now, the way the Father sees us,
We are holy, through our Jesus,
Thus selected, we're connected,
For we're in His family.
With His grace that won't diminish,
He will love us to the finish,
He protects us, and corrects us,
As he changes you and me,
From the lowly to be holy,
So at last when Christ we see
We are clothed in purity.

Verse 10 tells us that we have been "made holy" (past tense), and verse 14 tells us that we are "being made holy" (present tense). On the surface, these two scriptures seem to contradict each other, but there is no contradiction.

Verse 10 also deals with salvation. When we put our faith and trust in Jesus, we were declared eternally holy in the sight of God the Father, and made an eternal member of God's family because we had been given the holiness of Jesus. We were then set apart to do good works for the Lord. Verse 14 deals with Christians, already saved, in the process of becoming the kind of person the Lord wants us to be. This is the sanctification process.

This sanctification process is a life-long endeavor by the Christian, guided by the indwelling Spirit of Christ. Too often, we resist, procrastinate or even become rebellious. But the good news is that the Lord began a good work in us and will carry it on to completion until the day of Christ Jesus (Philippians 1:6). So if we're in Christ and Christ is in us, He changes you and me, from the lowly, to the holy and at last when Christ we see, we are clothed in purity.

December 10

PRAY CONTINUALLY

"Pray continually." – 1 Thessalonians 5:17

NEVER CEASING LET US PRAY

Is our love for Christ increasing,
Are we praying without ceasing,
As we're walking, are we talking,
With the Lord along the way?
With regard to our behavior,
Do we focus on our Savior?
Thus abiding, in His guiding,
Through His grace, as we obey,
Let our action, have impaction,
As we spread His love each day,
Never ceasing, let us pray.

In this section of 1 Thessalonians, Paul is giving instructions to the members of the church in Thessalonica, regarding godly living. One of his many admonitions to the Thessalonians, and to each one of us was, and is, to pray continually.

Numerous scriptures instruct us regarding to Whom we address our prayer, and these instructions include both God the Father and God the Son, but always offered in the name of Jesus. The scriptures never tell us to offer our prayer to the Holy Spirit, because the Spirit indwells us, and makes intercession for us. Our attitude in prayer should be the same as that of Christ Jesus as He prayed to His Father, an attitude of dependence and submission. As we continually engage in prayer, the Spirit convicts us of so many truths and we begin to grow in the Lord. As we mature in Christ, our spirit begins to work in tandem with His Spirit, and the result is a burning desire to please the Lord. Our prayer is that by His grace, we might obey and spread His love to others day after day. Never ceasing, let us pray.

December 11

CONTINUE TO LIVE IN HIM

"So then, just as you received Christ Jesus as Lord, continue to live in Him, rooted and built up in Him, strengthened in the faith as you were taught, and overflowing with thankfulness." – Colossians 2:6-7

LET US OBEY

Jesus Christ, our Father gave us,
He's our Lord, He came to save us,
Now He's living, in us giving,
Us His love along the way.
He is speaking, we can hear it,
The indwelling Holy Spirit,
We grow stronger, stronger longer,
For He feeds us day by day.
We're so grateful, truly grateful,
Let us thankfully obey,
Our Lord Jesus, day by day.

The young church in Colosse had become the target of heretical attacks, and Paul, in his letter to the Colossians, refutes this heresies and exalts Christ as the very image of God. The theme of Colossians is the complete adequacy of Christ as contrasted with the emptiness of mere human philosophy.

In today's scripture, Paul is encouraging these young Christians to be thankful for who and what they have in Christ, urging them to live in Him, and let Him give them the strength needed to stand firm, rooted in the truth of the gospel.

These words from Paul are as appropriate for us today as they were for the young Christians in Colosse. When we consider who and what we have in Christ, we should with all humility, be SO THANKFUL. Our prayer is that we hear what His Spirit is directing us to do, then by His grace, as He feeds us day by day, we become stronger and stronger in the Lord, being so grateful to Him for what He has done, that we thankfully obey, our Lord Jesus day by day.

December 12

GOD'S GRACE

"In accordance with the riches of God's grace that He lavished on us with all wisdom and understanding." – Ephesians 1:7b-8

GOD'S GRACE THROUGH HIS SON

Grace to us is God's decision,
Through His Son, He made provision,
Our selection, of direction,
Through our Lord, makes us secure.
From this earth, our final parting,
Sends us home, through our Lord's sorting,
Grace He's giving, as we're living,
And complete this earthly tour.
Through His tender, loving splendor,
We receive His grace, so pure,
Our eternity is sure.

In the first chapter of Ephesians, beginning with verse 3 and continuing through verse 14, Paul first tells us that we have every spiritual blessing in Christ, then he enumerates many of these blessings. We are told that these spiritual blessings are in accordance with the riches of God's grace that He lavished on us, so this scripture makes two things very clear: The abundance of God's grace through Jesus – an inexhaustible supply.

This grace through Jesus is all-encompassing. It is by grace that we are saved through faith. This, of course, is our salvation, and we are also the recipients of God's grace in our everyday life, a gift from God, never earned but always a gift. This inexhaustible supply of God's grace is ours and it is lavished on us. We thank God for the grace He's giving, as we're living here on this earth, and when we finish this earthly tour, by His grace our eternity is sure.

December 13

SIMPLICITY OF DEVOTION TO CHRIST

"But I am afraid, lest as the serpent deceived Eve by his craftiness, your minds should be led astray from the simplicity and purity of devotion to Christ." – 2 Corinthians 11:3

LET OUR LOVE FOR CHRIST BE BOLD

May we never have the notion,
To be changing our devotion,
But with passion and compassion
Let our love for Christ be bold.
Let whoever looks and sees us,
See our eyes upon our Jesus,
Never straying, just obeying,
Let His love through us unfold,
Make it simple, we're His temple,
And we're His, to have and hold,
Let our love for Christ be bold.

False teachers masquerading as apostles of Christ had infiltrated the Corinthian church. They were teaching a different Jesus and a different gospel, moving away from the simplicity and purity of devotion to Christ into other areas with additional requirements. They were teaching a religion instead of a personal relationship with the living Lord. In this scripture, Paul is warning the Corinthians against this heresy.

A great truth is revealed to us in these scriptures. We are never to be led astray by anyone or anything, which would distract us from simply loving the Lord. The simplicity and purity of our devotion to Jesus is not to be altered for any reason. Even within our church, as we attempt to work for the Lord, let us never substitute those works for the Lord. Our prayer is that we keep our eyes on Jesus and simply devote ourselves to Him, never straying, just obeying so that His love through us might unfold. Let our love for Christ be bold.

December 14

TO HIM WHO IS ABLE

"Now to Him who is able to do immeasurably more than all we ask or imagine, according to His power that is at work within us." – Ephesians 3:20

LET US USE HIS STRENGTH TODAY

In our Lord, we are abiding,
Let His Spirit do the guiding,
He's the tower, of all power,
He gives strength to us each day.
For He dwells within to guide us,
And He's walking here beside us,
He's so forceful and resourceful,
And His strength is here to stay,
While residing, in us guiding,
May we always ask and pray,
Let us use His strength today.

In this scripture, Paul is attempting to describe the indescribable power of the Holy Spirit who indwells each believer. Paul uses two "yardsticks" in an attempt to magnify the power source of the Spirit. First, the Spirit is so powerful that He can do more than we ask Him to do. Second, He is so powerful that He can do more than we can even imagine, and considering the magnitude of our imagination, that is real power. In this scripture, Paul also tells us that the Spirit is at work within us. So, we have this Dynamo of power at our disposal. The question is, "What are we going to do about it?"

Whatever our endeavor may be, we have choices as we proceed. The first and foremost choice is whether to proceed in our strength or in the Lord's strength. If our particular endeavor is not within the will of the Lord, our strength is all we have and we are getting ready to see exactly how puny we are. But if we are within the Lord's will, we have that Dynamo of power at our disposal. What a difference this makes. Our prayer is that we do the abiding, and let His Spirit do the guiding. His strength is here to stay. Let us use His strength today.

December 15

YOU ARE CLEAN, ABIDE IN ME

"You are already clean because of the word which I have spoken to you. Abide in Me and I in you." – John 15:3-4

YOU PROVIDE ETERNITY

Lord, You cleanse us, then You save us,
And Your very life, You gave us,
You're the answer, the Enhancer,
And You'll ever with us be.
Though the world may be deriding,
In You only, we're abiding,
Never straying, always staying,
That the world out there might see,
With Your living, loving giving,
You, not only set us free,
You provide eternity.

John 15:3 is a statement by Jesus, a truth concerning our salvation. He tells us we are already clean (already saved) because of His word (we have already believed). The word "already" is the key. This verse is a statement of fact, setting salvation apart from sanctification, because in the following verse (John 15:4), Jesus is giving instructions regarding the sanctification process, by admonishing us to always "abide in Him." He already abides in us.

As Christians, we possess the indwelling Spirit of Jesus. He is with us and will never leave us. However, the Lord has set us free – free to love one another and to pass His love on to our brothers and sisters and free to make choices. But with our freedom in Jesus, let us be sure that our choices are for Jesus. Unless we abide IN HIM, there will be no fruitful labor FOR HIM. Our prayer is that we never stray, but always stay within God's will, continually abiding in Jesus who not only set us free but also provides for our eternity.

December 16

THE GOSPEL

"I am not ashamed of the gospel, because it is the power of God for the salvation of everyone who believes." – Romans 1:16

THE GOSPEL OF SALVATION

By God's power, and His giving,
We're believing, and we're living.
Through God's giving, we are living,
And we'll live eternally.
God has made a declaration,
It's the Gospel of Salvation,
God now sees us, through our Jesus,
Who atoned for you and me,
He's the nearest and the dearest,
And with Him, we'll always be,
Throughout all eternity.

The gospel is the good news of the Kingdom of God, and of salvation through Jesus. According to Vines, Paul uses the word "gospel" to denote two associated yet distinct things: The basic facts of the death, burial and resurrection of Christ, and the interpretation of these facts. The basic facts reveal what happened, and the interpretation reveals why it happened and how it affects us.

In this scripture, Paul is telling us that the gospel is the power of God for the salvation of everyone who believes in Jesus Christ. As you will note, there are no other requirements. God has the power. He extended us an invitation and we either believe what God has told us, or we don't believe. Either we accept Christ as our Savior or we don't. It's that simple. Paul spent most of his time in his ministry defending the purity of the gospel. Men wanted to either add something to it or subtract something from it. But as he tells us in the first chapter of Galatians, that there is no other gospel. And we as Christians have believed and we know that Jesus is the nearest and the dearest and with Him we'll always be, throughout all eternity.

THE LOVE OF CHRIST

"That you may have the power to grasp how wide and long and high and deep is the love of Christ." – Ephesians 3:18

HIS LOVE IS FOREVER

It's the widest and the deepest,
It's the highest and the steepest,
Christ prevailing, never failing,
With His love for you and me.
For He loves with extra caring,
He's so special with His sharing,
His great ration, of compassion,
He extends to you and me.
And His living, loving, giving,
That He gives to you and me,
Is for all eternity.

With our finite minds, we can't possibly grasp the magnitude of the love that Jesus has for each one of us. In the eighth chapter of Romans we are told, "neither death nor life, neither angels nor demons, neither the present nor the future, nor any powers, neither height nor depth, nor anything else in all creation will be able to separate us from the love of God that is in Christ Jesus our Lord."

Most of us intellectually know that Jesus loves us, but many of us have to experience some special circumstance or pain in our life before we can begin to understand the extent of His love. We know He loved us enough to go to the cross and suffer for our sins, that we might have salvation in His name. But until we walk in the valley, we don't realize how wide and long and high and deep His love is. As we actually experience His grace, mercy and peace, we begin to understand to some extent how great His love for us really is. And the good news is that the great ration of compassion He extends to you and me is for all eternity. HIS LOVE IS FOREVER.

December 18

LOVE ONE ANOTHER

"A new command I give you; love one another." – John 13:34

LOVE—DEEP AND WIDE

When our love is thus directed
Is response to love expected?
With our caring and our sharing,
Is our love both deep and wide?
When we put our love in motion,
Does that love involve emotion?
Do we ration, our compassion,
If our efforts are defied?
Let our living, loving, giving,
Of His love not be denied,
Let our love be deep and wide.

In today's world, the word "love" has many connotations, but in this scripture Jesus uses the Greek verb "agapao" (the noun is "agape") in His command for us to love one another. We are to "agapao" one another. Agape-love can be described as an exercise of the will in deliberate choice, made without assignable cause, save that which lies in the nature of God, Himself. Agape-love is not an impulse from emotions, but is an exercise of our will. No reward is expected and none sought. The only reason any of us can love in this manner is because of the indwelling Spirit of Christ, the fruit of His Spirit. However, it remains a deliberate choice by the exercise of our will. Phileo-love is distinguished from agape-love, in that it more nearly represents tender affection. When we love others, if we are well enough acquainted, we might also love them with phileo-love. But that is not a requirement in our Lord's command. He didn't say like them, He said to love them. And our prayer is that in response to His command, we never ration our compassion, even when our efforts are defied. By His grace, let our efforts not be denied, LET OUR LOVE BE DEEP AND WIDE.

RECEIVE GOD'S GRACE

"As God's fellow workers we urge you not to receive God's grace in vain. Having nothing, yet possessing everything." – 2 Corinthians 6:1, 10b

OUR RACE IS WON

As we work for God we're knowing,
That His grace is surely flowing,
He has told us, that He'll mold us,
To at last be like His Son.
But, today, His grace let's treasure,
He has given us great measure,
Grace prevailing, we're not failing,
Let's not wonder, think, or ponder,
Let's just work 'til day is done,
With His grace our race is won.

God's grace, by definition, is the overflowing, unmerited favor of God, freely given. Romans 5:17 refers to the abundance of God's grace, and 2 Corinthians 12:9 assures us of the sufficiency of His grace. In the first verse of today's scripture, as fellow workers for Christ, we are warned not to receive God's grace in vain. In the tenth verse, we are assured that even though we might think we have nothing, if we have Jesus, we have it all.

God's grace, through our Lord Jesus Christ, flows from an inexhaustible supply and like love, the more it's used the greater the supply. We don't have to wonder, think or ponder as to whether we will deplete this supply of God's grace. Paul owned nothing. He was on the low end of the poverty scale, yet in Christ he possessed everything. The truth in this scripture for each one of us is that regardless of our circumstances, with the abundance, availability and sufficiency of God's grace, we are rich beyond measure. In Jesus, we have it all. So as this earthly race we run, let's not wonder, think or ponder too much. Let's just work 'til day is done – and, with His grace, the race is won.

December 20

OFFER YOURSELVES TO GOD

"But rather offer yourselves to God, as those who have been brought from death to life." – Romans 6:13b

WE'RE DEVOTED TO THE LORD

Our Lord Jesus did the giving,
Now it's our turn, while we're living,
While we're living, let's be giving,
Full devotion to the Lord.
Let our will be straight and stable,
As we let our Lord enable,
Christ-connection gives direction,
He has saved us – we're His wards.
Now we're saying, we're obeying,
Though to some, it may seem hard,
We're devoted to the Lord.

Our Lord is not looking for part-time Christians. He saved us, and we were adopted into the family of God, not on a part-time basis, but for all eternity. He brought us from death to life and paid the price on that cross at Calvary. We had a debt we could not pay, and He paid a debt He did not owe. While on this earth living, Jesus did the giving. Now it's our turn. Let each one of us offer ourselves to the Lord, never on the basis of fear, but always in loving recognition of what He has done for each one of us.

As Christians, we have the Spirit of Jesus indwelling us; even so, in our humanity we retain a sin nature (Romans 7:23), and this sin nature is like an orange peel which completely conceals the sweet fruit within. Just as an orange peel has to be removed before we can taste the sweet fruit within, our sin nature must be torn away before the sweet fruit of His Spirit can be revealed. This can be done only through Jesus (Roman 8:25) and, although He is the Enabler, we must make a conscious decision with our will in order to produce the sweet fruit of His Spirit. Our prayer is that by His grace, His will becomes our will, His Spirit becomes our spirit, and we become full-time Christians, devoted to the Lord, all for the glory of God, through our Lord Jesus Christ.

December 21

PREPARED FOR GOOD WORKS

"For we are God's workmanship, created in Christ Jesus to do good works, which God prepared in advance for us to do." – Ephesians 2:10

LET US WALK WITH CHRIST TODAY

We're created in Christ Jesus,
That's the way our Father sees us,
Let's be working, never shirking,
Let us walk with Christ today.
Let our joy not be depending,
On a special kind of ending,
For we're winning, from beginning,
As He guides us day by day.
Let our mission, be submission,
As we pray, and then obey,
Let us walk with Christ today.

There is nothing wrong with goal setting, because this helps keep us focused. However, in our endeavor to work for the Lord, there is danger of putting so much importance on the end result that we lose the joy of our daily walk with Jesus. As Christians, our desire is to do something for Jesus – something special. In obedience to Him and with our fervor for Him, we set a goal, then launch out to work and reach that goal. This endeavor for the Lord will have a special kind of ending. It will be a success – it has to be. The problem is that we are making God's purpose for our life dependent on our dreams of successfully reaching a goal. We are trading all of our "todays" for one successful "tomorrow," and this is not His purpose for our life.

God's purpose for our life is that we depend on Him, through our Lord Jesus Christ, that we rely on His power, love, mercy and grace, day after day, after day. Our prayer is that whatever our endeavor may be for the Lord, we never confuse our dreams with His purpose for our life. Let us do the praying and obeying and leave the outcome to Him, all for the glory of God, through our Lord Jesus Christ.

December 22

JESUS WEPT

"Jesus loved Martha and her sister and Lazarus." – John 11:5

"Jesus wept." – John 11:35

"Then the Jews said, 'See how He loved him.'" – John 11:36

HIS PASSION IS COMPASSION

We must never have the notion,
That our Lord has no emotion,
And He's stressing, this great blessing,
With His love for you and me.
His "agape" is directed,
But "phileo" is connected,
Love abounding, grace resounding,
Love as tender as can be,
For His passion is compassion,
That He has for you and me,
Loving us, eternally.

John 11:35 is the shortest verse in the Bible. It simply says, "Jesus wept." This was in response to Mary's weeping because her brother had died. Verse 5 tells us that Jesus loved (agape) Mary and Martha and Lazarus. Verse 36 tells us that Jesus loved (phileo), and verse 35 gives evidence of this phileo-love.

Agape love is the highest form of love possible, an unconditional love, the love God had for mankind that caused Him to send His only Son to die on a cross for the sins of the world. It was a deliberate exercise of His will, made without assignable cause to do good, without any thought of reward, but it normally is not an impulse from feelings, while phileo-love represents tender affections. In these scriptures, it is quite evident that the love of Jesus was the perfect combination of both agape and phileo-love. He loved them with the highest form of love possible, agape-love, but He knew Mary, Martha and Lazarus intimately, therefore phileo-love (tender affection) was added to agape-love.

Today, as Christians, Jesus knows us well; therefore, He wants the very best for us. He not only "wills us" His agape-love, but with tender affection, He feels what we feel. He's sad for us when we're sad, glad for us when we're glad.

December 23

BY FAITH WE HAVE HIS PEACE

"Grace and peace to you from God our Father and from the Lord Jesus Christ." – Romans 1:7

"The righteous will live by faith." – Romans 1:17b

LET US TRUST IN CHRIST ALONE

We desire His peace while living,
And by grace, it is His giving,
But progressing, to this blessing,
We must live by faith alone.
May there be no self-importance,
But by faith, in God's accordance,
May submission, be our mission,
As our Jesus sets the tone,
For God sees us, through our Jesus,
Who is sitting on God's throne,
Let us trust in Christ alone.

As Christians we are admonished to live by faith, and up to a point, most of us do. As long as we live by faith, we have the peace of God through our Lord Jesus Christ that surpasses all human comprehension. We have placed our trust in Jesus for our eternity, and we have confidence in His saving grace. But as we travel down this road of life, dark clouds suddenly loom on the horizon and we see a raging storm now brewing, soon to engulf us. At that point, we take our eyes off Jesus, and focus on circumstances. We become engrossed in how we can overcome, then realize we can't and, sometimes, panic-stricken then turn to the Lord for help. Our peace is shattered. We need help, Lord. Will You help us? He responds, and our peace is restored.

We can only imagine how the Lord feels when we don't trust Him completely. We trust Him for our eternity, but when a small crisis occurs, we seem to relegate ourselves to be the object of His words in Matthew 8:26, "You of little faith, why are you so fearful?" Our prayer is that, by His grace, we not only have faith in our eternity with Him, but we have complete confidence that He will take care of us in each and every situation. We desire His peace. May our mission in life be submission to Him in all situations. Let us trust in Christ alone.

December 24

MY CONSCIENCE CONFIRMS IT

"I speak the truth in Christ – I am not lying, my conscience confirms it in the Holy Spirit." – Romans 9:1

THE RADAR OF OUR SOUL

Through our conscience we're detecting,
If His Spirit is directing,
Always being, in us, seeing,
It's the radar of our soul.
It was once not so detecting,
When there was no Christ-connecting,
But His tender, loving splendor,
Now directs us toward our goal.
And we're caring, and we're sharing,
As we see His will unfold
Through the radar of our soul.

Our conscience is like radar. It is a detection device giving us direction regarding what we should or should not do, commensurate with the highest standard of behavior we know. Most of us have heard someone make the statement, "he has no conscience," referring to someone ruthless in nature. This is a half truth at best. Everyone has a conscience, but the compelling question is "What is the highest behavioral standard we are aware of?" Before we were in Christ, our highest standard was determined by our nature, which is, in fact, a sin nature. Now that the Spirit of Christ indwells us, our highest standard is determined by His nature, a holy nature, if we, in fact, have our eyes on the Lord. Before we became Christians, there were certain things our conscience would say "yes" to that now receive a resounding "no" from our conscience. This is because our highest standard is higher now than it was before we received Christ. We now have His indwelling Spirit to confirm or deny the validity of our actions.

Our conscience is truly the radar of our soul, with our Christ connection, by His grace, we have His direction, and He directs us toward our goal. Our prayer is that, as we are caring and sharing with our brothers and sisters in Christ, we will see His will unfold, through the radar of our soul.

FOR UNTO YOU IS BORN

"For unto you is born this day in the city of David, a Savior, which is Christ the Lord." – Luke 2:11

LET'S THANK GOD FOR CHRISTMAS DAY

Once upon a world so darkened,
Through His grace God's Spirit harkened,
Love unfailing, all prevailing,
And a babe was born that night.
Midst the turmoil and the danger,
Lay our Lord, within that manger,
And this gifting was God's lifting,
Of the darkness of the night.
Grace prevailing, God's unveiling,
To the world with all its plight,
Was His Son Who is "THE LIGHT."

To the shepherds, flocks attending,
Came an angel of God's sending,
And the story of the glory,
Of the birth of Christ was told.
And this little baby Jesus,
Would be changing how God sees us,
And forever and forever,
As we see God's love unfold,
By believing, we're receiving,
Saving life within our soul,
For the Lord has made us whole.

So the living life God gave us,
Jesus Christ, the One Who'll save us,
Is directing, and connecting,
Every step along the way.
And on earth as we're advancing,
Our dear Lord is here enhancing.
Our Enhancer is the answer,
And He'll ever with us stay.
He's the Sender of God's splendor,
And the One and only Way.
LET'S THANK GOD
FOR CHRISTMAS DAY.

THE BLESSING OF CHRIST

"I know that when I come to you, I will come in the full measure of the blessing of Christ." – Romans 15:29

THE FULL MEASURE OF HIS GRACE

As we go out on the highways,
Or on country lanes or byways,
The great blessing, we're addressing,
Is the Gospel, by His grace.
We now have the life He gave us,
For He gave His life to save us,
And His living, loving, giving,
Is the blessing we embrace.
The full measure, of this treasure,
As we run this earthly race,
Is reflected by His grace.

The full measure of the blessing of Christ is ours through the gospel. The gospel is a plan for salvation, promulgated by God the Father, and activated by Jesus Christ. Simply stated, the gospel is God's plan whereby when we believe in and accept Jesus as our Lord and Savior, we are cleansed, redeemed, reconciled, saved and sanctified through His blood. We immediately receive His eternal living Spirit, never to lose it, but to live forever, eternally with the Lord. We not only have an eternity with our Lord to look forward to but that eternity began immediately when we exercised faith in Jesus and the full measure of the blessing of Christ is ours today, tomorrow and forever. His indwelling Spirit will continually give us direction and comfort.

Just as Paul was giving assurance to the Romans, he is also assuring each one of us who is a Christian. As we go out in this world, we are assured of the full measure of the blessing of Christ. We know our eternity is secure, and we also know He will never leave us nor forsake us. As we run this earthly race, no situation is too difficult for the Lord. We have the full measure of the blessing of Jesus, and as we embrace this blessing, we see grace upon grace, upon grace, from our Lord. What a loving Savior we have.

December 27

GOD WORKS IN YOU

"For it is God who works in you to will and to act according to His good purpose." – Philippians 2:13

LET'S DO OUR PART

God is working in us, teaching,
And He's working through us, reaching,
A great blessing, we're confessing,
But we have to do our part.
He enables while assisting,
Let us not be found resisting,
Let our mission, be ambition,
To obey in full, not part,
We're selected and directed,
Let response be from the heart,
By His grace, let's do our part.

Today's scripture affirms the fact that God's Spirit is working in the lives of believers to do His will, but in verse 12, we are told to "work out our salvation." This does not mean to work for our salvation. Our salvation is free, but to "work out" means to obey God, and to live the kind of life He wants us to live. So when we combine these verses the message we receive is that God works in us, but we have to work it out.

In verse 13, the word "works" means to "energize or to provide enablement." So God, through His indwelling Spirit, enables us to do what He wants us to do. In fact, He even energizes us in order that we might obey. In one sense, we might say that we are partners with God, working together with Him, but He does not force us. We have choices. When our choices are not within His will, we may experience the discipline of God, which is not something to look forward to. Our prayer is that we, at all times, obey the Lord, letting His enabling Spirit energize us. As we respond from the heart, by His grace, let us do our part, all for the glory of God, through our Lord Jesus Christ.

December 28

AT THAT MOMENT THEY WERE TERRIFIED

"At that moment the curtain of the temple was torn in two from top to bottom. The earth shook and the rocks split. The tombs broke open and the bodies of many holy people who had died were raised to life. When those guarding Jesus saw the earthquake and all that had happened, they were terrified and exclaimed, 'Surely He was the Son of God.'" – Matthew 27:51-52, 54b

GOD'S POWER – AN AWESOME THING TO SEE

On that cross, bereft and lonely,
Jesus died for sinners only,
Our foundation, for salvation,
Gave His blood for you and me.
With His body beat and battered,
All around the earth was shattered,
And the tower of God's power,
Was an awesome thing to see.
No denying our Lord's dying,
But now lives through you and me.
He is our eternity.

This scripture records what happened the moment Jesus died. The curtain of the temple was torn from top to bottom, indicating God did it, not man. This was an indication that access into God's presence was now available for everyone, not just the high priest, and this access is through Jesus because He is our only High Priest (Hebrews 4:14-16). The earth shook, rocks split, tombs were opened and saints were raised to life. This was only a small preview of the awesome power of God, but this scripture tells us that those who saw what was happening were terrified. They were also convinced that Jesus was the Son of God.

With God's New Covenant in full force and effect, we now, by faith in Jesus, have salvation through Him. To the extent that we abide in Him, He now lives His life through us, and this is ours for all eternity. Let us never forget how awesome the power of God is. He can create and He can destroy. He hates sin and loves the sinner but without faith in Jesus, we never receive the manifestation of His love and we remain under eternal damnation. We thank God that by His grace we do have faith in Jesus and when we see or even think about His awesome power, we are not terrified—we are exceedingly thankful.

IF NOT, HE IS NEARSIGHTED AND BLIND

"For if you possess these qualities in increasing measure, they will keep you from being ineffective and unproductive. But if anyone does not have them, He is nearsighted and blind and has forgotten that he has been cleansed from his past sin." – 2 Peter 1:8-9

NOW WE'RE SEEING

We were blind, but now we're seeing,
You indwell our very being,
First our blindness, then Your kindness,
Caused our blinded eyes to see.
Now we know You are our Savior,
This has altered our behavior,
For Your ration, of compassion,
Saved our soul, and set us free.
Now we're reaching, with Your teaching,
That lost souls out there might be,
Saved by Grace, eternally.

Some Bible commentators teach that this scripture refers to unbelievers, but considering the context of surrounding verses, it seems preferable to say that Peter was writing about Christians who were and are spiritually immature. He goes on to say that they had forgotten that they had been cleansed from past sin. Some of the qualities they lack are enumerated by Peter, beginning with faith, then continuing with goodness, knowledge, self-control, perseverance, godliness, and brotherly kindness, which cumulatively produces agape-love. Unfortunately many Christians know the Lord in salvation, but lack the fruit of the Spirit, are not advancing spiritually and are either blind or nearsighted regarding what the Lord has done for them. They seem to forget the magnitude of God's gift of eternal life through Jesus. Thus they don't grow in the Lord, and their ministry for the Lord is hindered and greatly restricted in fact by their actions. It is sometimes almost impossible to differentiate between them and the unsaved person.

Our prayer is that we never become near-sighted or blind regarding what the Lord has done for us, but continually keep our mind and our eyes focused on Him, thereby making ourselves available for whatever ministry He has in mind for us.

HOW MUCH MORE GLORIOUS

"If the ministry that condemns men is glorious, how much more glorious is the ministry that brings righteousness." – 2 Corinthians 3:9

IN OUR JESUS IS GOD'S GLORY

We pass on the truth, God's story,
In our Jesus, is His glory,
And the story, of His glory,
Shows His grace has magnified.
For by grace the Father gave us,
Jesus Christ, the One who'll save us,
And believing, we're receiving,
Life through Him Who death defied.
Now we're knowing, His grace growing,
With His love, so deep and wide,
Keeps Him always at our side.

The law was given through Moses and came with glory because it came from God. That glory shone on the face of Moses, but he had to put a veil over his face to keep the Israelites from seeing that the radiance was fading away. The ministry of the law, even though it came with God's glory, was temporary, and it condemned men because they couldn't keep the law. In this scripture, Paul is explaining how much more glorious this New Covenant is, the ministry of the Spirit through Jesus that brings life instead of death and lasts forever. We are saved by grace when we put our faith and trust in Jesus. Not only is the glory of God not fading away. Verse 18b tells us that it is an ever-increasing glory. We never have to put a veil over our face, because this glory of God shining on the face of the believer through Jesus continually increases with the reflection of God's glory. In fact, we are told that we are being transformed into the likeness of Jesus, with ever-increasing glory.

As this year comes to an end, let us thank God for His glory, especially His glory of salvation. But in addition to our salvation, as we attempt to live the Christian life, we are knowing that His grace is growing, and with His love so deep and wide, we truly thank Him for always being at our side.

December 31

ABRAHAM OBEYED AND WENT

"By faith Abraham, when called to go to a place he would later receive as his inheritance, obeyed and went, even though he did not know where he was going." – Hebrews 11:8

LET'S LAUNCH OUT WITH FAITH

Now this year is surely ending,
And a brand new year is pending,
Let's be saying, we're obeying,
What the Lord tells us to do.
We may look back with inspection,
As we pause with our reflection,
But our growing, should be showing,
As we face next year anew,
Christ-connected, we're directed.
As He tells us what to do.
LET'S LAUNCH OUT
WITH FAITH THAT'S TRUE

This scripture reveals the faith that Abraham had as he obeyed God. At 75 years of age, at God's direction, he launched out on a journey to find his inheritance. He left the known to explore the unknown. He left comfort and ease to experience hardship. Instead of looking back, he looked forward. He did all of this without having any idea of where he was going. His reason for making this journey was his love for God and faith in the trustworthiness of God. God made Abraham a promise. Abraham believed. Abraham obeyed.

As this year ends and the next begins, by the grace of God may each one of us launch out with the same kind of faith Abraham had. We may pause as we look back on this year, reflecting on what has happened, but let us look forward instead of backward as we journey to our inheritance. Let our growth in the Lord show, as our faith in the Lord grows. God made us a promise. Let us believe, then let us obey. We are Christ-connected and Christ-directed. AS HE TELLS US WHAT TO DO, LET'S LAUNCH OUT WITH FAITH THAT'S TRUE, all for the glory of God through our Lord Jesus Christ.